A Product of Genetics
(and Day Drinking)

A
Product
of
Genetics
(and Day Drinking)

A Never-Coming-of-Age Story

Jess H. Gutierrez

An imprint of Penguin Random House LLC
penguinrandomhouse.com

TINY REPARATIONS BOOKS with colophon is a registered trademark of YQY, Inc.

LIBRARY OF CONGRESS CATALOGING-IN-PUBLICATION DATA
Names: Gutierrez, Jess H., author.
Title: A product of genetics (and day drinking): a never-coming-of-age story /
Jess H. Gutierrez.
Description: 1 edition. | New York : Tiny Reparations Books,
Penguin Random House, [2024]
Identifiers: LCCN 2023042409 (print) | LCCN 2023042410 (ebook) |
ISBN 9780593475072 (hardcover) | ISBN 9780593475089 (ebook)
Subjects: LCSH: Generation Y—Attitudes. | Coming of age. | Lesbians.
Classification: LCC HQ799.5 .G87 2024 (print) |
LCC HQ799.5 (ebook) | DDC 305.2—dc23/eng/20240207
LC record available at https://lccn.loc.gov/2023042409
LC ebook record available at https://lccn.loc.gov/2023042410

Printed in the United States of America

1st Printing

Interior art: Cocktails © Msnty studioX

BOOK DESIGN BY KRISTIN DEL ROSARIO

V,

I'll be your shotgun rider for as long as you'll have me

Contents

A Product of Genetics
(and Day Drinking)

Introduction

I recently saw an Instagram giveaway that included a collection of eight vibrators of varying shapes, sizes, and talents. Instead of thinking, *Wow, my wife and I would have a blast with those!* and signing up for a chance, I was like, *No way. That looks like a charging nightmare. I don't need that kind of responsibility in my life.*

I mean, you'd have to build a custom charging station and make some kind of written rotation schedule to keep all of those suckers juiced and at the ready. And don't even get me started talking about the cleanup of such a configuration. Sounds utterly exhausting. Truth be told, the only thing I'm into these days is the idea of eight straight hours of uninterrupted sleep. I tsked disapprovingly, blocked the original poster, and continued my online search for "the world's best pet stain remover."

My smokin'-hot wife has a libido less battered than mine. Nonetheless, she still would've fullheartedly supported my decision to keep scrolling. If those fuckers aren't dishwasher safe, they don't belong in our house. Vaginal happiness be damned, we haven't the time or patience for such recreational goodies anymore. My girl may be fit and ready to get it on at a moment's notice, but I know that secretly, way deep down, she just wants a nap too.

So, no kinks for me. I am about as far from masochism as a girl can get. Don't expect me to ask a stranger from the internet to don a diaper and throw a leather saddle on me and ride me anytime soon. My forty-something back hurts too much for such extracurriculars.

I'm just a tired-ass mom. I love these kids that I'm raising (trying not to royally screw up) with my wife of fifteen years, but they're kicking my ass. Every single day welcomes the renewed realization that I have no idea what I'm doing. I am an amateur in a vast pool of amateurs who are way better at pretending that they know what in the hell is going on than I am. These days I talk in exclamation points to a six-year-old who can only poop whilst wearing goggles and an eight-year-old who has already surpassed me in both intellect and maturity. My year-old son, recently adopted into this crazy mess, doesn't even try to pretend like he thinks I'm smart enough to parent and seems determined to learn self-care so that he can start handling shit on his own.

But this isn't a parenting guide. Read one of those somewhere else. I'm no Dr. Spock. I think Dr. Phil is a douche. I have no advice for you. I can't help you learn to be better through my mistakes (no matter my long track record of making them). What I'm saying is that I have little wisdom to lend. I've heard that carrots are good for the eyes and that you should read to your kids on the daily. You should limit screaming profanity in their presence unless you're keen on the idea of Timmy being sent home from kindergarten with a note explaining that they called another kid a "shithole." Other than that, I've got nothing for you. I'm treading water over here with a cinder block chained to my legs. And if you have advice, send it elsewhere—I don't have time for that shit either. I'm too busy microwaving processed food and explaining why our library books are two years overdue.

I wasn't always an exhausted parent, one tantrum shy of searching for a nearby manhole to fall down. I used to be someone different.

This is *that* story.

Disclaimer: Internet sources explain that "coming of age" is the attainment of prominence, respectability, recognition, or maturity. Disappointingly enough, I have achieved none of those things. Is it possible for someone to, I don't know, just not come of age? Or like, get halfway there and then stall around age fourteen? If you were looking for a heartwarming, inspiring story of a woman finding herself and coming into her own, you should do a quick scan of Oprah's book club list for a different tale. Your author here is, instead, a giant, messy work in progress.

A "memoir" is defined by Wikipedia (the very site god would reference if she were ever forced to use MLA formatting on a term paper) as "any nonfiction narrative writing based on the author's personal memories."

You might be curious/confused (as am I) as to why someone from Christ-only-knows-where, with no fame (outside of winning a three-hundred-dollar bingo pot when she was eleven years old), is writing a memoir. I have three Twitter followers, one of whom I'm pretty sure is a bot. Who in their right mind would read my life story other than my mom and her two friends that she'll strong-arm into buying it?

But you're here. You arrived at my story and are still reading. That seems like a really good sign.

Yeah, this is my personal narrative. But really, it's the story of many my age, our nineties frosted-lip-gloss-coated childhoods and the things that gummed together to turn us into the helicopter-parenting, gluten-damning, brunch-having, Amazon-shopping, selfie-stick-using, vain-as-hell cum bags that we all became. The details of how you got here might be a teensy bit different from mine, but in the end, we're likely still cruising the same path in our matching Cheeto-encrusted SUVs. Some of us have the leather package and sunroof. Some of us don't. Some of you may have become bougie bitches and gotten the third-row seating. Others may have even leveled up and paid for the ass warmers in their minivans. I got the Bose speakers to make sure that even though I look basic as hell, I can still thump like the badass I imagine I am. Upgrades notwithstanding, we remain the same. Every day consists of all of us struggling to avoid egocentric elder-millennial stereotypes and labels whilst stuffing down the temptation to ask to speak to the nineteen-year-old Starbucks manager to bitch about lukewarm pumpkin spice lattes.

My collection of tales may be unique to me, but my general story isn't. No matter our Facebook arguments or passive-aggressive grabs for the latest farmhouse trends at Target, we are a united group of early millennials trying not to turn into our parents or the asshole generation that came after us. It's a tenuous tightrope balance, but one we fight to maintain on the daily whilst gripping our White Claw seltzers and browsing Etsy's homemade wares.

I readily admit that there's a fair chance that this book will read like a three-hundred-page TikTok video. I apologize for that, but it can't be helped, as my brain actually works like a three-hundred-page TikTok video. Sorry in advance for the few fucks given and occasional lapses in judgment and political correctness that you are sure to encounter in the following chapters. Welcome to my shitshow. Please take a name tag and make yourself at home. Choose a spot far from this dumpster fire if you were heavy-handed with the hair spray this morning or if your clothes are made of flammable material. If you don't have your shit together or life figured out, you are about to feel a whole lot better about yourself.

Chapter One

Older Than Twitter

Being a nineties kid was an experience in and of itself. Every single generation can claim that their upbringing was unique, different, the ultimate challenge. Older generations remember walking up and down hills both ways to school sans shoes (I'm too lazy for that shit and would've remained illiterate for sure). They remember the good ol' days when they ate sticks of lard for dinner. Back then all it took was a handpicked willow branch to knock a kid in line. Screw childhood trauma. It wasn't even a thing. You weren't gay or autistic or different in any measurable way. Everyone had Barbie parts and babies were dropped by storks.

Older generations are wrong about having run the toughest gauntlet. Because being a child of the 1990s was, in fact, the experience of all experiences. Babies of the eighties turned kids in the nineties are the true survivors. Think about it like this: We were raised by folks who doped hard while listening to crap like Cheap Trick and Journey. Our own parents were brought up by one of the most rigid of generations. In turn, they refused to do things like cook or clean or even really discipline. We were the first generation to eat every single meal beneath the trans-fat-saturated golden arches of McDonald's. We played the shit out of Oregon Trail and died of diphtheria while our pregnant cows were trapped under broken wagon axles. We hacked away at our eyebrows on the instruction of heroes like Gwen Stefani and shook our asses to "Achy Breaky Heart" and "Macarena." From the wise advice of popular musicians, we knew to absolutely not go chasing waterfalls and to be suspicious of the comingled scent of sex and candy. By 1999 we knew to watch for scrubs, and under no circumstances would we be giving them our number. Understanding that many of us could never dream of being as goddamned cool as Lauryn Hill, we settled for homemade, slapdash basement choreography to Ace of Base's hits instead.

If you were a kid of the nineties, any sound resembling a velociraptor was enough to make you shit Frisbees. No one looked through your Halloween candy for drugs because no self-respecting person would waste perfectly good cocaine on kids. Those of us in states with bottle deposits recycled not because we cared about Earth but because every single dime dropped in your piggy bank inched you that much closer to the sweet BMX bike you'd been drooling over. Yearbook signing was the time of year when you found out if anyone was in love with you, and your favorite school lunch consisted of a square piece of pizza, a watery mess of fruit cocktail, and canned corn. If the hairnet-wearing cafeteria gals were feeling particularly frisky, the same meal might also feature a block of brownie (that, suspiciously enough, tasted exactly like the aforementioned entree).

My generation was allowed to play Donkey Kong until our thumbs were permanently crooked and our eyes bled. Sans chaperones, we ran around arcades and reserved games with a quarter steadied on the console. We chugged Surge soda even though the rumor in 1998 was that the stuff got banned and eventually discontinued solely based on its ability to make kids' hearts explode. We ate enough Pop Rocks, Hostess cupcakes, and Zotz to ensure prediabetes before hitting puberty (which came years early from all the hormones injected into our kids meals). An entire dinner could consist solely of the gelatinous goo of Cheez Whiz. Little Debbie may as well have been my auntie, because I was raised on her oversugared boxed delicacies. Nothing, and I mean nothing, tastes better than a Christmas Tree Cake chased by a swig of orange Fanta. Fight me on this.

In the nineties, there were no bedtimes to speak of. So long as when the streetlights flickered on your bike could be found in a heap on the front lawn, you were golden.

Police didn't care about seat belts, and pregnant women were prescribed small glasses of wine in the mornings to cure nausea. Parents hotboxed us in cars while they chain-smoked Pall Malls and threatened to "turn this fucking car around" at every stoplight.

It's a scientific fact that if your mom and pop weren't drunk driving on a Saturday, you weren't going anywhere. Whichever parent wobbled the least got behind the wheel of the station wagon and sideways squinted until you got home. If you wanted to go to goddamned Blockbuster, it was with the understanding that you very well might pay for the new release of 3 *Ninjas Kick Back* with your life. That's how weekends went.

When we weren't watching Steve Urkel on TGIF (which we had waited for all week), we were using homemade nunchakus to look as much like Michelangelo as possible. We saw toothless meth heads get tackled on bootlegged cable to the soundtrack of

"Bad Boys," had crushes on Randy from *Home Improvement* and Topanga from *Boy Meets World* (some of us on both simultaneously). Our parents thought they were actual friends with the cast of *Friends* and our moms all wore Jennifer Aniston's haircut in a rainbow of shades.

Don't even get me started on how I continue to suffer from very real night terrors from the scene in *My Girl* where Thomas J. lay in the kid-sized coffin while Vada screamed for his glasses. That was fucking brutal, and I was never the same after seeing it. The 1990s were full of such trauma. We just didn't know the word "trauma" yet, so it wasn't a thing worth worrying over.

It was a confusing time in history.

As a 1990s kid, once you could ride a bike without training wheels, you gained access to the entire universe. There were no rules about traveling distance or supervision when you were on your self-powered vehicle. The possibilities were endless. What did you say? You want to get your favorite kind of slushy, but they only sell them two towns over? Get on your goddamned bike and pedal your heart out. You are mere miles away from the icy deliciousness of Mountain Dew mixed with Wild Cherry.

A common problem for our generation of youth was the blatant lawlessness of it all. Without rules, without guidance, we got into some real scrapes. Sure, it was wonderful to be free to roam and play until the fireflies started twinkling, but some life lessons were hard-earned. If you ask many of my peers, they can recount tales of skirmishes that today would likely end up with some soft jail time for the involved parties. Perhaps a bit more supervision could've lessened the number of sessions many of us now spend hashing shit out with therapists.

So yeah, being granted full access to independence wasn't

without problems. No one knew where I was, and trust me, I was everywhere I shouldn't have been. My two younger brothers and I often tumbled with a set of ginger twins named Tom and Jerry (I shit you not). We didn't know which brother went with which name, but we did know that they were both fucking lethal. Luckily(?), I was one of the stockiest kids in the white-trash town we grew up in and a tyrannizer in my own right. Both Tom and Jerry and their asshole third rider, Phillip Filby, suffered my wrath more than once. The game was simple: whichever kid was still standing at the top of the sewage drainage ditch at the end of the fight, no matter the blackened eyes or dripping blood, was the victor.

Despite the dirt on my Umbro shorts, I was generally that kid.

My empire of bullying supremacy stood until a local sixth grader, the known overlord of the middle school and two grades my senior, heard of my reign. Unwilling to be outdone by a villainous little girl, he waited for me after school one day. Not giving a shit about my new-to-me hand-me-down-from-older-cousins pineapple culottes, he knocked me off my bike into the gravel parking lot. FFF (a moniker that stood for "Feral Fucking Frankie," gifted to him by local kids) then straddled me and allowed every pound of his weight to settle atop my nine-year-old body.

Feeling my ribs squeeze under his mighty bulk, I thrashed and yelped and dug my heels into the dirt until a bored-looking teacher pulled him off me.

Though I still kicked plenty of ass after that day, I was forever humbled. I continued throwing Phillip Filby into puddles of raw sewage, but he and I both knew after my encounter with FFF that I had been vanquished. The future wins that left my foes dripping in human feces were bittersweet at best. Once folks have seen you scream bloody murder for your mama beneath the beefy legs of a freckled ruffian, it's incredibly difficult to ever reestablish alpha status.

Childhood was death defying but fun. With few constraints over where my mind or body was allowed to roam, I, along with many of my generation, owned the universe. We rode skateboards, played pixelated video games, and threw dirt and curse words to our hearts' content. We were nineties kids, and we didn't have to give a shit.

Y2K was coming and there was a good chance we wouldn't survive it. We lived hard and fast.

The factor that made us true outliers was that we were the first wave of kids to have the internet at our fingertips. First, it wasn't there—we played with sticks and GI Joes—and then, all of a sudden, *BAM!*: fucking internet access. The whine of dial-up connecting changed the world as we knew it forever. Our parents had no earthly idea of the web's evils and capabilities, and we were allowed to roam AIM without supervision. I still swear as an adult that there is nothing in the entire world more exciting than the trilling notification of a message received from your best online friend from Lithuania.

Nothing says "please come decapitate me" like announcing that you're a thirteen-year-old girl home alone in a foreign chat room to bring the creeps (who figured out the evils of the internet far ahead of our naïve guardians) running.

With the insatiable thirst of a generation used to manually recording music with a tape deck and perfect timing, we reveled in using Napster and LimeWire to download and infect family computers with both terrible music and debilitating viruses. If one was fortunate enough to have siblings, one always had someone else to blame for the incapacitating malware. We had the luck of parents still not knowing shit about computers, thereby making it impossible to determine the true culprit, on our side.

The internet really didn't become a thing until the early 1990s. I mean, I'm sure it was out there for rich people on their rich-people yachts or whatever, but it hadn't yet graced the South's lower echelon of motley citizens, such as myself. It wasn't widely mainstream until 1999 (Wikipedia says, so it must be fact).

My mother, a registered nurse at a local hospital where she was professionally required to take care of all patients, even KKK members (think rural Arkansas), lugged our first computer into our house at the beginning of my freshman year of high school.

My brothers and I stared in awe as our mom, about as tech-savvy as an 1840s farmhand, squinted at the instruction manual and plugged in cords and cables. It took a fair number of tears and swearing, but at long last, when she depressed the front-facing button, the power light flashed green.

Let me tell you, the giant, humming box was fucking glorious. I had seen computers at school but had never, ever thought our family would own one. But suddenly, it was there, in all its plastic glory, settled on a secondhand desk in our living room.

The first time I heard the droning hum of dial-up in my own house, my heart swelled like the Grinch's during the part where he decides to save Christmas.

The world was officially at my fingertips.

As one of the first millennials (the generation is defined as those born between 1981 and 1996; I was born in 1982), I am a fluid mix of that generation and the one before (Gen X). My early-eighties peers and I have been dubbed "elder millennials" by a

bunch of dickbags who have no idea what it feels like to start receiving AARP membership offers in the mail. My younger millennial brethren consider me an antiquated dinosaur in desperate
need of makeup tips and a daily multivitamin. But once members
of the cohort before mine find out I am a loathed millennial, I am
shunned as a self-entitled jobless jagoff, which hardly seems fair,
because I have a job and I try to keep my self-entitledness in
check (which is precisely why I'm writing a book all about myself).

I am the voice of a fucked-up (but hilarious) generation.

Enjoy my rant.

Chapter Two

Her Village

I grew up in a quaint cottage in the countryside. It had sleepy English ivy slithering up the sides and a small courtyard in the back reminiscent of a secret garden found in an identically named movie from my childhood. Outside could be heard the soft lilt of twittering birds and the occasional nibble of a rabbit that lucked into a bit of clover. When I threw open the clapboard shutters to sing over the morning dew, a chorus of nature's most beautiful creatures echoed my gay melody.

Kidding.

I was raised in a series of trailers and dilapidated rental houses. Some were nicer than others but none of them had goddamned creeping ivy unless you count the thatches of poison oak that had inspired many a scrotal rash on my younger brothers. In lieu of a mystical garden, we had skinny dog runs that didn't dare grow grass.

My family moved a lot but never to anywhere exotic enough to brag about in new school cafeterias during auditions with prospective elementary friends. Not even a third grader is impressed to hear that you lived in eastern Oregon or that you've done a stint in Ogden, Utah.

Before I was eighteen, I had lived in twenty houses. Unbelievably, not a single one of them was a mansion. With little money and plenty of landlords ready with eviction notices for overdue rent, we relocated on the regular. In my youngest years, we flitted here and there in the Midwest, generally keeping near both sets of grandparents. Later, though, we wandered all over, including several moves following my parents' divorce. By the time I was fourteen, when my mom told us to pack again, I agreed but told her it would be my last time. The cardboard boxes, which were worn thin from overuse, were loaded into yet another beaten cargo truck and we went south. When we landed in Arkansas, I registered for school, unpacked my trinkets, and announced that I was finished with address changes. Like the spot or not, I was home.

"Here?" my mom asked incredulously, starting to regret the whim that had flung our family southward. "In Arkansas? Seriously? Of all places?"

"I'm done," I answered, maybe wishing I had taken my stand a state or two before. "I won't leave this place."

And I haven't and I won't. Short of vacations or a quick jaunt across state lines in my early twenties to buy better marijuana, I have kept my word.

But long before Arkansas, I had mostly lived in Kansas. When I was young, and when my parents were still together, we were broke. With a reputation tied to those little red notices on our doors, we had earned a bit of a scarlet letter and had run out of places to live. Luckily, my dad was a cunning fucker. He had risen above dealing in regular currency.

You see, there are a million different ways that people come to live in their homes. Some people stay forever in the neighborhoods they were born in. Others inherit. Those with a love for city life seek apartments to suit their specific needs. Many pinch pennies and visit open houses until they find a dwelling perfect for their wants and budget. People build, fix up, buy, trade, and rent. Whatever the way, they find homes and make them their own.

My dad's way was extra special. In 1989 he romanced an elderly woman into lending our family of five an extra farm she had lying around.

All of the aforementioned ways people happen into their dwellings are sweet enough, but being poor doesn't allow for such carefree browsing. When you don't even have enough money for a roll of coconut Donettes at the gas station, choice is no longer a luxury you get to exercise. You aren't pining over the right kind of neighborhood to raise kids in when you're worried you can't even afford walls.

We were in a pickle, and my father had a card left to play (and play it he did).

The exact details of how the deal was struck are controversial, as the sides involved (my divorced parents) have been feuding for the entirety of the twenty-first century and the latter part of the twentieth. With the few grains of actual truth I've been able to gather, I've pieced enough of the story together to be pretty grossed out.

The sprinkling of deets that aren't grainy have me convinced there was wanton nudity involved during the property transaction. The old woman basically exchanged lodging and land for biweekly rights to my father's naked ass and sexual talents.

The crude deal was simple enough. My dad would work the land (and the grandma's body) for a stretch and would eventually pay off the acreage with his acts of pants-less loyalty. Now, the farm was in a shithole county in the dregs of Kansas, but fifty acres is still a sizable plot for some raking and doing the naked dance with a senior citizen eight times a month. The old broad must've really had a thing for freckled redheads.

But you see, my pops was a ladies' man. He was something of a trailer park Casanova, resplendent in denim. No woman was immune to his charms—not even seventy-seven-year-old Deb Moorland of Topeka, Kansas. The woman, no stranger to trailers or denim herself, had gotten lucky in a Powerball drawing years before and had caught my dad's eye at a local bar. Any gal who could call for that many shots of the good stuff without blinking had to have the money to back the order. This interested my father. Greatly.

So, Deb and my dad did whatever they did (some things shouldn't be elaborated on, even in this book, even if kids aren't reading it). Our family loaded our few possessions into cardboard boxes and moved to a trailer house on a working farm in the middle of bumfuck nowhere.

We weren't farmers, nor were we country folk. We were just a Midwestern family lucky enough to have a patriarch willing to screw for a piece of the American dream. The trailer was so wind-beaten it was one hearty flatlands breeze away from demolition. My brothers' bedroom seemed a palatial suite to me when I, the only girl, was moved into the pantry closet adjacent to the kitchen. My twin bed fit wall to wall, making it impossible to open the bottom drawer of my built-in dresser. When we moved years later, I was thrilled to reunite with the toys that had been entombed inside.

"Raggedy Ann! Bitch, where you been?" I cried gleefully,

squeezing the recovered toy to my chest. I wasn't sure what the rag doll had been doing in my drawer with Teddy Ruxpin all that time, but I certainly had suspicions.

A roomy wonderland that trailer was not. My dad had shrunk the space even more one night when he started a fire after falling asleep with a burning Marlboro Red resting atop a Coke can next to him. The couch, eventually pushed away from the charred family room walls when Mom grew sick of washing soot out of our clothes, now took up an even larger chunk of the tiny quarters.

"Goddamned bullshit," Dad muttered, a fresh cigarette dangling from his lips, the next morning when reminded of the fire. "I barely dozed off."

My mom was understandably unimpressed with his paltry defense against almost killing a household full of children.

Our family matriarch might've thought my dad royally sucked. But there were others who wholeheartedly disagreed. Once Deb Moorland had a nicotine-flavored taste of Dad, she couldn't seem to get enough. Shortly after we settled in the stuffy space, the old woman began dispatching what my mom still refers to as "toothless meth thugs" to our front door on a regular basis. The visitors were sent with explicit instructions to threaten my mom to leave her stud husband, OR ELSE.

Or else what, boys? You'll make my bone-weary twenty-eight-year-old mother live in a rat-infested hovel sans air-conditioning with one toilet that's usually on the fritz while being threatened by parolees as her husband fucks the Crypt Keeper? She risked losing her life to tetanus every time she so much as washed a plate in that kitchen. She once fell through a rusted heating vent in the floor and broke her ankle. I mean, it would've been a real stretch to deal my mom a shittier hand at that point.

She likes to call them our "rough years," while I less affectionately refer to them as the "Why in the fuck did you allow this, I can't believe we survived" years.

With nary a streetlight in sight, a station wagon with a faulty starter, and an absent husband who didn't believe the stories about the menacing goons, my mom quickly decided she had to build herself a support system. Coincidentally, she didn't have to look far. A couple of hundred feet behind our trailer, just over a rickety fence line, Mom discovered an entire co-op of single women. Conversations sailed across the fence as underwear and holey socks were hung on clotheslines. Before long, Mom's new friends were ducking through a split in the fence to join her for a glass of refrigerated boxed wine. While Dad was busy screwing around, Mom created a village of female friends.

Admittedly, the lady companions shared some oddities. Despite the shabbiness of their homes, their nails were always done and their wardrobes of silky robes and nighties impeccable. They smoked long cigarettes out of holders like in the movies and could never accept invitations after dusk. Refusing to meddle in the affairs of the only friends she had, Mom didn't ask many questions.

Considering the arrangement of their trailers—a semicircle with front doors facing the center—she assumed the five women were religious zealots belonging to a commune or lesbians living on the outskirts of the city limits for discretion. Oddly enough, despite her Anne Rice obsession, she never once considered that they might have been vampires. Whether they were Jesus freaks or top secret clam divers, it made no difference to my mom. Whatever was happening behind those thin tin walls was of no concern to her. The ladies next door who curiously always had to scurry home before the sun set each day had become the most reliable people in her life.

One day, when mom was trying to kick-start our shit car in the snow to take my middle brother and me to school, one of the women popped under the fence.

"Girlie, don't take the baby out on those dangerous roads," she said, stroking my youngest brother's curls. "I'll watch him until you get back."

The well-meaning woman looked like she hadn't slept in a month of Sundays, but my mom, in her sweats and too-thin coat, was relieved to have the help. She slammed the car door shut (not giving a shit about seat belts because they were basically just décor back then) and hugged her friend.

"I'll be right back."

She watched Maureen coo over the baby as she carried him across the fence back to her own trailer.

Morning babysitting became a routine. While Mom loaded us, one of the do-gooders would join us car-side and claim the baby. Soon thereafter, my brothers and I were spending occasional afternoons at the community of trailers while Mom dashed to the grocery store or bank. The five women always had dark rings under their eyes, but they smelled nice and were good to us, with a never-ending supply of chocolate chip cookies. During our visits, there were frequent knocks on the front doors and frequent redirecting of visitors, but we didn't think much of it. We imagined they were running a fancy hotel and pretended to be bellhops in charge of make-believe luggage. One of the ladies would disappear in a cloud of perfume, to be replaced by another sitter, and we'd go back to nibbling sugary snacks.

One afternoon, a few of the girls were lounging on our front porch with my mom when my dad's van rolled down the long drive. Having likely been off on a kinky adventure with his cougar girlfriend, he hadn't been home in days and hadn't been expected.

Upon hearing the crunch of the tires, the women, who had never seemed shy before, scattered. They defied the laws of gravity and the confines of their satiny lingerie when they catapulted off the porch and ran toward the hole in the fence.

My dad, with a look of sheer confusion on his face, stood frozen for a minute.

"What in the hell were those whores doing here?" he barked when he finally recovered his voice.

My mom, gathering the half-drunk plastic cups of wine, glanced at the group of trailers across the fence.

"They're my friends!" she sang, still merry from their camaraderie. "And how dare you call them whores considering how you've spent the last few days? They're all the help I have," she continued, tossing cigarette butts from an ashtray into a planter. "They watch the kids while I run errands and are lovely company."

My dad shook his head in bewilderment. He balled and unballed his fists.

"They're actual working fucking whores," he said slowly. "Christ almighty, Trish, they're running a cathouse."

Realization slowly dawned on my mom. She considered the other five members of her newly established book club, thought about their flimsy negligees, nocturnal schedules, and frequent visitors, and the two a.m. headlights that would shine in our bedroom windows.

She recalled one gentleman late-night pounding on our trailer door, waking her up, and she remembered his grinning and drunken companions (who were apparently lost), who told her they were "looking for a good time."

Admittedly, Mom was doing a lot of things in the latter part of the 1980s. However, offering a good time wasn't one of those things.

Maureen, Nell, Carolyn, Nancy, and Peg were not clandestine lesbians. They weren't a broken-off sect of a bizarre cult or church. They weren't even big-city escorts dripping with diamonds.

They were goddamned Kingman County prostitutes running an illicit trailer house brothel two hundred fifty feet from her kids' bedrooms.

"M-motherfucker," my mom stammered as her dreams of discussing Oprah's latest pick over a dish of cocktail peanuts went up in flames.

Shooing away us kids—who were begging for piggyback rides from a parent we hadn't seen in days—my dad shook his head.

"You've been letting hookers babysit our kids?" he asked.

"You knowingly moved us next door to a goddamned bordello? Seriously?"

At that second, something else occurred to my mom.

"Wait, how in the hell do you know they're hookers?" she frothed, knowing the answer all too well.

My dad once again pried us off him and crossed his arms over his chest.

"Which one?" my mom spat.

The look on Dad's face was clue enough.

"All of them? Goddammit, Maureen! You bitch!" She stormed off.

Later, when my dad dug in on the argument whose fire wouldn't die, he told my mom that it had been all of them and that since they knew we were broke, he had gotten a deep discount for their specialized services.

Like I said, my dad was a ladies' man. Apparently, even the hookers of Sissy's Trailer Court were not immune to his wiles.

Later that night, after my dad had flown back into the saggy-armed, Oil of Olay–scented embrace of his mistress, my mom seethed. She was so mad, in fact, that she took out some paper and scrawled an angry note.

"Book club is canceled. Give me back my fucking blender."

From that day on she swore that her Cuisinart never blended the same.

Mom was only able to hold her grudge for as long as our station wagon's carburetor held out. A few weeks after the brawl, with nary a husband in sight, she found herself (and a trio of kids) at the hookers' front door asking for a ride to the grocery store. A box of wine later, we were allowed to accept our neighbors' cookies again (not in the same way that their clients did, of course). To this day if you ask my own kids who makes the most kick-ass seven-layer chocolate cake, they will unblinkingly chorus, "Aunt Maureen!"

Now, as a mom of three myself, I understand my mother's plight well. I don't have an unfaithful spouse (she's too tired for piddling around and also quite afraid of me) and I live in a house that my mom could've only dreamed of in 1990. But on a fundamental level I get her thirst for community, for people, for glasses of wine shared whilst bitching about arbitrary everyday bullshit.

Because even as a hermit-esque introvert who has no desire to crawl out of her troll hole, sometimes even I just need to be around goddamned people. It's annoying but it's biological. After a five-minute fix—the moment I've grown tired of wearing pants with a zipper—I've had my fill and am ready to slither back into solitude. But the urge for contact always eventually resurfaces.

I have never (again) found myself in the company of an entire prostitution ring, but I think sometimes maybe such a circle of friends wouldn't be the worst thing. Instead, I'm sprinting to keep up with all of the brushed-hair moms who check their Apple Watches and sigh with judgment when I rush into PTA meetings ten minutes late. Maureen wouldn't have given a shit. She would've patted the chair that she had saved for me before whispering all of the gossipy shit I had missed. At least the ladies of my childhood knew how to have a good time.

And no, I'm not likely to look for a roundup of trailers hosting a roost of hookers on Care.com for date-night babysitter options. But I well understand how the desire to go to the grocery store alone could make a woman crazed enough to consider it. My mom wasn't wrong to leave us with the central Kansas concubines, she was just a bit desperate.

Riding on two hours of sleep and gas station coffee fumes, today I feel the fuck out of that.

The women were engaged in the oldest profession in the world. Their regulars would've said they were doing it rather well. Those bitches were enterprising AF when they opened their business in the rural prairie land and tapped into an (apparently) unmet need. They had steady paychecks, four walls, and a roof. It stands to reason that my foster mothers weren't the poorest examples of strong women that I could've had in my young life. Perhaps they shouldn't have screwed my father or fucked up our fancy blender, but again, I'm not here to hate on anyone's journey.

Chapter Three

F-Bombs and Holy Psalms

Before I was an out-and-proud flag-waving lesbian, I was an entirely different kind of zealot. I grew up Catholic. Like, really Catholic. I was of the knee-socks, *Jesus Christ Superstar*, punch-the-devil-right-in-the-kazoo, plastic-WWJD-bracelets-stacked-to-the-elbow, love-letters-to-the-almighty religious variety. When I won my fifth-grade spelling bee, the victory was dedicated to the (oddly) very Caucasian Jesus Christ that the very white nuns at my school had taught me all about. God himself had abandoned the Bosnian War for long enough to float down to Sister Ann's elementary classroom to remind me to add the "w" at the end of the word "yellow." Sure, I had some serious questions linked to the story of an Empire State Building–sized hand-built boat stocked with opposite-sex animals of every species. (Why the fuck weren't they eating each other? What if the farmers or ranchers or shepherds or whatever the hell they were had picked a gay camel?) I was similarly concerned about all the good book's raising of the dead (seemed messy and a problem for population control), but other than that, I was happily buckled into my front seat on the

Bible Bus. A raucous round of "Amazing Grace"? A murmuring of the rosary? A quick lighting of prayer candles or a spirited sign of the cross? I was there as fuck for it.

Thrilled with my piety, my grandparents happily forked over the monthly tuition to the same Catholic school my mother had grown up in. They did this never minding that the hefty sum could've likely funded a year of clean water for one of the suffering nations we learned about at the end of each Sunday sermon. We didn't have time for worrying about such silliness—there was stained glass to pay for and potluck honey hams to bake for funerals.

Though I'm sure you've guessed, religion didn't stick much beyond my thirteenth birthday. If you've read even a few pages of this delectable literary snack I've written, you know that this sheep has strayed far from the Vatican. But before I developed a colossal stiffy for Topanga from *Boy Meets World*, I was god's girl. He and I were one six-month anniversary away from getting matching neck tattoos together. Religion was my boo, and I was a faithful mistress.

My unshakable devotedness led me straight to the scene of a story I'd like to share. Like the other tales from my early childhood I've vomited onto the page, this one doesn't need to be embellished for the sake of entertainment.

There are certain rites of passage in Catholicism. First, you're baptized with holy water as a wailing baby, then each Sunday you're made to wear a dress so gaudy that you look like one of those trumped-up pageant tots. If you're especially unlucky, there's a matching damned hat made of some sort of pokey wicker material that could only have been forged in hell. If you survive the early childhood attire and move forward through the religion, you're certain to get whacked in the back of the head for chewing gum during church. When you're seven years old and in second grade (provided all went well scholastically in earlier years), you begin the holy journey to first communion.

Catholics may be loosey-goosey about a lot of things (e.g., drinking and background checks on clergy) but are not so laissez-faire when it comes to feasting on the body and blood of Christ. Such a sacrament is handled with the utmost ritual and routine. You are not allowed to simply fuck around and then march to the front of the church on Sunday for a taste of Jesus. Nope. You can only do so once you are well versed in the whys and the what-the-fucks of how the entire sacrament came to be. One of the major steps leading up to first communion is the first confession.

The purpose of confession is to fess up about your cache of sins. Once they've confessed, Catholics consider themselves forgiven by god. With a clean slate, you can get back to your sinful shenanigans without the weight of all the former unpleasantries pulling you downward.

It's okay to dirty that shit up again because you can hop right back into the confessional for another go.

It's actually a pretty handy ritual if you think about it.

Like, sorry about that drunken brawl. Even on my nine-thousand-dollar Sleep Number bed I barely got a full eight hours last night with all of the bloody details popping into my mind every time I closed my eyes. I'd like to go ahead and confess and cash in on a pristine conscience to start next week out right.

The rationale behind confession before communion is that Catholics are only to partake in the latter rite when they are as clean from sin as possible.

Yikes. There would be six days between my inaugural confession and first communion. The number of things that could go awry and land me right back on the damned sin wagon were staggering.

Like my seven-year-old peers, I had been attending Confraternity of Christian Doctrine (CCD) for months. Basically, CCD is a religious education program for children that shows the divine sacrifices of the lord our god via macaroni pieces glued to crosses. I think the theory goes that if you paste a chunk of dried penne to cardstock while listening to Bible stories, the lessons stick for life. The details are a bit blurry as my brush with CCD was thirty-four years ago, but I do remember that the hour-long class was painfully boring and that it really fucked with my Wednesday evenings. No matter; each week I was trotted into the basement of the church and handed over to a nun who looked as miserable about the whole situation as I felt.

For weeks, CCD prepared me for my first confession. I learned the reasons why, the steps I would take, and the potential penance I would be forced to pay. Having grown up in the church, I had known Father Tom my whole life, and boy, was he about to get an earful. Given that he'd be listening to my endless inventory of transgressions, I fervently hoped that he really did drink leftover communion wine as reported in the church ladies' rumor mill. Perhaps his being booze-soaked would soften the edge of my self-incrimination.

At seven I was mindful enough to know that I was a bit of a dick and fully expected to serve maximum terms for my many missteps. Luckily for me, the Catholic Church hands out recitations of prayers instead of jail sentences for confessed crimes. Sure, I might have been saying Hail Marys for the rest of my life, but I figured it was better than becoming a gang member with a teardrop inked under my eye in maximum-security prison.

As a Catholic kid, I had been raised with an overabundance of rules. Within the church, families were watched closely. No matter how devout the household, blunders were considered scandalous embarrassments. We were told how to dress, how to behave, how to address an audience of clergy. We were also told to pretend our families were perfect no matter their strife, and of course, what to believe. We were not to question biblical stories or rubrics. Those goddamned tales and rule sets were written in literal stone and not to be monkeyed with.

By the ripe age of seven, I was reasonably exhausted by the demands of the male-controlled church. I didn't know what patriarchy was exactly but processed what I was seeing as utter bullshit. What better time than one of the most sacrosanct ceremonies of my religious journey to rouse a bit of rebellion amongst my peers?

The plan for our protest was simple: We'd promised each other that we would refuse to go face-to-face with Father Tom. Instead, as a group, we had determined that we would go into "the box."

There are two choices for confession. You can stare straight into the eyes of the priest (counselor-client style), or you can creep into the private confessional box like a stone-cold murderer. Slinking into the box suggested a certain amount of culpability.

A child's first confession is usually done face-to-face with the priest to make the experience more personal and less scary. Second graders, already hopped up on accounts of sin and eternal damnation, are not expected to kneel in a dark confessional booth. Especially not on their first run. Sure, confessing in person may seem braver for an adult spilling their sins, but it was the opposite for kids. The room was well lit and nonthreatening. The environment was much less monster-in-the-closet terrifying than the incense-scented closet we had heard about for as long as we could remember. During our last CCD class, we toured the in-person space where we would sit knee-to-knee with Father Tom to unveil our darkest secrets.

"You don't have a choice," Sister Ann sneered to our fidgeting class. The pointed words made my hackles rise. "You will confess in here for your first time. Do not go into the private confessional."

It was another fucking thing being forced on us. Fantastic.

Now, don't misunderstand: other than a few arguments with my brothers and a recent use of the word "shit" when I dropped an M&M in the cathedral, I didn't have much to report to Father Tom. I wasn't the type of person in dire need of a private booth to ask for forgiveness of my mortal sins. In grammar school I wasn't into heavy gambling, nor did I have any marital indiscretions that needed explaining, but I still wanted the choice of confidentiality. Sure, there was no real privacy when confronting a priest who had known my voice since I uttered my first words, but that wasn't the point. The idea of anonymity for anyone in our small parish was laughable. Nonetheless, the adults who had ushered me through my religious education didn't understand that it was still my own path and that I wanted some autonomy in the decisions. Besides, I was antiauthoritarian as fuck and didn't want Sister Ann's grouchy ass controlling me.

I was on board with the religion but unimpressed by the incessant bossing. For years not much had happened to me as a Catholic. I attended church each Sunday and went to Arby's for a hot beef and cheddar directly after. That was kind of it. Suddenly, I was being commanded to confess and commune, and it felt like a lot.

I had sold my CCD classmates on the idea of stealing back our independence. We would confess. We would commune. We would do all the shit. But we would do it on our own terms. Fuck the nuns and our parents, who were trying to strong-arm us once again. And with that, we all agreed that we were going in the box for our first confession.

On the evening of my first confession, I was nervous. I had been shortsighted and hadn't even practiced good behavior that day.

Goddammit, Jessie, I thought, *you couldn't have pulled your shit together for even one afternoon?*

I certainly could've passed on smacking my brothers around after school and maybe should've held back some of the f-bombs that I had dropped like Molotov cocktails.

As my grandmother drove me to the church I silently considered lying to Father Tom. I was sure the guy had enough on his plate without hearing about my bullshit too.

I couldn't lie though. I had heard far too many stories of good Catholics fibbing during confession and then immediately being zapped with bolts of lightning. Others had been decapitated for similar transgressions. The nuns had prepared me well for the possible punishments that could come with deception during confession.

It's well-known that as far as confession goes, the priest is sort of like a mall Santa. Like, you know he's not really the one you're trying to get to, but he's an employee of the North Pole and a direct channel to the almighty. Basically, the priest is the main line to god. He's the bouncer outside the bar prescreening to make sure no one who looks like they might mess the place up gets in. He handles all the grunt-ass horseshit on the front end so that the

actual maker can focus on pestilence and scheduling the apoca-
lypse (or whatever).

Because of an unfortunate incident involving a fast-food orange drink that had left my fries, dress, and panties soggier than
I preferred, Grandma and I were running late to the confession
shindig. When we scurried into the church and I slid into the pew
beside the nine classmates I'd been attending CCD with, things
were already well underway.

"Who's already gone?" I hissed in an exaggerated whisper loud
enough to make Grandma cluck her tongue from across the aisle,
where she and a small group of parents waited.

"Jen, Sarah, Chris, and Emmett so far," Abby, my favorite of
my compatriots, muttered back. Perspiration beaded her brow,
and her hands shook where they were folded on her lap.

"They're going in the box, right? Like we planned?"

Her lips tight and eyes averted from mine, Abby shook her
head.

Fucking balls.

It was our one act of rebellion and my classmates had foozled
it. While I was busy mopping fluorescent soda out of my hoo-ha,
the fuckers had all caved to the pressure of an oppressive nun and
ditched our well-laid plan.

Now, at the time, with my Christ-washed vernacular, I really
tried not to swear excessively, but what a bunch of butt-sniffing
dickholes, I thought. I gritted my teeth and muttered the only
word that could describe my cowardly peers at the moment.

"Pussies."

I knew the word wasn't church appropriate, but it was the only
term that accurately summed up the situation at hand. Considering all the cockamamie happenings that I had read about in the

Bible, I was sure the good lord understood that there are times that necessitate some down-and-dirty vulgarity, and this was just such a case. My baby-faced allies had bailed the second things had gotten sticky with the grown-ups, thereby annihilating our mini-insurrection.

Well, I wasn't them and I wouldn't have it. Even if I had to go it alone, I would ignore the nun and our parents' insistence that I meet face-to-familiar-face with Father Tom. I was going into that dark, private confessional if it was the last thing I did.

"Jessie, it's your turn," Sister Ann said, her knotty hands gripping the back of the pew. "Remember, we decided as a class that face-to-face is the most appropriate method for our first confession."

Her brow was furrowed, and she squinted as she assessed me critically. It was clear that in my absence I had been ratted out as the ringleader of the mutinous operation.

Sister Ann could smack her lips disapprovingly as much as she wanted, but a girl's walk to confession is one she must do alone. She couldn't force me into the well-lit closet-sized room.

I'll admit that part of my anger was likely from the fitting of my communion outfit I had had the day before. I felt reasonably pissed about the garb, which consisted of shiny shoes that pinched at the toes and a lacy white dress so itchy that it set my skin afire whenever I stood within six feet of it. The only part of the sanctimonious costume that wasn't completely off-putting was the filmy veil, which I suspected made me look exactly like lady legend Cyndi Lauper.

Screw them. The defectors be damned, I was still going in the box. In a town as rough as the one I was growing up in, I needed my peers to see that I was not one to be fucked with. Sure, my acid-washed jeans embroidered with daisies and permed hair might've said I was soft, but that was dead wrong.

The life-hardened third graders who had come before us had passed down the local lore that no first-timer had ever gone in the box. Several of our elder antecedents had crossed their hearts and promised that they would, but as soon as their name was called, they spooked and skulked to the shared room.

Ignoring the nun's piercing gaze, I approached the two doors to the confessional. My chest heaved and lip quivered as I tried to slow my pounding heart. I felt the nine pairs of eyes of my classmates boring into my back. If for nothing else but street cred, I had to choose the private confessional. My sweaty palm slipped as I twisted the metal doorknob. I heard a sharp intake of breath from my grandmother as I stepped over the carpeted threshold.

Inside it was dark. Really dark. It had the smell of the cedar closet from our basement mixed with the waxy scent of candles. I also sensed a slight muted (but present nonetheless) meatball aftertaste.

I inched forward toward the interior wall until my foot bumped into something. Trembling, I dipped down as I had been taught. Immediately the lip of the thinly padded kneeler bit into my knees. I shifted uncomfortably, feeling the darkness of the confined space press down on my small back.

I won't say that I have brass balls, but compared to the other namby-pamby wusses in my CCD cohort, I was practically Stallone. Despite my nervousness, I felt a hint of self-satisfaction sidle into my smug little heart.

I was a girl of legend. I was making history. With my feathered bangs sweat-pasted to my forehead, I was saying, "Fuck the patriarchy!"

I made the sign of the cross and quickly recited the words that had been drilled into me: "Bless me, Father, for I have sinned. This is my first confession. These are my sins: I ignored my mother when she asked me to clean my room. I fought with my younger brothers. I swore. A lot."

I thought for a moment. Goddammit. I had to be completely transparent. A decapitation would really suck. FML.

"I said the word 'pussies' just before coming in here. Father, I am sorry for all my sins and for those I cannot remember."

I sucked in some of the dank air and awaited Father Tom's response.

That was the instant in which the scariest thing in the history of all scary things happened.

From far above my bowed head (from the sky, I daresay), a voice boomed in the blackness.

"Bless you, child," it said, its timbre guttural and entirely, un-expectedly, terrifyingly unfamiliar. Every hair on the back of my neck stood up, and the air felt hot and electrically charged. My throat dried and my tongue thickened. I could feel a grand pres-ence in and around the booth, and it shook me down to my trem-bling toes. The teensy room squeezed in around me. I needed water. I needed my mom. I needed to get out of there.

What in the hell was going on? What had I gotten myself into?

It wasn't Father Tom speaking. I knew his voice well and that wasn't it. The voice from the pulpit that I had heard every Sunday morning since birth had been replaced by another.

Comprehension flew over me like a vat of ice water. God was talking to me. God. I had been expecting to talk to Father Tom, my god go-between, not hear the booming voice of the actual lord himself.

Instead of being honored that the almighty had taken time out of his busy schedule to attend my first confession, I was fucking terror stricken. My heart was racing in the presence of this miracle and I was suddenly seeing stars. My breathing quickened. Each exhalation escaped in tiny puffs. Shit had gotten really real very quickly.

"As your act of penance, recite two Our Fathers and three Glory Bes," the giant voice thundered on. "With these prayers, I absolve you of your sins."

Now, Catholics have a complicated relationship with god. From an early age, you are taught to adore him but to also fear him. Being on the wrong side of the supreme ruler could get your ass roasted like a Costco rotisserie. The hierarchy was clear, and I wasn't meant to be conversing with the big guy without my priestly buffer. Grandma had been attending church for seven damned decades and had never had direct contact with god. There I was in a dark room with no sign or sound of my childhood priest. The realization that my accumulation of sins had been so egregious that Christ had bypassed his helpers to deal with my shit personally hit me like a ton of bricks. Middle management had been pushed aside and corporate officers had entered the building. Sure, it may seem like a dream come true for someone so devout to have such a holy visit, but I didn't take it to mean anything good. Mary, the last young girl that I knew god had personally called upon, had birthed a baby in a barn because some prick at the local Courtyard by Marriott refused to rent her a room. If I had been handpicked for the next immaculate conception, I was in for a hell of an end to my second-grade year.

Oh Christ. Where *was* Father Tom? How did it work when god took over in a confessional? The only frame of reference I had was the few alien abduction movies I had seen. Things rarely went well for human hosts.

I made a hurried sign of the cross, squeaked out a quick "amen," and tumbled out of the door through which I had come. When the light of the church hit my face, I began to sob hysterically. So much for street swag. I was losing my shit. Their mouths agape, everyone gathered on the pews gawked at me in bewilderment.

Unnerved by the mounting magnitude of my public drama fit, my grandmother football-carried me out of the church and shoved me like a weeping pile of dirty laundry into the back seat of the car. I was inconsolable for hours thereafter. Not even a VHS showing of *Sister Act* turned to max volume was enough to wake me from my hiccoughing mewls. Whoopi Goldberg could shake her ass as much as she wanted, but it wouldn't soothe my utter devastation. From the spilled drink to the abandoning coconspirators to having actual god moderate my first confession—the day had been too damned much.

Once my mom, altogether surprised by my hysterics when she arrived home, coaxed the origin of my wild panic out of me, she explained that Father Tom was away having emergency surgery. The voice I'd overheard hadn't been god but instead a visiting priest from two towns over who had agreed to sub. I'd missed being prepped with the rest of my class because of the ill-timed soda debacle.

Goddamned orange drink.

"No, Jessie," Mom said, raising her voice over my bawling. "Now, you definitely shouldn't be saying 'pussy' in church, but you weren't being punished. It wasn't god. It was Father Cliff."

I can't say that I believed her. Her story sounded like some shit parents made up to make their kids stop being psychotic.

The truth was I believed that god had visited me in that confessional. He came to set me on the straight and narrow. Message fucking received, Your Grace. I would not be dropping any more cusswords in church anytime soon. Staple some wings on my back, toss me a harp, and give me a thorned crown for how saintly I was about to act (for like two-ish weeks until the terror wore off).

Though I'm no longer Catholic, or religious at all, some of the guilt and tendency to fear god remains. For example, I won't utter aloud that nuns enjoy witnessing others' pain. I'm not at a point in my life where I can afford a lightning bolt to the brain. No matter though, I still believe in my heart of hearts that Sister Ann relished my confession that day more than any other in her holy career. If she were alive today, she would most certainly still be cackling away at my expense while doing quiet nun chores and eating flavorless nun food.

Fuck the patriarchy indeed.

Chapter Four

Small-Town Safari

The loud crackle of the school's PA system made me jump in my seat. My seventh-grade peers, scattered at desks nearby, were in varying stages of wakefulness, likely wishing that they hadn't traded a night's worth of sleep for PlayStation marathons. I was tired too, but not for the same reason. I had been up into the wee hours doing something actually worthwhile—making Backstreet Boys fan art.

"Fellow Grizzlies, I need y'all to take a moment from your studies to listen up for a minute," our principal boomed, his Southern accent stretched long and slow as molasses. True to the ways of small-town redneckery, he was also the middle school's football coach and worked part-time as a game warden.

With ears perked curiously, we straightened in our hard-backed chairs. We lived in the South and had been taught that when a coach (especially the head coach of the lord's sport) spoke, we were to listen.

Ms. Mays, our homeroom teacher, pressed a finger to her lips to shush those of us alert enough to be whispering.

"It's been brought to my attention by the authorities that we've got a bit of a situation with some local predators," he continued, clearing his throat noisily.

Wait. What? Predators? Like sharks? Imagine my confusion at that moment. Geography wasn't my strongest subject, but I was pretty sure that we were landlocked in Central Arkansas. Unless some true aquatic wonders had learned how to swim upstream via dirty river, we should've been in a pretty good position to never have to worry about such dangers.

"Y'all, it seems that there was an incident at Mama's Rescue this morning which resulted in the escape of several of its predatory cats," the principal continued, his voice as casual as if he were reading from the day's lunch menu. "A few of the runaways have been spotted around campus. Considering these developments, we will handle today differently than usual. Your teachers have been briefed and will go over the plan with you."

Whew. No sharks. That seemed like a bright note. Predatory cats didn't sound like a much better alternative though. I was pretty sure the animals hailing from the Pride Lands weren't only about singing and dancing like Disney wanted us to believe.

As local kids, we had all visited Mama's Rescue a time or two. In the tiny, one-stoplight country town we lived in, one so small and convenient that our single gas station also served as a bank and a Chinese food buffet, there wasn't much else going on. A gathering in the dollar store parking lot was considered a hot Friday for local high schoolers, and the only thing we had more of than trailer houses was meth dealers. Truth be told, Mama's was the one thing that made our part of the boondocks (a destitute, scabby blight on the American countryside) somewhat special.

Because of all the void acreage nary a business wanted to

purchase, a nonprofit had swooped in and claimed a hunk of land on the cheap for a displaced animal refuge. Because where do African elephants want to live more than the red-dirt backwoods of the Ozarks? Probably for a parcel of rat poison, a soft pack of Camels, and four boxes of decongestant (this is what I think methamphetamine is made of), the do-gooders had bought themselves land enough to build their altruistic haven for misfit creatures.

Though perhaps well-intentioned, Mama's Rescue was less outback oasis and more crawdad sewer hole. The facility wasn't exactly state-of-the-art. Even at thirteen, when I should've been enthralled by the wonder of a makeshift zoo so close to home, I knew the compound left much to be desired. Polar bears lay prostrate on boiling concrete on 108-degree days. The baboons looked suicidal. The bald eagles were actually bald and hadn't the energy to consider escape. Every animal on the inside looked like it needed a loading dose of Prozac paired with a baker's dozen of counseling sessions.

The poor upkeep wasn't just cosmetic either. There were gaping holes in the fencing and gates that leaned haphazardly. There were frequent reports in town that a set or two of rabid gazelles had cleared the barbed wire. We were occasionally asked to call the local authorities if we spotted a wayward emu in the grocery store or a lost-looking wallaby pumping gas.

No wonder the poor feline bastards had decided to make a break for it that Tuesday. As a middle schooler confined in a building that reeked of overheated bologna and puberty-stricken armpits, I could sympathize.

The overhead system clicked off, leaving our class in stunned silence. I gnawed at the electric-green poster paint wedged under my thumbnail and eyed Ms. Mays. She was twisting her hands in the fabric of her cardigan and swallowing hard.

"Erm, uh, like he said," she said loudly. Sweat beaded her upper lip. "Things are going to be a bit odd today. We have been given instructions on how to move from class to class. I need you all to listen carefully."

Wait a goddamned minute. We were staying at school? This wasn't reason enough to cancel classes for the day? We had just been notified that our campus was being stalked by pumas and our homeroom teacher was talking about the game plan for how she was going to carry on and escort us to algebra. If there was any time in the history of mathematics when it was okay to say fuck quadratic equations, right then seemed like the moment.

I thought of faking an illness and asking to call my mom. If she'd had any inkling that morning when she was sending me off to school that I was headed into dire danger, would she still have handed me five bucks for lunch and made me run for the bus?

Yeah, probably. It was 1995 and parents didn't care much about their kids getting mangled on the playground, be the attacker a school bully or a wildebeest. Having kids stay home from school could really get in the way of watching *Ricki Lake*.

My attention reverted to the teacher. Her throat clearing was making me nervous.

"We are going to walk in a pack. It's safer that way," she said. "Those of you that are larger than the others are going to walk on the outside of the circle as we all move together."

Giving more detail than the principal had (he had likely since returned to scratching his balls whilst reading *Sports Illustrated*),

Ms. Mays explained that an assorted quintet of panthers, lions, and cheetahs had outsmarted the park's electric fencing and was on the prowl in town.

I was a fucking goner. In mere minutes I'd be a dead girl. I had a foreboding feeling that there was zero probability I would make it to the end of the school day.

Ms. Mays glanced my way as I shifted uncomfortably and tugged my too-tight flannel top downward to cover my belt loops. There was no question that I was one of the bigger kids, and both she and I knew it. I glowered at my size-ten sneakers and thought about the note that had been sent home tattling to my parents that I had failed the school-mandated physical assessment the week before (because that was another fucked-up thing they did to the youth of the nineties). I lived in goddamned Arkansas, a place where people fried fucking macaroni and cheese. What did they expect? According to the fat-shaming educators, my Crisco-coated heart was just a few double-cheeseburger-addled ticks away from its finishing move.

I sunk deeper into my chair.

"We are gonna go slowly and not make any sudden move-ments."

Seriously?

My classmates and I were about to be released into nature with the expectation that we would battle for our lives, gladiator style. A *Hunger Games* mentality and a thirst to live would be our only saving graces. As a pale, freckled kid better at Super Mario than distance sprints, I was royally fucked. The outdoor transit from first period to algebra had never felt so foreboding.

"Everybody understand?" our teacher intoned. "Do those of you on the outside of the circle have questions?"

I swallowed hard. *Fuck yes, I have questions, bitch*, I thought maniacally. *I'm about to be slaughtered and have my eviscerated intestines eaten on the middle school playground.* I knew from multiple viewings of *Jurassic Park* that I could very well still be alive when my attacker started gnawing at my gallbladder. I assumed my insides would taste identical to that orange ooze that makes Big Macs so irresistibly delicious. So yeah, there were plenty of questions I was suddenly very eager to have answered.

"Okay," Ms. Mays said, clapping her hands together. "Let's go."

Our hearts thumped. We knew that in the next few moments, we would either be eaten or handed over for fifty-five minutes of math (neither prospect was attractive). We walked through the side exit of the school, and the smallest members of my class quickly claimed their spots in the gooey center of our humanoid pack.

Lack of prepubescent hygiene be damned, I envied their security. For them to be murdered, several of their much larger classmates would have to be disemboweled first. I liked their odds far better than my own.

"Keep moving," Ms. Mays murmured. "Stay close together."

Now, if you're thinking, *Wow, this is a real fucking problem! Children could get hurt!*, please congratulate yourself on having an appropriate response to the aforementioned situation. However, in 1995, well-reasoned thoughts involving harm to minors weren't in vogue. It hadn't yet become trendy to give an actual shit about your kids. In a year where the world had just been introduced to movies like *Billy Madison* and *To Wong Foo, Thanks for Everything! Julie Newmar*, a good old-fashioned mauling delivered by a half-starved exotic animal could only serve to strengthen character. If you made it to Y2K unscarred, you surely had missed out on some pertinent life lessons.

Ergo, instead of canceling classes as goddamned sane people would have done, we forged on. It wasn't even a consideration that perhaps we should avoid changing buildings until animal control had a grip on the situation. With my teacher tucked safely inside the inner circle of a mobile meat wall made of frightened students, we inched northward on campus.

"Jessie, move forward! Close the gap!" Ms. Mays hissed.

The balls on that woman were dazzlingly gargantuan. Teacher of the year she was fucking not. Nuzzled in safely like a queen bee guarded by her drones, she was speaking with the confidence of someone who knew she would survive the morning—a luxury I hadn't been afforded.

The desire to be obedient overcame my inner voice, which was vehemently protesting the cross-campus death march. I blew out a held breath and closed the gap as instructed.

The life I had lived thus far hadn't necessarily been impressive, but it was the only one I knew—which is precisely why the blood froze in my veins when I heard what I thought was a guttural growl from a nearby patch of trees.

The dawn of my death had arrived.

Piss on me for being a fucking 192-pound seventh grader. I was the size of our well-rounded homeroom teacher and had consumed a breakfast of pizza rolls that had settled like a rock in my gut. A half gallon of Sunny Delight, an orange so bright that it occurred nowhere else in nature, threatened to climb its way back up my esophagus. At my tender young age, I didn't have the life experience to realize that the cellophane-wrapped chocolate donuts I had chased the Totino's with had been a bad choice, but they most certainly had been.

In short, I was in no shape to outrun anything in the wilderness. My breakfast mishmash of processed foods and years of evading physical activity would guarantee that I'd be the first one intercepted by the stalking animals. I was unprepared to clothesline a lion that could tear my throat out with its incisors.

I mean, really. Who was I to battle a goddamned cougar? I was a kid who ran a twenty-four-minute mile while sucking on an inhaler between desperate wheezes. Every fucking chance I got I presented debilitating period cramps as an excuse to get out of gym class. I was willing to produce blood-soaked pads if it meant I could avoid a torturous hour of dodgeball.

My wide-leg jeans paired with dainty patent leather Easter shoes (that I had hoped would get me out of gym class) suddenly felt like very bad decisions.

And the ominous growling continued.

"Blaine! Stop joking around!" Ms. Mays snapped, jabbing his ribs while he was nestled close enough for her to breastfeed. Blaine Adams was small for our age and had been dubbed too weak for combat on the outside of the clump of kids. He would've been picked off like a diseased, elderly, cataract-riddled zebra the moment we hit the door. Safe and sound, he was in the perfect position to poke fun at all his linebacker-sized classmates who had been chosen to protect his scrawny ass.

I tried to slow my breathing and heart rate. The entrance to the trailer that housed our math class (truly) was in sight.

We continued our perilous trek onward. Apparently, the stars of fortune had aligned in our favor that day as nary a one of us had life or limb amputated. Minutes later we were able to still have a pop quiz and lived to be blessed with lasagna and creamed corn for cafeteria lunch.

I could laugh now and say that once again my proclivity for

drama may have overinflated a nonthreatening situation, but fuck that. Absolutely not. The entire web of faculty members (and my parents, who were abreast of the situation—thanks, Ma) had dangled me in front of five carnivores like I was a piece of prime rib on a fucking fondue fork. I simply cannot forgive the time I was almost eaten.

Also, just for the record, I want it to be known that if one of those bloodthirsty wildcats had knocked on the trailer door looking for an afternoon snack, I would've gladly punted Blaine's simpering ass right into their unhinged jowls. That kid was a motherfucker who went on to torture me for the duration of high school. Sure, he might not have been the meatiest morsel, but starving animals in captivity aren't often given the top-tier selection. Chef's choice (had I been cooking) would've been that little bitch of a kid smeared in honey mustard and hog-tied for convenience. Fortunately for him, the wild animals were apprehended within the week. He had enjoyed his many cross-campus commutes tucked away as safely as a fetus in utero.

Because I hold a grudge, I check my former classmates' social media from time to time. It would seem that his lucky streak didn't glimmer much beyond high school. Other than going to a few out-of-town Korn concerts in later years and winning a fair prize on some gas station scratch-offs, things have been pretty uneventful for him in the last several years. He didn't get eaten by any of Mama's residents, but he did eventually fall victim to the allure of our quaint small town's abundance of meth. He has had a myriad of girlfriends, with whom he had a myriad of children. None of those children who are school-aged today face the threat of animal refuge absconders though, as the compound was shut down years ago when a black bear was found dining on leftovers in a local kitchen.

I am happy to report that we were excused from outdoor kickball that week, as disbanding for play wouldn't have left much protection for the feeblest amongst us. Though it was the nineties and blood sport was all the rage, the school board thought it would be in poor taste to allow students to be dismembered for the sake of recreation.

Even more frightening? Because we lived in rural Arkansas, the land of guns and Civil War reenactors, word of loose wildlife unleashed a slew of eager hunters thirsting for a shot at exotic non-indigenous species. Though the armed hillbillies were threatened with jail time and fines for rogue, unlicensed poaching, the excitement in a sleepy town was too much temptation. Before long, we weren't only worried about being filleted by leopards but equally concerned about stray buckshot from Billy Bob and his second cousin Chester who had taken in one too many Busch Lights.

Perhaps weaving betwixt bullets and sharpened claws gave us just the lesson we needed though. Per my Facebook research, which yields the faces of my very much alive former classmates, we did survive our childhoods. Somehow. Furthermore, I have yet to see one account of my peers of yesteryear subjecting their own children to running a gauntlet of defector man-eating mammals. Honestly? That feels like a win.

Chapter Five

Midnight Toker

Cody and I had been holding each other for an hour, wailing uncontrollably into the soggy fabric of his bed pillows. I was pretty sure the world was ending and that Cody, two years my junior, was leaving home for good.

My eleven-year-old brother was addicted to the pot. Our mom had caught him with a bag of weed and he was being sent to rehab.

"Caught" is a bit dramatic. No crime scene investigation had unfolded. My mom didn't do much sleuthing. She didn't have to uncover any clues or grill any suspects. Cody had left a dime bag of schwag (low-grade marijuana, for anyone who didn't go through this particular phase) in his jeans pocket, and it fell out when Mom was sorting laundry.

We cried harder as we listened to our crazed mother pacing outside Cody's room, on the phone long-distance with one of her many sisters. Our terror mounted as we heard the words "police" and "gateway drug" as her voice grew more and more manic.

I choked on my sobs, thinking about my brother's guaranteed

future of panhandling alongside a highway off-ramp, doing anything to get enough money for his next toke. I had seen *The Basketball Diaries* and the murky depths that Leo DiCaprio was willing to go to for a fix, so I knew the trajectory of such things.

"Yes, rehab," my mom said, her voice glacial. "I've already called the police and he's going to rehab after he spends a few nights in jail."

Jail? The fucking clink? The goddamned slammer? By dawn my brother, who was less than five feet tall, would be linked up to a chain gang, cleaning the public sewers (I think that's what they do).

Now, as an adult looking back on this story, I of course realize how utterly full of shit my mom was. The phone call outside the room was meant to scare the ever-loving piss out of us. My mom had not, in fact, called in the cops or the DEA, nor did she have any intention of sending Cody to rehab.

But at that moment? Oh, Trish's threats were real as fuck. I knew for certain that my druggie brother was about to be carted away by the goddamned FBI to an undisclosed location to have the marijuana waterboarded out of him.

"I love you so much," I whispered into his sweaty hair, memorizing the feel of his hug. My nose ran and slick tears slipped down my freckled face as I felt his heaving cries intensify. "I'll help you pack, okay?"

I tossed a new dental floss from the bathroom drawer into his Ninja Turtles suitcase. I'd never seen my brother floss before, but I was sure he'd have extra time in rehab to develop new habits. The very thought made me burst into a fresh set of tears. I envisioned Cody's skinny arms sticking out of a rehab-issued jumper holding a harmonica to his cracked lips (he didn't currently play an instrument, but, like flossing, I was sure he'd learn).

"Buddy, I know you have a problem, but I'm here for you and I will help you through this," I said bravely.

I wondered how the situation had happened to our family, to my own little brother. Hadn't he listened to a single fucking thing the DARE people said when they visited our school? Christ almighty, was he in a gang too? Was he one street kill away from a fucking teardrop tattoo? Had he gone against everything those safety officers had taught us?

I stared at his fifth-grade form with regret, admitting to myself that the current situation wasn't his first brush with deviance.

There had been other infractions.

He'd recently been caught lying about being on X-rated sites on the internet. When my mom accused him, he denied the charges with the sincerity of an innocent man. As soon as she produced a stack of freshly printed pornographic images, he balked. I don't know what he had planned on doing with all of those grainy images of boobs and vaginas, but I assume he was planning a scrapbook with a spread-eagle theme.

When he'd left the printer to grab his nuked snack out of the microwave, he'd completely forgotten about the print jobs. He inhaled his lavalike, mouth-blistering Hot Pockets (or some such nineties bullshit), fell into a game of *Mortal Kombat 3*, and never returned to claim his hedonistic treasures.

I also knew for certain that he had taken my new copy of *Teen* magazine with Alicia Silverstone on the cover. When I had found it wedged between his mattress and the wall, some of the pages were stuck together with god only knew what (as an adult, I now have a pretty solid idea of what made my commandeered periodical stiff enough to stand on its own).

The minor transgressions were in the past though. Magazine theft suddenly seemed like a petty crime. My brother had moved on to the hard stuff (still talking about pot).

The only other drug addict I had ever known was *Saved by the Bell*'s Jessie Spano during her three-day caffeine pill addiction. Horrified, I had watched the honor student's dangerous spiral. If it had gone on much longer, viewers would've likely had to watch Jessie offer Mr. Belding a BJ for a twenty spot to buy more drugs. I can't even begin to imagine how much that would've fucked up A. C. Slater, not to mention what it would've done to the show's ratings. What if Belding had been into butt stuff? How far would Jessie have gone for the caffeine equivalent of a double espresso? It goes without saying that that had been a very bad week at Bayside High.

If it could happen to every parent's dream, Jessie Spano, it could happen to anyone. If Jessie had really been as smart as her GPA boasted, she would've, like, drunk two cups of coffee instead of taking the pills, but that wasn't the point. The point was that the pills owned her ass and she lost control.

Because that's obviously how addiction went. One second you're in a girl band singing your little heart out, the next you're the evening's headliner at the sex shop glory hole, welcoming cum shots for spare change.

"The police are almost here," we heard Mom shrill into the phone's mouthpiece. "Yes, they'll definitely handcuff him. Only bread and water. Uh-huh. Uh-huh. Yeah, a huge rat problem too."

It was about to be full-tilt *Jerry Springer* in our house and there wasn't shit we could do about it.

Fear made my stomach clench as Cody's hiccupping cries

filled the room. I folded his Spider-Man underwear into tiny triangles, focusing on the task at hand. If my brother had to leave, it would be with neatly arranged cargo pants.

"People survive this stuff, Cody," I said. "You don't have to become another statistic of marijuana."

I gave his hand a reassuring squeeze as he nodded numbly.

"That's right, they said he'd have to share a cell with a murderer tonight because the jail is so full," my mom said, her shadow flickering beneath the door. In an age when cell phones hadn't yet been introduced, Mom was tethered to the wall. Nonetheless, she was making damned good use of the phone cord's length to stomp back and forth in the hallway.

"I don't know for sure what happened," she commented. "Something about killing a kid in a drug deal gone bad. You know how those things go."

My brother turned a grayish color and swayed where he sat on the bed.

"Fuck this. This bitch has gone too far," I said, my tears drying. No goddamned brother of mine, junkie or not, was going to be sleeping next to someone capable of homicide.

I turned toward him.

"I think maybe you have to run away," I said.

I scurried through the Jack-and-Jill bathroom to my dresser, where I had a roll of dollar bills I had saved from my birthday; rushed back to Cody's room; and thrust the money at him.

"I agree that you need to go to rehab because of the addiction," I whispered. "But the jail part isn't right. You've gotta get out of here before the cops come."

A decision made, I tugged shut the zipper on his suitcase and stood up.

"Now, Cody!"

I hugged him tightly and pushed him toward his window.

Just as Cody was about to sling a leg over the sill to begin his life as a transient, our mom burst through the bedroom door.

Her face was red. The phone she held in one hand dangled at her side. She stared into our swollen, tear-streaked faces and sighed.

"I called the police back and told them to hold off," she said. "I'm going to give you another chance."

Cody and I exchanged a look, and we both exhaled all of our pent-up air.

"He can stay?"

"For now."

"Do I still have to go to rehab?" Cody asked.

"Probably," our mom answered haughtily. "We will talk about this more tomorrow."

Goddammit, Trish and whatever asshole sister you were talking to, that was some cold-ass, next-level, evil-as-hell, mean-fucking-mom, shank-in-the-prison-yard, dirty-fighting bullshit.

Before I left Cody's room that night, I asked for my money back. Birthday cash was a hot commodity, and if he wasn't going to rehab, I wasn't giving it up. Besides, now that he was addicted, I didn't want to be responsible for funding another one of his drug runs. I wasn't sure how all of it worked, but I had a suspicion such things required a donkey and a surreptitious border crossing. I didn't want any currency that could be linked back to me involved in such criminal undertakings.

A new sort of bond formed; Cody readily handed back the cash I'd gifted him for a life on the run. We hugged again and went to our respective beds for a fitful night of sleep. Cody fell asleep glad to be on his own mattress instead of blanketless on a hard cot in county lockup. Relieved to still be able to afford the Girl Talk game board with bonus zit stickers I had been saving for, I passed out as well.

I'm going to be honest here: the fear from my mom's threats only had a temporary effect. A few years after the Great Drug Debacle of 1995, Cody reunited with his old pal Mary Jane.

What I'm saying is, just like with Jessie Spano, who eventually went off the tracks again when she played the naked lead in *Showgirls*, the threat of life ruination by drugs only lasted so long. Soon enough my younger brother was back to smoking and toking and a pot-littered life. I'm happy to say that though he crossed certain thresholds our DARE coach warned us about, he manages to keep a full-time job. To my knowledge, he has never traded a rim job for weed.

A valuable lesson *was* learned that fateful night though. He never left his shit in the laundry again.

What Mom couldn't find, Mom couldn't send him to prison for.

Chapter Six

Pizzazz AF

The sharp tang of imitation leather stung my nostrils. My borrowed motorcycle jacket crackled as I moved around. My eyelids felt heavy beneath caked layers of eyeliner and shadow. I could feel the thick coat of hair spray in my hair rustle. I tugged at the miniskirt cinched like a python around my thighs and let out a long breath.

Over the course of my outfit changes, I had sported sequined tube tops, bangle bracelets to my elbows, an off-the-shoulder neon sweatshirt, and enough stonewashed denim to outfit a Kid Rock concert. I had been picked at, prodded, plucked, and painted.

I fluttered my mascara-thickened eyelashes, feeling glitter rain down. I was sweating and painfully aware of the orange-hued foundation that had been spackled to my face as it streaked in rivulets.

Being so goddamned gorgeous wasn't easy.

"This is my favorite look," a woman intoned, a finger to her chin as she examined my twelve-year-old physique.

"Oh yeah," my mom gushed, practically bouncing on her chair. "This one is *so her.*"

I glanced down at the cheap moto jacket and the plunging black tank top underneath it. To my horror, the pleather skirt squeaked against the stool. As a sixth grader, I had very little expertise in makeup and beauty. If my mom and the Glamour Shots style artist said that my trademark look was biker girl, I had little choice but to believe them.

I squinted at my friend Rose where she sat in front of her own stylist two booths away. She had also been made up to resemble a lady of the night, albeit a different version. Instead of the gunmetal, studded look that I wore, Rose had been swathed in a gauzy coral-colored wrap. When she twisted to glance back at me, yards of organza bunched in what looked like a perpetual shrug. It was all very grandma chic (another look that had been intentionally accomplished but that I didn't entirely understand).

Rose appeared like she'd had the shit beaten out of her by the Golden Girls' closet. Earlier in the session, I had listened to her beg to wear the ivory feather boa that was slung across a nearby mirror. The adults in the room had unanimously decided that the feathers were inappropriate for girls our age. Prior to the discussion, I'd had no idea that plumage was so slutty. Though still mildly confused, I was glad to now be informed enough to avoid such overt sensuality in the future.

I had pitched my case for a rhinestone-covered cowgirl hat but was told that we were going in a different direction with my look. As it turned out, the specific direction they were referring to was modeled on the style of a woman committed to being pinned on the back of a Harley behind a beefsteak of a man called Bubba. I was nervous about the way I looked, but what did I know? Again, I was only twelve; I certainly wasn't the expert on aesthetics in the room.

Either way, Rose and I both looked sensational, even though we seemed ready to offer Friday night specials on a street corner. With enough Exclamation perfume to kill a dolphin drizzled on my throat and wrists, I even smelled like a call girl.

I had never been assigned my own personal stylist before, so when Tiffany, wearing an apron brimming with makeup brushes and powders, had approached me at the beginning of my session, I was sure I was in good hands. The snowy frost of her lipstick and the impressive height of her bangs were sure indicators that she knew what in the hell she was doing.

"Pizzazz," she had whispered, nodding her head with her lips tight around her front teeth. "We're going for pizzazz."

The words had inspired terror in my little heart. I had never considered myself a pizzazz kind of girl and was worried about the steps it would take to get me there. The woman may have sensed my hesitation.

My mom, herself a confident queen routinely dressed in animal print and glitter, had immediately taken the side of the Glamour Shots employee.

"Pizzazz!" she parroted in an awestruck tone. "That's exactly what we need!"

Granted, my mom needed pizzazz more than anyone I knew. She was perpetually tired from working the graveyard shift in the emergency room, where she spent her nights helping detox drunks and being screamed at by drug seekers. She needed some pep. Even more, she needed sleep, fewer bills, and, in the moment, a daughter who wouldn't resist a chintzy makeover.

"Do it," I grumbled, the warble in my gravelly voice betraying my fear.

Tiffany had taken my permission and pizzazzed the hell out of me. In the hour that I had been under her control, I had completely transformed into an entirely different twelve-year-old.

The adults in the room were thrilled with the results. They oohed and aahed over my hair (formerly flat and mousy), my face (previously freckly and pale), and my costume. I had been metamorphosed into a big-haired, ginger-faced, scantily clad courtesan and they couldn't have been more pleased with their work.

In all fairness, I was lucky that my mom had taken notice at all. Early in the makeover session, Rose's mom had parked herself in a nearby chair to chain-smoke and devour a romance novel. I was curious about the long-haired man on the cover who was wearing a shirt that looked as though it had been torn to shreds by a ravenous wolf pack. With his head thrown back in what I now know was a look of ecstasy, he didn't appear bothered by his state of disarray. Rose's mom, her cheeks tinted pink and her lips partially parted, was enraptured by the creased paperback on her lap. The Glamour Shots employees could have outfitted her daughter in a candy thong for all she cared.

"Are you ready to take your pictures?" Tiffany asked.

I was definitely not ready. Nonetheless, I let the bubbly stylist lead me by the hand to another part of the large room. My nerves gurgled in my belly as I spied the makeshift photography studio.

Near the far wall was a set of stairs carpeted in material that closely resembled my grandmother's velour couch. The steps, a photo prop as it turned out, led to nowhere. Behind them, a backdrop had been erected. The canvas was so glitzy, and such a contrast to the discombobulating carpet, that it was hard to take in all at once. From what I could tell, someone had shot a unicorn point-blank in front of the wide canvas. The unicorn's insides (which were obviously made up of pink bubbles and candy and happiness) had sprayed across the backdrop, creating a quagmire of shooting stars and rainbows.

What could be a better complement to my studded leather jacket and mass of frizzy hair frozen in place by an entire can of LA Looks hair spray?

"Get comfortable on the steps," Tiffany ordered.

Get comfortable? For Jesus's sake, Tiffers, my adolescent brain shouted. *My vagina is seconds away from popping free of this skirt.*

I was certain that neither Naomi Campbell nor Cindy Crawford had to take such crap at photo shoots. Tyra most certainly wouldn't have stood for such nonsense.

I shot a pleading glance at my mom.

"Listen to her, Jessie," she said, nodding. "She's a professional."

It was in that instant that I realized what a tradeswoman my stylist really was, because lo and behold, Tiffany was not only a gifted makeup artist and fashionista, she was also the person in charge of taking photos. It hardly seems fair that in a world of so many people, the Glamour Shots employee was so rich in talents.

She did a quick check of the film in her camera while she waited for me to comply.

"Climb up, sweetie," the stylist-turned-professional-photographer said, checking her bedazzled watch.

I froze as I assessed the three steps in front of me.

"You're fine, just hop on up there," she urged again.

With a hand strategically shielding my ass, I half-shimmied, half-squirmed my way onto the faux staircase. The garish rug burned the miles of exposed skin on my forearms and upper thighs as I awkwardly settled into position.

My mom nodded approvingly. I could see the pride of having a daughter-turned-biker-babe twinkle in her hazel eyes as she watched my every move.

"Do these ever get looked at by professional modeling agencies?" she wondered aloud.

"Oh, absolutely," the photographer bragged. "One of our girls actually ended up on a commercial for the local Refrigerator Barn not that long ago."

A wide grin splitting her face, my mom gasped in awe.

"Act natural," the stylist said, her face eclipsed by a large camera.

Because what could be more natural than a prepubescent teen wearing full leather while draped over a shag staircase?

Accompanied by a trickle of sweat that had slid its way down my waistband, the microskirt began to roll upward. I grappled with the synthetic fabric, my hands fumbling with the hemline, which seemed intent on exposing my lady goods.

"Show more teeth," the photographer barked, growing impatient with my wriggling.

"Jessie, stop fidgeting," my mom chided. I could see written all over her face the fear of losing her dream of me posed in front of discounted appliances.

Sucking in a deep breath, I bared my teeth to the lens in front of me. For the next thirty minutes, I twisted and posed and tried not to lose my stifling costume to either the pull of my gut or the tug of my legs. I grinned and fluttered my eyelashes and tilted a shoulder seductively.

When I was finally allowed to dismount the staircase, I did so with utmost care. The fake leather had become progressively less forgiving with each pose I was ordered to strike. When I was finally allowed to change back into my Ninja Turtles T-shirt, I breathed a sigh of relief. I knew I had been the very beacon of beauty, but the entire act had been utterly exhausting.

As the photo package my mother had purchased whirred out of the printer, I stared at the images of a face completely foreign to me. My hair, still stiff from product, and my makeup, which had begun to dry and flake, were the only reminders I had that I was indeed the girl in the photographs.

"Do we leave a picture with you for talent scouts, or how does that work?" my mom asked, handing Tiffany one of the photos. The glossy image featured me presenting as many of my pearly whites as possible, which caused me to look startlingly similar to a feral hyena freshly emerged from its cave. "Will they call us if they want her to model?"

I touched my lips, crusted with frosty pink lipstick that felt way too dressy for my culotte shorts. I was a twelve-year-old girl but felt somehow changed into a woman by the power of that scintillating Glamour Shots studio.

I waved goodbye to Rose as she finagled her way onto the steps that I had conquered before her, and I clutched the photo packet to my chest. I stared longingly back at the leather jacket flung over a chair, wishing I had savored my time as a biker goddess a bit more.

"Thank you so much," I whispered to Tiffany, feeling the coats of makeup shift as I mouthed the words. "Thank you."

Shockingly enough, I never did get a call from Refrigerator Barn or any other discount outlets for a modeling job. My mom and I were certain that they would see my photo pinned on the shop wall and line up for an opportunity to feature me in commercials pointing to dented microwaves and advertising kids' toothpaste.

Alas, such dreams never came to be.

Today, I don't know any women my age who didn't have a Glamour Shots photo shoot. If you ask nicely enough, all my forty-something-year-old friends can dig up pictures equally embarrassing and equally garish as the ones that I took in that studio in 1994. We felt pretty and worthy and desirable in the pictures, where we were made to look like baby hookers. We were sexualized before we even knew what being sexualized was.

So let the forty-one-year-old me speak up for a hot second here to address how ridiculously fucked up all of this is. As a mom now, I am certain that I am screwing my daughter up in all kinds of creative ways, but dressing her like a sex worker isn't one of them.

In my mom's defense, I had begged for the makeover. Rose and I had plotted and planned and had even made a pretty convincing poster board presentation highlighting why we deserved the day of beauty. Our mothers hadn't put up much protest against the request either, because, well, we were right—everyone was doing it. The exploitation was wrong, but it was a societal standard of the time, and my best friend and I were happy to leap lemming style for it.

And sure, so long as I'm being fully honest, maybe I would be less negative about the situation if I had indeed made it to stardom via a Refrigerator Barn commercial.

Later in life, I bought a biker jacket of my own, in real leather. It was fitted like the one I wore when I was twelve. It even had the same dizzying number of zippers at the elbows and a zigzag collar. No matter; it never did hold the same magic (even when paired with Fizzy Peach Bellini frosted lipstick).

Leather jacket or not, I learned that you can't just re-create the kind of sparkle I had in that Glamour Shots studio back in 1994. Even if I could find Tiffany and her apron of congealed brushes wherever she's probably selling insurance today, that type of pizzazz just isn't reproducible.

Today, in a modern age of selfies and vanity videos made for social media, I am now well used to being a star (at least of my own life, until I had kids). Sadly, my sixth-grade counterpart would be both shattered and horrified that I have given up on glamour altogether. The little girl who ardently prayed that she would grow up to be as bewitching as the novice vixen at the mall photo shoot would shed some dramatic tears over my modern-day uniform of stretchy-crotch sweatpants and fire department T-shirts stolen from my spouse's side of the closet.

Despite her grave despair over the state of her future, I know she would be secretly glad that we never mounted that bike behind Bubba and his skullcap. She would also be pleased that we became a writer instead of a prostitute. Being a lesbian though? That might really surprise her. Young me wasn't a homophobe but she had pretty fucking high hopes of marrying Devon Sawa. Had my first-choice heartthrob not been readily available I would've gladly settled down with my backup draft pick (Jonathan Taylor Thomas) so long as we lived in a hot-pink house with baby-blue shutters.

Yeah. The gay stuff might've taken a minute to settle in.

Chapter Seven

First Love

I had finally made it. Fourteen years without romantic love and I had arrived. My dry stretch was over. As I leaned against the round hay bale, my home-bleached hair the same texture as the scratchy straw behind my adolescent back, I grinned into the Arkansas sun.

The scene was nearly perfect. I wore my favorite set of dark-wash overalls with a shiny new pair of hunter-green Doc Martens laced to the calf. The melon and green stripes on my long-sleeved thermal popped. My highlights were on point, freshly done by my best friend with a four-dollar L'Oréal Paris Chunking kit, and my sexiness was unmistakable.

"Jordan, get the angle right," I sniped at my brother, who I was certain was royally screwing up all the body shots he was taking. Forgetting to be breathtakingly gorgeous for a moment, I glared at him over the shuttering click of the disposable camera I had bought at the gas station that morning. I couldn't be sure that the photos would be bad, but I guessed I would have plenty of reason to kick his ass in a few days once the local Walmart developed the film.

"I'm trying. Gimme a break," he griped, flicking greasy strands of his bowl cut out of his eyes.

My youngest brother, unused to being deemed useful by me, grunted from where he lay on his belly in the grass, angling for the perfect shot.

Huffing, I tilted my freckled chin toward the sun, hoping that despite the amateurish talent of my help, my true beauty would speak for itself.

Jordan's lack of skills and the cheap disposable camera would just have to do. It was the 1990s and instant photos were rare. My family wasn't fancy enough for a Polaroid camera, so there was no shaking of fresh snaps for us. Luckily for me, OutKast hadn't yet released "Hey Ya!" into the world, so I had no real grasp on what I was missing. Instead, we filled out paper forms at the photo center, watched the pimpled clerk smack Big League Chew as he reviewed the information, and waited seventy-two agonizing hours to see the prints.

It wasn't even that Jordan was necessarily a shitty photographer. At ten years old, with no pressing engagements of his own, he was just the best option out of limited choices to serve as my assistant for the afternoon. But without any formal photography lessons, he had proved to be more trouble than he was worth.

I wasn't being picky just to be a bitch. The pictures were important. I wanted my internet boyfriend, Mark McDowell, to see what a true catch he had reeled in from the vast pond of online options. I knew the cyber world was teeming with plenty of dating choices for an Australian grocery store clerk and I wanted to prove myself worthy.

Even more? Mark was twenty-seven years old. Thirteen years his junior, I was certain that our age gap made our relationship even more special. I mean, how many adults find their soul mate in grade school after they themselves graduated nearly a decade prior? What are the odds? In our time spent together in a seldom-occupied chat room entitled "Belarus," we shared our hopes and dreams. I wanted to pass algebra. Mark wanted to find discount beer after work.

Never was there a more beautiful, fitting match. If only sweet Mark had lived closer than nine thousand miles away . . .

Now, as an adult, I realize the abhorrence of this relationship. I mean, obviously. I have young children, and if a grown adult even looked at them sideways, I would make short work of removing their genitalia with the unopened melon baller I received as a wedding gift fifteen years ago.

But we were not so enlightened as kids in the nineties.

I can't count the times I received an online message from a strange handle to the effect of, "I'm 13f too. What color are your panties?"

Even then it seemed like a weird-ass question coming from another pubescent teen, but who was I to judge other girls my age? I just assumed that we were all weird in our own quirky ways. I was glad to divulge this if it would help my new friend with her social development. Sure, the young voyeur appeared weird as fuck, but I wasn't going to throw shade on her journey.

Mark was different though. He told me he never talked to such young girls on the internet, but there was just something magnetic about me. Of the millions of adolescents swarming the web in droves, I was truly unique.

I believed him because I was pretty sure he was right.

Our daily talks were the highlight of my ninth-grade life. I anguished as I counted the hours until our conversations and couldn't wait to see his screen name pop into our private chats. LuvfromMark1 knew exactly how to talk to me in a way that kept me gripped in awe of his superior intellect and chat room finesse.

Keep in mind that this relationship occurred in the days before emojis and memes. We had to converse with real words. It was next-level shit, and my teenage mind was blown.

The real pain in the ass was finding time to talk. Mark had a busy schedule, and ninth grade in the United States was rigorous (lies). I felt lucky for every minute I could steal with him. His Australian social life appeared to be packed, and the demands from his friends that he attend parties and outings really interfered with our blossoming relationship. Not to mention the perils of the grocery store. He was, like, mere years away from being promoted to assistant manager. The pressure was huge.

Alas, when you find your adolescent true love living half the globe away, still very much under her mom's rule, things can be tough. Of course, Mark could commiserate about my plight as he too still lived at home, in his parents' basement.

As my little brother plucked the twigs off his cargo pants and bellyached about not wanting to miss that afternoon's episode of *Family Matters* because of "some dumbass photo shoot" for my "dumbass fake boyfriend," I let my thoughts wander to the care package that Mark had sent me in the mail. His gift, full of pictures of himself, Australian candy, stickers (as grown men often gift their girlfriends), and a key chain (which wasn't super useful considering that I was still several months from being old enough to get my learner's permit) had thrilled me to the core.

In his letter, scrawled on purple stationery, was a passionate declaration of his love for me and an invitation to fly to Australia to live with him.

Because I was a jobless bum of a fourteen-year-old and about $1,692 short of the $1,700 I needed for a one-way ticket to Oz, I settled on sending him a care package of my own.

My ninth-grade school photos were far too babyish for such a sophisticated man. Hence the field, the Doc Martens, the layers of dollar store mascara, and the photo shoot being sullied by my bitching little brother.

"Just a few more," I snapped back, bristling at Jordan's mockery of my relationship. LuvfromMark1 was many things—suave, gorgeous (per the blurry photos he'd sent), noble, full of integrity—but he certainly wasn't a *fake* boyfriend.

My brother shrugged and snapped a few more photos to pacify me.

"Are you really gonna move to Australia?" he asked.

"Probably. If Mom says yes."

My reasoning that there was a chance that my mom would let me live out the rest of my youth in a foreign country with a strange man wasn't entirely unfounded. Though Mark had suggested we keep a lot of the details of our romance between just us (it was more romantic that way), she did know I was spending odd hours chatting with a "boy" on the computer. She just didn't know that the boy had a five o'clock shadow and a drinking problem.

In hindsight, I think maybe she should've thrown a few questions my way.

"Hey, kiddo, is your internet boyfriend in junior high too, or has he aged into an auto insurance discount?" or "Do you know better than to send half-naked pictures across the world?" Perhaps even a warning worded like, "You know that it would be very dangerous to give an online stranger our address, right?" would've sufficed.

Maybe during the conversation with my mom when I asked for money to send a package to my damned-near-senior-citizen virtual lover, I should've been told no. Perhaps she should've stripped me of my internet privileges and detailed the potential repercussions and dangers of talking to people online.

But my mom was no cockblock and never one to stand in the way of love. Besides, the hypocrisy of ripping my relationship at the seams would've been criminal considering the current state of her romantic affairs.

You see, even though this may sound crazy, my mom had also found love online. As if by magic, one late night, between electronic shuffling of solitaire, she had stumbled into Richard Stonebreaker. Several private messages later, she and the well-muscled fireman who lived in a mansion in Key West were practically engaged. I hadn't met many millionaire firefighters in my day, but as a juvenile, my experience was limited. My mom didn't think it was odd that she couldn't call Richard at certain times and had to send a private code word to his beeper before he could talk. Apparently, there are a lot of super top secret elements to working at fire stations (especially for those who also work as part-time spies).

What's crazier still? My aunt had also been blessed with an internet boyfriend that year. Her virtual beau, coincidentally another Australian, was also a millionaire who had earned his money as an internet mogul. The details as to why he always needed my aunt to send him money transfers on Fridays were a bit grainy to the rest of the family. Nonetheless, we were thrilled for her.

Now, I'm not saying my family is special, but it certainly seemed as though the true-love gods were working in our favor that spring.

I had Mark. Mom had Richard Stonebreaker. Aunt Susan had

her boyfriend, whom my grandma affectionately referred to as "the male gigolo." We had all seen pictures of him in a Speedo swimsuit that covered little of the parts that my aunt spent most of her hours imagining. Again, I was no expert in things like male anatomy at my young age, but I certainly didn't think that my aunt's gentleman caller had what it took under that yellow thong to make a living from his manly services.

In the days while I waited for my photos to develop, I gathered mostly household items to send to Mark. My lover from down under would be gifted with a collection of Lisa Frank stickers, the first love letter I had ever written, some perfume samples from a magazine, and a homemade frame featuring a picture of yours truly.

Seventy-two hours later, I begged my mom to drive me to Walmart to grab my photos (this would've been another excellent opportunity for her to intervene). When I picked up the snapshots, I was furious to find several images featuring my younger brother's thumb and even more that featured what appeared to be a ball sack. When I asked him what the mystery photos were of, he laughed maniacally and ran away.

What can I say? Little brothers are asswipes.

Luckily, there were a couple of shots that showed the true magnificence of my slightly pudgy, awkwardly posed, acne-littered, fourteen-year-old frame. I chose the best of the lot, painted my lips with a layer of sparkly Lip Smacker, kissed the glossed photo, and taped it into the frame I had painted.

Three weeks later, when Mark got my package, he messaged me right away. I had been waiting on pins and needles when his screen name flashed in my instant messenger.

Mark thanked me for the stickers, the love letter, and the

perfume samples. He didn't say anything about my picture though—even when prompted. In the same conversation, he apologized and told me that we needed to break up. He had met another girl who lived in his own time zone and she was crazy jealous. Sure, she was a little younger (than me even), but she was definitely mature for her age.

When Mark signed out of our Belarus chat room that night, it was the last I ever saw or heard from him. My heart broke as I searched more heavily populated rooms for someone else to talk to.

I guess I wasn't the pinup of a ninth grader that he had hoped for. I mean, even I was realistic about the fact that I was no Brooke Shields circa *The Blue Lagoon* or even pouty-lipped teen star Jennifer Love Hewitt, but come the fuck on, LuvfromMark1.

That was pretty damned cold. It certainly didn't do much for my already rickety self-esteem. Some internet predators are ill-mannered as fuck. I'm putting the blame for that on poor upbringing.

Today, with nearly thirty more years of experience under my belt, a few things are painfully evident to me about my first romance. Here I sit in the twenty-first century equipped with a safe-driver discount and life experience enough to know how truly fucked up the entire situation really was.

I am lucky as shit that I didn't end up on a milk carton or nailed into some creep's basement. What in the fuck was my mom thinking? What the fuck were all our parents thinking? Trust me when I say that I wasn't the only damned ninth grader with a serious online boyfriend.

I wish Mark nothing but male-pattern baldness and the burning acid reflux that comes with age. If he isn't totes bald, I at least hope his comb-over is super uncooperative.

Furthermore, I'd like one more crack at a chat room conversation with my Aussie admirer. Once I logged into our Belarus meeting spot (after listening to the telltale whine of dial-up) for a final go, I would say something akin to:

Mark, you are a true fuckling and a bit of a child molester. I hope with all my heart that you experience some sort of genital rash each month that makes it nearly impossible to wear pants. If the To Catch a Predator *show had existed in 1996, you and that Chris Hansen guy would've had a very uncomfortable on-camera conversation.*

I have said what I needed to say. May your penis have trouble rising and your beard always be sparse. Good day, sir.

One nice thing about me? I don't hold on to bitterness. As a result, and because I'm totally over it all, I'm not still mad at my internet sweetheart or my younger brother. It would be silly to still be holding such a grudge three decades later. I mean, what a waste of goddamned energy and headspace.

But, if I'm really going to reflect on what happened, I still blame Jordan and the fucked-up pictures he took. If he had gotten my perfect angle, with the right amount of sunlight glittering through my hair . . . if his photos had highlighted the green lace-up boots and the zing of my freckles against the melon shirt . . . things could've been different. I might not have lost my chance at becoming a child mail-order bride.

Like I said, little brothers really are asswipes.

Chapter Eight

My Heart Barely Went On

Disclaimer: If I were a normal girl, writing a normal book, there wouldn't be a whole chapter entirely focused on fictional film characters of the late 1990s. But, as you've come to learn, there's no direction in which this story is afraid to wander. The movie discussed in the subsequent paragraphs was a formative cornerstone for the person that I have become. Sure, I'm embarrassed as shit that I must admit such things, but the truth is the damned truth. If I were going to practice any restraint or decency in this history-making literary masterpiece, I would have done so several pages ago.

If you're a woman of a certain age (my age), you'll readily admit that the most erotic moment in cinematic history was when Rose and Jack stood at the stern (helm? Bow? Who fucking cares?) of the *Titanic*. The wind in her face, dress fluttering, Rose DeWitt Bukater spread her arms like a woman ready for crucifixion and rode the front of that ill-fated ship like it was a sticky mechanical bull at a dive bar—all with the hottest man of the decade gripping her waist behind her. Talk about every female member of my generation popping a big ol' lady boner. Imagine how confusing that was for me, a budding bisexual at the time. I mean, goddamn, I was left cripplingly confused over the giant lust chub I had for both Kate Winslet *and* Leo DiCaprio. Whoever would I have wet dreams about that evening? That shit isn't exactly easy to navigate at fifteen years old.

I remember moments of hiccoughing sobs shared between my best friend and me after watching the movie at the theater for our sixth time. We weren't sad about the actual people who died in the actual 1912 tragedy. No. We were far too vapid for that. We were, however, entirely consumed by the freezing of the iconic star that we had fallen madly in love with over the three-hour drama. We were living on a planet so cruel that it would dare splinter the truest love we had ever seen. Caroline and I would lie prostrate on Caroline's bed, clutching each other when we had strength enough, and relive Rose and Jack's story over and over.

In the way that teenagers do so well, we writhed in the histrionics of it all. Wailing like milk-starved infants at the severing of the doomed couple's love, we would try not to be angry at Rose for not making room for her newfound lover on the palatial door on which she had taken residence. Their relationship (though less than ninety-six hours long) was one for the stars. That fucking dickbag of an iceberg ruined it all! Goddamn you, punishing ocean and your subzero temperatures! Why couldn't the *Titanic* have had a more tropical destination? Screw New York! Barbados is nice as fuck. The most dangerous thing on that route would've been some frolicking porpoises and maybe a sprightly pirate or two. Jack was young and healthy. He could've slapped on some baby oil and treaded until help arrived. A run-in with a cheery dolphin or jaunty buccaneer would've resulted in little more than a quick song-and-dance number (as detailed by Disney). The point is that the moviemaking dreamboat most certainly would've survived. Had the *Titanic* headed into hospitable waters, Jack and Rose could've lived the American dream (instead of crushing my teenage dreams).

Needless to say, the movie shattered both Caroline and me emotionally. I'm not saying we were wholly healthy in the mental department to start with, but the film was the final straw to send us on drama spirals. In my third theater viewing, with my arm elbow-deep in a tub of popcorn, I cried so hard that a movie theater usher shone a flashlight in my face. The poor minimum-wage worker's mouth fell slack when he saw my mess of tears, wadded tissues, and butter-sludged fingers. I couldn't bear seeing the ship sink into the abyss (again), but still I watched. As Rose promised to never let go of Jack (while quite literally letting go of his frozen hand), I keened in the darkened cinema.

"Are you okay?" the theater employee asked.

I wasn't.

Since we're on this particular topic, another thing must be said: it's indisputable that there was room for Jack on the door. Like, no sane person is ever going to fight you on this. The door was goddamned ginormous. Beyoncé, her backup dancers, and a baby grand piano could've easily fit. But that's not the point. The point is that Jack was so enamored with the ruby-haired heaven-sent treasure (Rose) that he wouldn't dare disrupt her comfort. He wanted his lady comfy as fuck and was willing to freeze to death or have his balls eaten by a shark to maintain her agreeable position. The man was made into an ice cube by the Atlantic, but he set the bar high as hell for all future suitors before he succumbed.

I mean, Christ. Instead of doing what everyone else would've in the situation and saying, "Bitch, I'm gonna need you to scooch over and be the big spoon for a minute. I'm cold as shit," he was all, "Here, my golden sparrow angel, rest your hallowed brow on this pillow that I wrestled from a deep-sea piranha while I tread water until I die."

And it must be said, so that I don't get harassed by movie-buff fanatics shouting facts from the comfort of their mom's basement, even though everyone on the planet calls the thing that Rose floated to safety on a door, it actually wasn't. It was, in fact, according to Director James Cameron and a ten-second internet search, an ornamental wood panel. But screw facts. In my mind, it was a giant-ass door with plenty of room for two.

No matter, goddamned late-nineties romanticism can't be beaten. That's another thing that shouldn't be fought.

I have little doubt that my wife loves me, but she won't even fucking share an order of Nachos BellGrande with me. I promise you that if we were in a situation similar to Rose and Jack's, she would hop on that door right next to me (splashing water everywhere) and demand that I muss my hair so that she could survive.

Fucking ridiculous.

Again, I readily admit that there are some embarrassing elements here. The fact that I could twaddle on for an entire chapter about fucking *Titanic* is a real problem. An even bigger issue? I'm not alone in this passion (nor has it ebbed with the advancement of my age). I have an entire army of female members of my generation who share said obsession. It's fucked up, we know, but as we are all still trying to regrow our eyebrows, which were taken by the early 2000s, we have more pressing problems to address.

When *Titanic* finally came out on VHS, like everyone else I knew, I bought it immediately. As it was super long (two hundred minutes), the entire film wouldn't fit on one cassette; therefore *Titanic* was sold as a beautifully packaged duology. If you're wondering if I displayed that shit in my living room like it was a piece of fine art, I can confirm that I most certainly did. I'd also like to put this here, and I'm going to say it with pride: I was a Tape One person. Tape One contained everything before the iceberg. All the fun and smiling and sexing and naked artistry and flying on the boat front (aft? Stern? I still don't fucking care) happened on Tape One.

Tape Two people, who liked the sinking and relationship-crushing parts, were and remain fucking monsters. If you are a Tape Two person and loved the part of the movie that made my teenage self catatonic for weeks on end, I can say with certainty that you are likely the same kind of person that kicks kittens for fun and tells three-year-olds that there is no such thing as Santa. I will not sully this story further by saying more about this type of person.

Nowadays, there are people on TikTok making very real, very impressive amounts of money driveling on about *Titanic*. I'd say few of the followers of such fact traps are historians. Instead, they're women like me. A small, slightly ashamed group of ladies nearing forty are starting to give in to the fact that we need strict skin care routines and that we no longer belong in tanning beds. At our advanced age, many of us are now realizing that we have the unfortunate ability to smack other people in the face with our newly developed bat wings. Not so unlike Jack Dawson, we are now treading unfamiliar waters.

A recent reshowing of *Titanic* in theaters made all my memories of fierce loyalty to the movie return. People who had still not emerged from the pandemic unearthed themselves, paid the outlandish price for a movie ticket, and reclaimed their spot in front of the big screen for another go at the iconic romance and all the nostalgia it promised. Forty-somethings dragged their own teenagers, the same age now that we were when the film was first released, to experience the awe inspired by the most illustrious movie of our time.

And sure, we may no longer have young bodies hot enough that anyone is willing to draw us like one of their "French girls" for a dime, but we are now old enough to not give a shit. It goes without saying that if Jack Dawson showed up from his watery grave with charcoal and drawing pad in hand and gestured toward that velvet sofa, all bets and panties would be off.

Draw us, Jack. Just be kind about our wobbly bits. It has been nearly thirty years since you sketched your last muse, so it'd be wise for you to note that nowadays we rely heavily on filters, touch-ups, and Photoshop.

Chapter Nine

Dental Dam

If what I was seeing on MTV was a true representation of society, I had it on good authority that men were sex-driven scallywags. In a world where artists like Eminem and Nelly were prime examples of the fellas whom we would soon be dating, we needed to do some very real prep work. Ergo, my two friends and I were nail-biting in my rusted Chevy Cavalier in front of the local health department trying to psych ourselves up enough to go in.

I was the ringleader of the afternoon trip to a town near our high school. As the daughter of a night-shift emergency room nurse, I knew all too well the perils of having unprotected sex. On mornings after the ER had been swarmed by underage girls with abdominal pain of unknown origin who turned urine-dipped pregnancy tests positive, my mom would shake me awake to go over the fundamentals of intercourse. Before I hit my teenage years, I had the details down. I knew to be terrified of sex and understood that the very thought of sperm or penises could yield nine months of gestation. An underwater penile emission resultant in Jacuzzi jizz? Well, that could buy you a lifetime of parenthood. Touching a penis? A surefire way to become some-body's baby mama. Putting a penis in your mouth? You were guar-anteed throat herpes that would eventually give you esophageal cancer and kill you.

Crazed by sleeplessness and pregnant teens, my mom would flip on my bedroom light and quiz me.

"Jessie, can you get pregnant from the first time of having sex?"

I would rub my bleary ten-year-old eyes and nod. "Yes, Mama."

"Does it have to feel good to count as sex?"

"No, Mama."

"Should you ever, ever have sex without protection? Ever?"

"Nope. Can I go back to sleep please?"

"Take a quick look first," she said, holding out visual aids I was all too familiar with. She had a tattered stack of homemade flash cards that bore gruesome pictures of a variety of sexually trans-mitted diseases. She flicked through them, flashing each picture, awaiting my response.

"Late-stage genital herpes," I said robotically, my mind waking up to the oozing image.

"Good girl!" she'd say, beaming.

"Chlamydia." I grimaced, staring at the angry, reddened penis tip jeering at me from the matte surface of the card stock. "HPV, syphilis, trichomoniasis."

"Good, good, good," she replied.

"Bed? Please?" I begged, feeling my skin crawl from the image of pubic lice she had paused on.

Mom tucked the cards into her scrubs pocket, nodded, and kissed my cheek. "Birth control is power. Abstinence is even bet-ter!" she would pump her arm and sing before letting me snuggle back into the bedsheets.

The graphic flash cards and roundtable talks were precisely why I was sitting with my terrified friends in an idling car outside the ominous-looking health department.

"We need birth control, girls," my sixteen-year-old self stated wisely. "If we're going to have sex we have to be prepared."

My fretting friends, usually willing to go along with whatever plan I set forth, shifted uneasily. I tried to ignore that they both looked like they wanted to puke.

Truth be told, we were a bunch of dorks. We wrote articles for the school newspaper and snorted over inside jokes that didn't even make much sense to us. We were our own group of utterly misunderstood weirdos. I wore a pair of nonprescription thick-rimmed glasses and pencils poked through the messy bun atop my head. My shirts were mostly polyester blends that I'd handpicked from thrift stores. The look I had meticulously achieved was "poorly dressed elderly man circa 1964." I made no attempt to tame the wildfire of frizz that was my hair. My girlfriends weren't far behind me in style or sleekness. No one, and I mean no one, was offering the three of us sex. There was no chance of any of us being propositioned, thereby making the birth control (and the after-school trip) entirely pointless.

The one time that the trio of us thought we were being catcalled by a couple of plumbers outside a local gas station, we felt repulsion and flattery in equal parts. We were more than a little disappointed upon realizing that the crass louts were directing their attention to a different, long-legged, blond woman, directly behind us.

Nonetheless, we had called the clinic number and used pseudonyms to set up back-to-back appointments.

"I'm not ready for this," my friend Elle whispered miserably. "I'm sorry."

"Are you ready to live below the poverty line because of an unplanned pregnancy?" I quizzed her, hearing my mom's lectures buzz in my ears. I pictured a brochure that she had recently left atop my pillow that had bulleted statistics referencing as much. According to my mom and the pamphlet, once a teen's pregnancy test showed a little blue plus sign, life was officially over.

"Do you want to forget your dreams of higher education and marry our high school quarterback, who'll work for minimum wage at Dave's Pizzeria for the rest of his life while you breastfeed a set of triplets?" I prodded.

"Our quarterback is, like, uber-hot," Elle answered.

He really was.

"That's not the point!" I practically shouted, my voice shaking from my passion for the topic my mom had crammed down my throat over the years. "Everyone can carry incurable STDs! HIV doesn't turn a blind eye just because the quarterback is hot as shit!"

"I think I might just not have sex," my friend whimpered, staring at the foreboding building before us. Our other friend, Sara, nodded in agreement.

"Maybe we should just join that abstinence club at school," she added helpfully. "If we don't do it, we can't get STDs."

My heart raced harder as I realized that my friends wouldn't be entering the building with me. It had never occurred to me that they might wimp out of our birth control pact.

"Are you with me or not?"

Both girls avoided eye contact with me as I flung open the car door and stalked into the building.

Once inside, I took a page from Sara and Elle's book and averted my stare when anyone glanced my way. My eyes skimmed over the waiting room occupants as I walked to the front desk to check in.

"I'm Myrtle Poppins," I said through the receptionist's window. "I'm here for my appointment."

The middle-aged receptionist stared at me over her bifocals and arched an eyebrow. "Myrtle? Poppins?" she asked incredulously.

"That's right. Eighteen-year-old Myrtle Poppins. That's me."

With quivering hands, I signed my fake name on the paperwork she held out.

On the desk next to my elbow sat a giant tub of condoms. Thinking of my chickenshit, unprotected, chaste-for-the-moment friends hunkered down in my car outside, I looked back at the secretary.

"Are these free?"

"Yes, dear."

I shoved handful after handful of the free rubbers into my purse, nearly emptying the jumbo bucket. Pretending to ignore me, the receptionist typed furiously, likely thinking about the wild orgy I had planned for later that night.

"You can never be too prepared," I commented, nodding curtly as I dropped two of the condoms back into the bucket. I didn't want the entire state of Arkansas to have to freeze the extracurriculars of their genitalia because I had been a glutton.

"Myrtle Poppins," a nurse called from the door. No one moved from their plastic seats. She scanned the lobby and called the name again.

"That's you, honey," the receptionist reminded me.

Once inside the exam room, I was handed a scratchy paper gown and instructed to remove everything, panties included.

That was when I really started to sweat. Why in the hell hadn't I asked my mom to take me to our family doctor for my first Pap smear? She was the biggest birth control advocate on earth and would've been elated at the responsible request. Mom would've eaten that shit up and probably would've even swung me by the smoothie shop for a celebratory drink afterward. Instead, I was posing as Myrtle goddamned Poppins on an exam table that I was certain hadn't been sanitized in the current century.

No matter and no regrets; the deed was nearly done. All I needed to do was survive the exam and collect my arsenal of protection. No penis would be my emotional or vaginal health's undoing. (If I knew then what I know now . . .)

"Okay, Myrtle," the doctor said. "Are you ready?"

"Ready to be prepared? Ready to be responsible? Yes, ma'am, I sure am."

To this day, I swear that the weary-looking physician rolled her eyes before inserting the metal speculum that I prayed had been cleaned better than the room.

The health department doctor, who likely had gone into the business to help people but had encountered one too many Myrtle Poppinses to still care, examined and scraped cells from my cervix with an itty-bitty spatula. The appointment was as horrible as I had expected.

"It's easier if you relax, Ms. Poppins," the doctor said tiredly.

Sounds great, Doc, I thought. *But it's a little hard to deep breathe when you're grating pieces of my nether regions off with something that should be used exclusively to flip pancakes in a fairy garden.*

Before I knew it, the speculum was out of my vagina and the doctor was out of the room. I lined my panties with one of the clinic pads that Dr. Personality had left to catch the drippy lube goop, put on my clothes, and walked back to the parking lot. My friends' eyes bulged at the overflowing bag of prophylactics I lugged into the car. I waved a three-month supply of birth control, condoms, and shrink-wrapped dental dams (whatever the fuck those were) in their faces.

"You two are a couple of fucking traitor wusses," I spat, shifting uncomfortably on the mountain of cheap sanitary napkin digging into my ass.

"Was it as bad as we thought it would be?"

I refused to dignify Elle's question with an answer. Her price for backing out on me was to wonder. Forever.

But hell yes it was as bad as we thought it would be.

Even though there was still no one who wanted to have sex with me, I popped a little white pill into my mouth and chased it with a swig of Mountain Dew. My friends stared in awe at the womanly act, their mouths ajar in pure wonder.

I had been the first of us to get my period. Now I was the first of us to harness it with a pharmaceutical lasso. I was woman (sort of), hear me roar.

I'd follow the same daily pill routine for years before I had a chance to see if the oral contraception (or any other) worked. Regardless of the protection I had, no one was eager or willing to bed a girl with my particular quirks and clothing choices. I was a virgin due to a lack of outside interest for years after my visit to the clinic. I still regularly fell victim to my mom's barrage of grotesque visual aids and invasive questions for years to come. After my first Pap smear, I answered her with the wisdom of a woman on the pill. I had grabbed my reproductive future by the horns.

You may be interested to know that Elle did marry the high school quarterback, RJ. The happy couple didn't end up having triplets, but he is celebrating his twenty-second year at Dave's Pizzeria in the town where we graduated. Sara is a neuroscientist and likely has had her first Pap smear by now. The fact that my two old friends are now mothers is a strong indicator that each engaged (at one point or another) in unprotected sex, thereby completely ignoring my and our fifth-grade health teacher's warnings. Like my high school friends, I too have engaged in the debauchery of bareback sex since my inaugural appointment all those years ago. The world did not end, nor did I end up with syphilis.

I recently had to pay a visit to another health department to have a health check and lab work done for my current job. Though a Pap smear wasn't part of the requirements, often people who visit hospitals, like I do, have to undergo yearly screenings and immunization updates to ensure that they're safe to be around patients. The thought of entering the building was enough to make my palms sweat.

I was still quite afraid when I walked through the flaking-painted double doors of the ominous building. Unable to use a fake moniker as I needed the results to go to my employer, I allowed Myrtle Poppins to remain retired and whispered my own name when asked. Gay for most of my adulthood and monogamous with my spouse for a decade and a half, I was still tempted to load my pockets with the free offering of condoms scattered across the receptionist's desk. With a plethora of prophylactics at my fingertips, I was awash in the memory of the young girl who was convinced someone, someday, would want to have sex with her.

Someone did, and it was fucking awesome.

Also, even in my brilliance earned from years of experience, I still don't really understand how a dental dam is supposed to be used.

Chapter Ten

————————

Unbeknownst Queer

Let me clarify something: There was never a time when I wasn't queer. There was, however, a superlong stretch in my life during which I had no idea that I was. My friends were gay, most of the people I admired were gay, my family was pretty sure I was gay. I was super attracted to women and androgyny in general. Even with all of that, it never occurred to me that I was queer.

It's quite baffling, to be honest. It's like this secret that I was keeping from myself that I was completely unaware of. I wasn't opposed to being lesbian. Not at all. It just didn't cross my mind.

My opinion about the few penises I encountered was lukewarm at best. I thought that they generally smelled like lunch meat (I've since been made to understand that that was likely due to the hygiene routine of the penis's owner) and avoided them at all costs.

If you have a penis of your own, good for you. Please continue to use it to your liking with absolute pride. I don't mean to impugn what is possibly one of your favorite features. It's just not necessarily for me. I'm not anti-penis or anything. I don't pump signs up and down outside of grocery stores that say "Down with Dick" or throw paint on the pants fronts of male strangers. I'm just super stoked that I have a vagina instead. Truth be told, if I woke up with a penis in a freak accident one morning, I would likely scream until I died.

Again, I like my subcompact vagina. Everything is basically contained on the inside and I rarely worry about her misbehaving against my orders. There's no unexpected rising or falling or boning. What can I say? I'm a girl who appreciates predictability. A penis, with all its unruly habits, would send me spiraling into panic over its eventual unanticipated next move. I can't have that kind of unpredictable craziness in my life with all these Toaster Strudels I'm making for breakfast and Lunchables I'm lovingly stuffing into my refrigerator.

Anyway, the blatant misunderstanding of my own sexuality made my dating life very, very funny. I liked hanging out with guys—doing dinner, catching movies, singing karaoke, taking shots, and talking to them—but when it came to the ends of dates, I fervently wished for a spontaneous, oozing cold sore to save me from any potential expectation of a make-out sesh. I was made fun of for years by some of my closest friends for my habit of high-fiving guys at the end of the night. While my date was anticipating the opportunity to touch my boobs, I was busy cementing my scheme of sliding out of his car with a goodbye fist bump.

Don't get me wrong. No one has to kiss anyone. Ever. Furthermore, sex is up to the parties involved and should never be expected. No one should feel pressured. But sometimes it *is* expected and sometimes there *is* pressure. On a fifth date that goes exceptionally well, like when you discuss the hobbits' Shire at length and connect on a fundamental level of nerdiness (just an example), people start anticipating a more naked outcome than "Great dinner, dude. See you on the flipsies!"

I think I wanted to be someone who made out. I wanted to be less awkward. I wanted to want to hook up. I dated a lot. Like, a lot, a lot. But I didn't have one-night stands. I didn't even have sex with the people I dated even though all signs pointed to the fact that we had arrived at that point in our dating relationship. The train had stopped at Doing It Station, I just wasn't punching any tickets. My best friend, Caroline, always talked about how I always had one boy or another around. They sort of trailed after me until they realized they were more likely to get to third base with their own grandmas than their girlfriend (me).

My deliberations on the whole sex thing sort of circled around the thought: *You want to put your what where, sir? Oh no, no, no. That sounds terribly unsanitary.*

When I was twenty-two, there was one guy—we'll call him Nick—and he was karaoke-bar famous. Now, that might not seem like a huge deal in a town with more stoplights and fewer hillbillies than ours, but for where I lived, Nick was, like, McGriddle big. He worked at the only karaoke spot in town and drew a decent Saturday night crowd. In between announcing the next gaggle of singers and reminding patrons to tip their bartender, he reserved plenty of time to croon some covers of his own.

He was pretty good. The voice that came out of him was a complete, velvety surprise. Just a few years older than me, he was tall and bald and cute in a way that was endearing but that you didn't really want to admit to your friends. He wore a leather jacket and drove a motorcycle without a helmet. I guess my younger self found something thrilling about a guy willing to risk brain damage to look cool. Each night Nick had plenty of girls who paid the door cover charge mostly to swoon over him.

He barely glanced their way.

For whatever reason (it certainly wasn't my charm), he started paying me special attention at the bar. He waved away my friends' and my five-dollar bills for admission. He began sending over drinks. I'd catch him grinning at me between song sets.

Goddammit, is that fuckwaffle staring at me again? I'd think irritably, trying to hide behind my pyramid of Smirnoff Ice bottles.

Here's the thing too: I could've done worse than Nick. In fact, I had just recently done worse than Nick when I dated a guy for two months who spent his weekends playing Ghostbusters with his friends. Not the video game. Like, they actually wore jump-suits and homemade power packs and ran around the woods hunting Slimer.

The relationship ended shortly after a day in my apartment when my then boyfriend asked me which of the original cast of *Ghostbusters* he reminded me of. When the only name of the original cast I could remember was Egon, I knew we were over.

He had been hoping for Peter Venkman, and let me tell you, he was no fucking Peter Venkman.

At the point in my life when I came onto Nick's radar, I was bitter about the recent breakup. I didn't care about much other than the free rum and Cokes that he sent my way. I begrudgingly laughed when my friends teased me about him and slurped my grenadine-infused liquor good-naturedly.

"He's not looking at me. Seriously, stop!" I'd whine, sincerely hoping that I was right. I didn't have time between my binge drinking and sleeping in to be the crush of the local karaoke guy.

But something about my awkward rendition of Britney Spears's "Oops! . . . I Did It Again" made poor Nick sweep into a hurricane of Jess lust.

What can I say? It happens.

Despite my lack of encouragement, Karaoke Nick zeroed in on me. Not one for subtlety, he pursued me like a rat after a slice of supreme pizza in a dumpster.

Though mildly flattered, I did my best to dissuade him from liking me. I grimaced when he addressed me and insisted on paying my way into the bar despite his insistence that my money was no good there. When he wouldn't take my five bucks, I would roll my eyes and pass it to whoever was in line behind me. My friends, enjoying my discomfort, encouraged him at every opportunity because they were (and remain to this day) total assholes.

"If this gets weird, I won't be able to come to this bar, and I happen to love this bar," I bitched to them.

Well, despite my meager efforts, shit eventually got weird.

It was Saturday, and Caroline and I had made our rounds at the local strip of bars. We had done shots out of glasses made of ice. We had dunked cheese pizza in ranch. We had drunk so many margaritas that our throats were sore from the cheap tequila.

"Karaoke bar?" she suggested, lifting an eyebrow in question.

"Dammit, fine, whatever," I groaned. She knew me well enough to know that I was excited to visit the bar but she also understood my complaining.

"He's sweet, Jess," she answered. "Be nice."

"He's a dipshit."

Caroline rolled her eyes and steered me toward the neon lights of the karaoke bar.

"Nick's girl!" the bouncer exclaimed, his face red and breath beer scented.

"What? No!" I said, my feminism flaring. "I'm not his girl."

Caroline smirked at the bouncer as he looped wristbands around our outstretched arms.

Though he was performing for his small-town tangle of lady fans, Nick waved and winked at me from where he stood gyrating on the bar's stage. Acid from my swirl margaritas climbed precariously up my throat as I ducked my head to avoid the stares of the people looking to see whom he was grinning at.

Because I was a major-league drinker and it was payday, I hit the bar hard. Caroline and I ordered shot after shot of things that tasted like apples and licorice. I tossed a glance at Nick and was happy to see him stuck behind the turntable frowning at piles of song requests scrawled on paper napkins.

Whew. He was occupied and I could drink the rest of the bar's offerings in peace.

That was the case until it wasn't.

I recognized Nick's voice mumbling in the microphone and blissfully ignored whatever the hell he was saying. Moments later I regretted that decision.

His throaty timbre belted out the lyrics to "You and Me" by Lifehouse. Caroline, who had been busy talking about what a jerk-off the bartender was, had stopped midsentence. Her eyes were saucer sized and her jaw had dropped as she stared at the space behind my shoulder. In the same instant, I felt the back of my neck heat up.

"And I don't know *whyyyy*, I can't keep my eyes off of *youuuuuuu*!"

The sultry string of lyrics floated into my ear.

Horrific realization turning my blood cold, I slowly rotated on my barstool.

What in the actual fuck is happening?

Nick was kneeling on the ground in front of me, his fingers encircling the microphone. His blue eyes were sparkling like goddamned glittering stars as he stared at me adoringly.

Oh, Jesus Christ. My face flamed as thoughts tore through my brain. *Is he fucking singing to me?*

Indeed, he was. He was serenading me like Michael Bublé in his prime-time Christmas special on NBC.

The entire audience was captivated as the love story unfolded before them. The handsome singer discovers the biggest mess in the bar (one desperately in need of a capable knight astride a trusty steed) and woos her with his vocal stylings. It's a tale as old as time. I was seconds away from throwing up my night of strawberry-flavored concoctions.

I am a person who loves attention, but I like it on my own terms. Nick had steered me right into a situation that made me want to run into oncoming traffic.

As polished as ever, I tried to swivel my chair back around. I don't know precisely what my plan was, but I do know that the need to escape was great. Caroline, who was seldom helpful in such situations, giggled uncontrollably and shoved me into the spotlight. I tumbled right into the arms of Nick as he huskily glided through the wholly humiliating lyrics.

His eyes twinkled like freaking celestial starlight as he held me tenderly. The Sinatra-smooth power ballad of my nightmares wouldn't end though. He continued singing, dipping into the lyrics about all the things I did being beautiful and right, as I lay mortifyingly limp in his embrace.

But nothing in that moment was right or beautiful. Least of all me, the drunk girl with a spinning head, mere seconds from puking on a grinning audience.

The spotlight burned straight into me like a lamp in an interrogation room. My frozen blood was being heated to the temperature of molten lava.

The romance that I had skirted for months had plucked me from my bitter bunker and thrown me onstage. The margarita swirl undulated in my gut again, threatening to make Nick's performance one of the most memorable the bar had ever hosted.

The song lasted what felt like a million years. The clapping that echoed from the bar walls lasted at least three times that long.

As the last chords faded, Nick delivered me back to my stool like the blushing damsel that I was (limp from sheer shock and humiliation) and strode back to center stage.

"Do you think she'll finally agree to go out with me?" he warbled into the microphone. His comment was met with amiable chuckling from the jolly drunks around him.

Before the next smile he flashed my way even made it across the room, I was already pushing Caroline through the exit. Bar tab be damned, I hauled ass out of there like I was on fire.

The next morning, when I woke amid a confetti of fast-food wrappers and an unforgiving headache from tequila mixed with Captain Morgan, there was plenty on my mind. Of all the craptastic people I had recently dated (they weren't having to take numbered tickets like at the DMV, but there were plenty), why was I so opposed to Nick? Sure, he and his particular anatomical configuration weren't really my cup of tea, but I didn't know that then. Instead, I'd spent the summer courting a guy who asked for gas money when he picked me up, and another who wondered aloud if I was jealous of Caroline because she was so much prettier than me.

Another winner had quite literally ditched me for a dude (a cute dude, but it still sort of pitched my suddenly nonessential vagina and me into a bit of a shame spiral as we stood there holding the new couple's drinks while they danced).

"I think I'm gonna go now," I called from the sidelines, hating to disturb their explicit club raunch grind to "My Neck, My Back" by Khia. "Gonna head on home."

They didn't mind. They were too busy having a fully dressed public hump sesh to notice the silly girl trying to find a table to use to stow their half-drunk vodka tonics.

I'd given all three of those jackasses more chances than they deserved, so why not Nick? Why not a guy who had tried to woo me in a totally endearing rom-com meet-cute she-gets-the-nice-guy-at-the-end sort of way?

After careful thought, I can only conclude it's because I was once a self-punishing dumbass. I wanted to have a good time. I wanted to drink and hang out with my friends. But apparently I also wanted to bitch about the planet being a mean place devoid of love. I couldn't do that if congenial guys with good intentions were serenading me adoringly. Sweetness didn't go with my brand.

As a drama queen, I didn't need a decent guy fuzzing the lines of my cynicism. I didn't want nice. Nope. Instead, I wanted to suffer happily and singly.

But it maybe would've been okay to hang out with someone who would've opened doors for me instead of slamming them in my face. Sure, I would've lectured him about my being a strong woman perfectly capable of letting herself into a coffee shop, but

I would've done so whilst in awe of how utterly not terrible he was. Accolades to his mom for not turning out an absolute fuckhat of a human.

Slow clap for that lady.

And sure, for one million reasons (top ranking being my fondness for clam diving), Nick never would have been it for me. But I should've taken note of his kindness instead of ducking in embarrassment.

If time travel existed and I could zap myself back in time, that night in the bar with that kneeling singing guy might've gone differently. If forty-one-year-old Jessica could pop back into that scene, I would most certainly embarrass my young adult self by reminding her to stay put and have some goddamned manners. I would finish the lecture by calling Nick a nice young man and reminding him to drive safely. I absolutely would slide in a lecture about the extreme dangers of motorcycling without helmets for good measure as well.

Capitalizing on the stolen time, while there I would pull former me into the bar bathroom to fill in her eyebrows.

Before leaving in a plume of time machine exhaust, I would gift my early-aughts historical self with some wise advice to the tune of, "Girl, no one needs to wear three fucking camis. Stop with the layering already. You're generating way too much dirty laundry for someone who doesn't even own a goddamned washing machine."

Before snatching the ever-present plastic bottle of liquor out of young Jess's hands, I would say one last thing: "And you don't have to marry this guy, but be decent to him. Stop and see that this nerdy karaoke bro with a crush is being far kinder to you than you've ever been to yourself."

And fuck it. To save that confused girl some trouble I would just get down to the nitty-gritty before returning to my present-day house with three kids and a mortgage. Because lord knows that time-traveling me has to fix all the messy shit.

"Boo boo, maybe take a gander at why all these relationships with boys are dead ends. Can we please skip to the good part and start touching boobs already?"

Chapter Eleven

Cruising for Ladies

When I came out of the closet it was no surprise to anyone (except me). As soon as I realized it though, I wanted a fucking announcement of billboard proportions.

You know how people at stores wear name tags that say, "Ask me about our money-back guarantee!"? I wanted to sport a sign plastered across my face that said, "Ask me about my gayness!"

Rooftop shouting wasn't enough. I wanted to soak in my new-found queerness. I wanted to swim in it. If someone wore Birken-stocks or rainbows (before sorority girls descended on them, they were both sole property of first hippies, then the gays), I wanted to run up to them and do a secret handshake. I was the queer club's newest inductee, and I was thrilled about my membership.

In the way other people ask for organic spinach at the grocery store, making sure others around them are aware of how wholesome and health-conscious they are, I did the same with my sexuality.

"Were these grown on a lesbian banana farm in Kansas? I only buy homosexual-raised fruit. You know, because I'm gay."

I'd say it all to the poor guy stocking produce, hoping that my phone would ring so he could hear my Ani DiFranco ringtone in case he wasn't 100 percent convinced that I was lesbian.

"What's that, ma'am? What side do I want with my chicken-fried steak? Well, whatever the gay folks are having. I'll have two of the queerest side salads you can find."

In short, I was not fucking around with outing myself.

But the news was just a blip on the universe's radar. Because, you know, compared to all the global warming and genocide and things that actually fucking matter, not much had changed.

My years of listening to Tegan and Sara, the Indigo Girls, and Melissa Etheridge had forewarned my family like a flaming siren. To say that they were flummoxed by my declaration is a gross understatement.

"I sort of assumed when every single boyfriend you brought home was gay that you were too," my mom said offhandedly directly after I revealed my newfound status to her. "I've known for years."

She went right back to reading her copy of Oprah's magazine.

Well, shit. I hadn't wanted to be thrown out of the house or spur on a hysterical Old West–style shooting scene, but I had certainly expected my news to be more interesting than whatever goddamned Oprah bloody Winfrey's favorite brand of linen pants was. For Jesus's sake, Trish. Give me some kind of reaction.

My bestie was the only one who provided the satisfying fanfare that I so craved. She hadn't been surprised either but was still good to go on the abundance of coming-out celebrations.

She was so supportive, in fact, that when we went on a cruise for my twenty-first birthday, she agreed to spend the entire five days trailing after a group of lesbians who were vacationing together. We didn't speak to them (as normal folks would've done).

Instead, we watched them from afar like they were exotic animals. We ducked behind pillars and avoided all eye contact any time they looked our way (which was often, because we were fucking following them). I studied their movements, laughter, and grazing habits. I learned that lesbians love piña coladas any time of day and eat a lot of buffet pizza at two a.m.

I had been thrilled to learn that there were actual gays mixed in with the throng of elderly people in Bermuda shorts on our trip. To say I obsessed over them isn't saying enough. By the second day of cruising, I had fallen madly in love with one in their ranks. She was a tall blonde with short spiky hair and muscular arms. Caroline and I were certain that I was destined to spend the rest of my gay life with her. The blonde, whom I assumed was unpartnered, was vacationing with what appeared to be two female couples.

Please note that at this point, I had never even kissed a girl. Beyond my watching *But I'm a Cheerleader*, I had little idea of how the whole lesbian thing worked. I knew I was one, but the logistics (especially where legs went whilst scissoring) were all a bit foggy to me.

On one of the last nights of the cruise, while we headed to the top-floor nightclub, I decided I would make my move. I swore I wouldn't disembark that fucking glorious boat without making out with the tall blonde.

My hype girl and best friend forever agreed.

"This is the night!" she said, running a lip gloss wand over her lips and smacking them together. "You're going to mug down with that bitch before we leave this boat or I'm pushing you over the side!"

I adjusted my push-up bra and accepted her offered tube of

peachy gloss. Fuck yes. Mugging down (early 2000s for "making out") was in my very near future.

Caroline and I were bikini cute and in our early twenties, and, admittedly, a minority on the ship. Most of the other passengers operated under full Medicare coverage, so, to the few other younger people on the boat, we were golden unicorns.

My bestie and I settled in a corner of the club to strategize. Project Integrate Jess into Full Lesbianhood had begun. I kept the blonde, my uninformed future victim of awkward fumbling, in my peripheral vision as we plotted.

"Crap," my best friend said, interrupting our scheming. "Dammit, I think Mustache is coming over here."

Ugh. Unfortunately, while we had spent the week stalking the quintet of lesbians, I had developed a devotee of my own. Caroline's boyfriend had joined us on the trip (we generally ditched him early in the night in pursuit of my lady lover), so she was mostly safe from the charms of onboard admirers. But me? One of very few single female travelers stuck on a boat with a sprinkling of young, vacation-horny fellas? I was fair game.

"Fuck!" I said loudly as I watched a guy with a thin mustache wind his way through the crowd toward us. "Not now, you fucker!"

We had spent the week dodging his winks and attempts to converse, but apparently, he had vowed to make his move that night too.

Caroline giggled and I panicked as Mustache crept closer. I had psyched myself up to lay my lesbian game down and I'd be damned if I let him squash my mojo.

"Act like you're crying!" I growled at her.

"What?!?"

"Act like you're freaking crying, dammit!" I whisper-screeched. "Please."

Stalling her laughter, Caroline began howling as if someone had shot her dog. Like an Academy Award winner, she sniffed and wailed and rubbed her eyes dramatically. Just as Mustache made it to us, she laid her head on my shoulder and let sobs rack her frame.

"Hi," Mustache said with a tawdry grin as he bobbed his head to the beat in the club. "I'm Bryan."

Caroline's artificial sobs heightened.

"Hi, Bryan," I answered, distracted by the choked mixture of giggle-wails on my shoulder. "This isn't the best time. My friend is really upset."

Twisting his mustache with a finger, Bryan squinted at Caroline's theatrical scene. "Do you wanna dance?"

What the hell? I was clearly dealing with a mental crisis and this douche thought I wanted to goddamned waltz.

To punctuate the situation, Caroline wept louder, yowling like a toddler robbed of his blankie.

"Bryan, my friend is crying."

"How about a drink?"

Goddammit, Bryan, you and your mustache are fucking clam jamming me like nobody's business, I thought. *Get the fuck out of here.*

"No," I answered. "I'm going to take care of my sad friend."

"But—"

At his protest, I yanked Caroline and her lunatic laughing onto the dance floor. My courage crushed, we ordered a lineup of shots and danced our asses off until I was drunk enough to find my bravery again. The night was ending when I saw the blonde stand up from the booth where she and her friends had been sitting. The two couples beside her began gathering their things.

"It's now or never," I slurred. Caroline nodded staunchly and nudged me toward their table. Both our lipstick and my inhibitions were long gone.

Looking like I do at the end of a night of drinking like a sailor and dancing like a *Footloose* cast member, I ambled my way toward the table that the lesbians were quickly vacating. My sweaty hair was pasted to the sides of my face and my pit stains were on point.

Unable to meet my crush's gaze, I instead looked at the older couple she was with. They were adorable, with near-matching haircuts, and wore similar utility shorts and polos.

What the fuck were early-aughts lesbians keeping in all those pockets? Screwdrivers? Dental dams? Pocketknives? Travel-size cans of Axe body spray? I still had so much to learn.

My stomach tilted nervously as I licked my lips and mentally drummed up my delivery.

"I just have to say that you two have inspired me all week long," I finally gushed after a painfully long period of staring blankly at them. "I think you're both so beautiful and I just came out of the closet and seeing a couple like you two together and obviously so happy and in love makes me hopeful."

I was painfully aware of my Bud Light–scented breath as I rushed through the ill-rehearsed speech.

The five lesbians at the table exchanged bewildered looks. They stared at my flushed face and fidgeting hands.

One of the women in the couple I had just addressed finally

spoke up. "Sweetie, we aren't gay. We're all married with husbands at home. This is our annual girls' trip."

The others nodded as my heart ceased to beat. Feelings of ice and fire and the urge to vomit tornadoed through my keyed-up body as I stood there, unable to move. I wished for a medical emergency to steal me from that moment, in front of those five women. For the first time as an adult, I nearly shit my pants, and genuinely would've welcomed the messy distraction.

Caroline, standing a few feet behind me, just out of earshot, sensed my panic.

"Time to go," she sang, whirling me around on my heel.

At the sound of her voice, my body reengaged. I used her interruption of the most mortifying moment of my life to sprint the fuck away. Grabbing our purses, my ride-or-die clacked after me in her heels.

"What happened?" she screeched. "What just happened?"

"Not gay!" I shouted back. "Not even sort of gay. They're all fucking married!"

"To men?" Caroline puffed, leaning forward to catch her breath.

"Yes!" I hissed.

We spent the rest of the trip doing the opposite of what we'd dedicated the beginning of the vacation to doing. Instead of hitting up the two a.m. pizza buffet and stalking the piña colada bar, we avoided anywhere that the group of women might frequent. We no longer haunted their spots. We avoided their schedule like a nun avoids STDs, like a spring breaker dodges sobriety, like a . . . well . . . you get it.

I learned that night to never, ever assume anything about anyone's sexuality. It's like asking someone if they're pregnant. Just don't. Unless a woman is delivering a set of triplets on your dinner table, don't ask unless the information is offered.

Short haircuts, cargo pants, and the habit of tipping quarters to bartenders may be clues that a woman is gay, but as my embarrassment taught me, they can't be considered surefire indicators. I tucked this life lesson into my memory for later use. In the future, unless a woman was offering me a round of cunnilingus in a gay bar whilst waving a rainbow flag, I would never assume again.

Chapter Twelve

Dental Debacle

I cracked the window of the car and stuck a few fingers out to feel the rustling wind. I was pretty sure I was going to be sick.

"You might have to pull over," I said, groaning at the curdled fast-food breakfast burrito stewing in my stomach, which was threatening to rebel. The extra dollops of salsa had been a shitty idea.

"Are you kidding me? I swear to god, Jess, if you destroy my car . . . ," Matt seethed.

I glanced around the interior of his hunter-green Pontiac Sunfire and kicked an empty bottle of 99 Bananas.

"Your car is already destroyed," I muttered, swallowing against some potential vomit.

"Whatever, it has a sunroof. It's green. It's awesome," he answered.

His points had merit. Besides, his shit bucket of a car was a veritable limo compared to my busted-ass Camaro. My classic car, with flaking paint and a hole where the stereo had been stolen, could never have made this trip. My stick-shift rattletrap couldn't even turn right anymore without making an excruciating squeal when the tires rubbed against the wheel well. I had learned how to get everywhere in town by only making left turns. The side mirrors had both been knocked around, but they were not yet completely disconnected. Before I drove anywhere, I had to make sure they were hanging next to the car by their cables. Honestly, the entire arrangement was a real bitch when it rained.

In short, Matt's car was the better choice if safety and arriving at our final destination were goals for the day trip. And they were, because love it or not, we were heading an hour and a half away from home to the only oral surgeon who accepted my insurance.

The dire necessity of the drive was ridiculous, but it couldn't be helped. For my whole life I had been terrified of the dentist. When I was six, I had obeyed a dental hygienist's order to "chomp down as hard as you can and don't let go no matter what" during an X-ray. As a super-literal kid, I had listened, and wouldn't let go despite the shrieks of pain when her finger slipped betwixt my rear molars. The dentist and my mom had jumped on top of me and pried the hygienist's finger out of my mouth just before I ate it. That kind of imagery doesn't ever flee one's mind.

I had listened to the bitch and had almost made a cannibal of myself. My courage to return to the dentist never resurfaced. I'm pretty sure the entire scene fucked my mom up as well, as she never made me go back. I guess there's something about seeing your angelic first grader gobbling a person's digits that really sticks with you.

Anyway, my wisdom teeth needed to be pulled and the only one who would put me under for the procedure was the aforementioned far-flung oral surgeon.

I heaved into a greasy McDonald's bag, the smell of petrified French fries making the experience even more excruciating.

"Fuck me," my driver groaned, cracking his own window.

Way sooner than I was ready, the Sunfire lurched into the Happy Smile Dental Group's parking lot. I shuddered at the cartoon image of an incisor dancing with a top hat and cane painted on the clinic's sign.

"I can't go in there," I whimpered. Matt rolled his eyes and risked shattering his decrepit car by slamming the door shut dramatically.

With my nerves already tottering on tenterhooks, the sound jarred me enough to make me reach for the fast-food bag again.

For once, I wasn't battling a hangover. I was nervous AF. There had been a lot of frightening things in my mouth over the years (questionable leftovers, ninety-nine-cent tequila, expired yogurt, a live cricket when I was two), but a dentist's drill (or whatever the piss they use to pull teeth) seemed like the scariest.

My ass was clenched so tightly, I was likely to produce a rare gemstone. I slapped a quivering hand on the receptionist's desk.

"Laughing gas, please," I screeched. "They promised I could have it the second I walked in."

"Not exactly how this works," the secretary said, matching my friend's eye roll.

She learned quickly that that was a mistake. I was no normal nervous patient. As a former child who had nearly eaten a person's right hand, I was next-level crazy. My waiting room pacing and muttering hurried the process right along.

Within minutes I was cowering in the oral surgeon's chair, an IV in my hand and a drool drape around my neck.

For good measure, I went ahead and choked back my vomit again.

I tried to not look horrified when I met the oral surgeon for the first time.

I failed.

As soon as he walked in, he gave me the skeeves. I was already freaking out; the presence of the man, who looked like he enjoyed wearing lady-skin suits and rubbing himself in Elmer's glue, almost made me bolt from the chair.

"Fuck," I whispered. The dental hygienist gave me a sympathetic look, probably feeling the same way about her employer. I guessed she was thrilled that I would be the one under his care instead of her. Either way, we wordlessly agreed that he was definitely the kind of fella a girl wants to have her eyes wide open around.

"It's okay," she said, patting my arm.

Fuck if it is, lady, I thought. *I'm about to let this shitbox creep put me to sleep while he diddles around in my motherfucking mouth. It's not okay. Not at all.*

Because I'm a bad person, I'm just going to say that he looked like the sort who would've only ever seen a vagina if he'd gone into a different field of medicine. He had the unfortunate head shape of a *Simpsons* character and wore pants with a deep crease along the front that told me he spent an abnormal amount of time with an iron. His hair had been greased and side-swept. He wore a tiny pair of wire-rimmed glasses that would've been a perfect fit for a Cabbage Patch Kids doll. The few hairs he had rallied enough to grow on his upper lip made a sad, sparse mustache. From his incessant sniffing, I surmised that he had a favorite brand of nasal spray. I stared at his long, pale fingers and nearly gagged again at the thought of them fluttering around in my mouth.

You're about to be sedated. Don't think weird shit, I repeated over and over inside my head. *You're about to be sedated. Don't think weird shit.*

But I couldn't help myself. The longer I sat staring at the little man and his miniature mustache, the weirder my thoughts got.

The last thing I remember thinking before drifting off is, *There is no chance this virgin of a dentist isn't touching my boobs while I'm out.*

Thirty minutes later I woke up *Exorcist* style, blood spurting from my mouth. Something somewhere somehow had gone super fucking sideways. Pain jolted through my jawline as I hosed the office with the breakfast burrito they had warned me against eating that morning (oops, apparently that "nothing by mouth before surgery" thing is a hard rule).

Because I wasn't being gorgeous enough at that very moment, I made the quick decision to humiliate myself further with tears and yelling. Anesthesia has never been my friend; I either don't wake up at all or I come alive like a Karen moose barreling through SuperTarget on Black Friday. There's no in-between. Like everything else in life, I practice no moderation when it comes to sedation. You either kill me with it or I kill you.

"Get her friend in here to calm her down," the oral surgeon barked to his assistant. "Now!"

Her clogs thumping as she scurried away, the hygienist disappeared, only to return with Matt seconds later.

My friend (refer to his lack of compassion earlier in the story) walked in reluctantly. When he made it to the door and surveyed the room, which looked like a murder scene from *A Nightmare on Elm Street*, his mouth dropped open.

"What in the—"

Apparently, seeing Matt did calm me down, as the surgeon had hoped. Unfortunately though, because I'm an idiot, especially under the influence of fentanyl, my mood shifted to an entirely different, much more giggly version of me.

I laughed at Matt's gawping expression and pointed at the doctor who had just removed my teeth.

Cackling like a maniac, and acting like Matt and I were alone, I whispered theatrically, "There's no way this guy didn't touch my tits while I was out. AMIRIGHT?"

My friend's eyes flew wide open as he began to shake his head. "No," he said. "Stop."

"We'd prolly better stop to get me a pregnancy test on the way home!" I crowed, missing my leg as I tried to slap it. "Because I'm 'bout to be my skeevy dentist's baby mama!"

Matt was too horrified to laugh but I couldn't stop. Slurring around the gauze stuffed into my cheeks, I hammered my point home.

"Sorry, sir! I should've worn cuter panties."

The dental hygienist made a choking sound behind the hand that had flown upward to shield her face from the horrifying scene.

"Get her out of my office," the doctor seethed, his itty-bitty khakis shaking in anger. "Take her now!"

"She's spurting blood!" Matt argued.

"Spurting! You said spurting!" I shrieked hysterically. "Oh god! What if he spurted in my mouth when he pulled my teeth! Can you die from that? Can I get some antibiotics?"

Blood continued to rocket out of my mouth. I was completely out of control.

"OUT!"

Matt, who had been an unwilling participant in the trip ever since I had begged him to take me, didn't seem to know what to do. Truth be told, if his own hangover had allowed any such swiftness, he probably would have run for the door and left my ass. Instead, he looped an arm around my neck and pulled me out of the chair.

"I don't expect to be charged for this!" I called behind my shoulder. "Pretty sure you already extracted my payment. Right, Doc?"

I winked and jabbed an elbow into my mortified friend's ribs as he manhandled me toward the exit.

For some reason unbeknownst to me I left the room chanting the word "cock" over and over. It's not something I had done before, or, to be truthful, have ever done since.

"Cock! Cock! Cock!" I laughed as I dribbled blood on the Formica countertops and floor tiles.

What in the actual fuck? Who does this? I get that I was under the influence, but somewhere deep inside of me lives that person from that day. Inside my subconscious is a fucking moron who thinks repeating "cock" is hysterical. I belong in the back row of a sixth-grade classroom to mingle with others matching my maturity level.

I am a total, horrible, monstrous beast of a person. I don't deny (nor have I ever denied) this fact. This incident and my totally unfounded accusations are not amongst my proudest moments. Believe me. I think about that poor doctor all the time and would guess I haunt his worst dreams as well. He didn't deserve my post-op stand-up routine (even if it was his fucked cocktail of sleepy juice that induced such a state). I feel even worse about the whole thing when I think about his expression and the horror on his assistant's face. Looking like you shouldn't be allowed within 250 yards of a grade school doesn't necessarily mean that you really shouldn't be allowed within 250 yards of a grade school.

I mean, no matter, I still wouldn't let the dude babysit my kids, but I certainly shouldn't have behaved like such a douche.

With me still bleeding profusely, Matt and I staggered to the car. My driver had been right earlier when he had claimed his car wasn't destroyed. With my hemorrhaging mouth and melodramatic flailing, I made short work of remedying that. If you've never seen a pint bottle of 99 Bananas filled with blood, try to keep it that way. It isn't an image easily forgotten once obtained.

By the time we reached home, the sedation grogginess was mostly gone. More than once, Matt gleefully repeated to me what I had said to the doctor. My friend laughed louder and harder each time he parroted my one-woman show.

"Oh goddamn," I kept repeating. I certainly hadn't grown into the polite damsel my grandmother had hoped I would. I stared at the inside of Matt's car, which looked not unlike a cattle slaughterhouse.

But at twenty-two years old I quickly got over the indignity of the entire situation. I soon received a call from the local pharmacy telling me that my penicillin and pain med prescriptions were ready to be picked up.

Matt and I stared at each other in shock. I'm not saying that the doctor's filling my request for antibiotics means he was guilty of ejaculating on my open wounds, but it doesn't speak well of his innocence either.

"You were right," Matt said. "You're gonna be your dentist's baby mama."

He glanced around my apartment and tapped a toe against a bucket that served to catch rainwater under the spot in the ceiling where the roof leaked.

"You'll probably have to let him fondle your junk again, but he'd probably get you a nicer place."

When the dentist's office told me to take it easy for the next forty-eight hours, I don't think they meant for me to go to the club that same night and hand out my hydrocodone prescription like I was Willy fucking Wonka.

That being said though, the discharge paperwork (which Matt had gotten before the post-surgery theatrics) hadn't been specific about that exact scenario. I was in my early twenties; I needed more explicit advice if I was meant to actually follow it.

For as long as my pain meds lasted that night, I was a fucking dance club celebrity. Through the blur of my hazy memories, I have a vague recollection of a stranger helping me trade out my blood-soaked gauze for hunks of gas station toilet paper. The burrito I gripped in my hand during the exchange was still frozen but had a large bite missing from it.

I have to say that possibly the worst part of the entire situation was when I got the bill in the mail. As it turned out, I had been misinformed. The oral surgeon's office was out of network for my shitty dental insurance. Apparently, if I had used the doctor about five miles from my apartment, the procedure would've been covered in full.

Dr. Jizz had the last laugh when he sent me to collections over $936.

Chapter Thirteen

You Had Me at Fellatio

I idolized the first woman I ever fell for. I wish the truth was a bit less embarrassing, but it isn't. She was an absolute asshat who treated me like monkey shit, but I thought she hung the moon. I gave her credit for seeming way more awesome than she really was.

But what can I say? I was a lovestruck twat and nothing would deter me. My newly outed beaver was calling the shots and she couldn't be steered away from the mistake she was intent on making.

Like any good parent, I patted myself on the arm reassuringly and said, "You have to let her make mistakes, Jess. Otherwise, how will she ever learn? We all have to kiss a few frogs before we find the real deal."

As a lovestruck twenty-something, I had tossed aside my urge to be a twatswat (beaver dam?) and started letting my vagina roam free.

My first girlfriend (I wasn't actually allowed to call her that) was my best friend's other best friend. For the most part, our mutual bro had kept us apart intentionally. He liked having options. He liked having something to do and someone to do it with and didn't necessarily want his worlds to converge. And for years, they didn't. He would go to parties with her. They would do drugs together. They would drink, eat mushrooms, and kayak. On Sunday mornings he and I watched movies rented from a Blockbuster that always smelled like pee. We binged trashy food. We mixed fruity drinks and made special trips to the store to buy umbrellas to garnish them with. I was his only "straight" friend and our relationship was complicated.

Holly was an absolute pain in the ass who had ignored me for years until the moment that she stopped ignoring me. Life got messy from there.

With our mutual bestie out partying with his third best friend (remember, he liked options) for the evening, Holly called me one night. Even though it was painfully clear that I was the last person on a long list of rejecting invitees, I told her yes when she asked if I wanted to go out for a drink (well, hello there, low self-esteem!). We'd go together with the intention of meeting someone, anyone, else out.

We visited a bar that she frequented first. She was an alcoholic and we lived in a small town. So, I suppose it's fair to say that she frequented all the local bars. After minutes of awkward silence came friendly banter. We chuckled watching the bartender reject a fake ID from an underage frat boy. I bought more beer. Suddenly, we realized that we didn't mind each other's presence so much.

When Holly eventually touched my palm, heat flickered up my arm and rocketed through my body. All the things I had never even thought, imagined, or considered were real in that one instant.

That's when everything changed. I was unlike a lot of people who spent their youth questioning their sexuality. I didn't have much opinion of mine at all until I got the zing. (Not to my heart, I'm not that romantic. The zing went straight to my vagina.)

So, the abovementioned vag flash that I now refer to as the Big Bang (trademarking this term) was a game-changer. It woke up my relatively dormant vagina. Unbeknownst to me, my girl had been napping through life. Suddenly, she was awake as fuck.

And per the message little Jess had just emailed me, I was about as gay as a girl without a mullet could be.

Truth be told, when Holly grabbed my hand later that night to lead me up the club stairs, I was done for. The moment our fingers connected I had the thought: *Oh shit, there it is. The thing I've been missing.*

So, much to her amusement, I followed her around like a puppy. We kept our tryst a secret from our shared friend and snuck around. In retrospect, I realize that the sneaking likely stemmed from her embarrassment over dating me.

Asshole.

Honestly, I was probably a bit off-putting. I wasn't exactly a model lesbian. I had no idea what I was doing and had fallen under the tutelage of an unwilling teacher. My Abercrombie ripped-knee jeans and blond highlights were unwelcome visitors in Holly's ultracool world of thrifted graphic tees and buzz cuts. I smelled like Triple Berry Splash from Walgreens instead of patchouli and angst. There was little doubt that I was Team Jacob all the way (the very fact that I had a *Twilight* team preference was a real fucking problem).

Holly listened to edgy lesbian music while I did my best to hide old 98 Degrees CDs under my bed before she came over. She cared about real-world issues. She raised her eyebrows when she saw that I didn't recycle. She sighed intolerantly when she realized that I had cable. The bitch watched it; she just expressed her utter disgust first.

I was a joke to her. Knowing that she was the puppeteer of my heartstrings, she reveled in the fact that she was my first female relationship. She cackled with her snotty friends (who all wore matching faux-hawks) over my bungling ineptitude.

I tried to be a different kind of lesbian than I was. I gave it a good effort. I thought when I came out that I would immediately be welcomed into this amazing gay fold. Like I was a new member and would automatically have a ready-made group of people who wanted to be *my* people. I thought once I joined the community, I would be, I don't know, more a part of it.

But Holly's people weren't my people.

The house parties we went to had signs taped across from the toilet that said, "If it's yellow, let it mellow. If it's brown, flush it down."

Unwilling to leave my pee rippling there for all to see, I always flushed. As I left the bathroom, I'd get glares. I suppose some of the lesbians thought I was afflicted with some sort of gastrointestinal disorder that made me crap at parties twice an hour. The ones who really sneered in my direction were the girls who suspected I had just peed and was slaughtering the planet one flush at a time.

"Does your girl have diarrhea, or does she just hate Mother Earth?" one of them asked Holly as I emerged from the bathroom, blotting my lip gloss on a shred of one-ply. I knew that a real lesbian never would've used toilet paper. Instead, to save Asian mountain yaks from extinction via deforestation, she would've air-flapped her beef curtains. As a failing new homosexual, I was neither conservationist nor agile enough for such an act.

"Probably the latter," Holly sighed, her disgust thickening the air.

Diarrhea would've been a better answer for the laser hate stares I got.

I hid my brand-name deodorant and dodged into darkened rooms to smear it under my arms. I stopped wearing as much makeup and started checking the labels of the products I did have to make sure they weren't sourced from baby kangaroo hearts. I'd eat quinoa and kale and wheatgrass spritzers at "family-style" gay buffets and then load up on as much processed fast-food macaroni and cheese as possible on the way home.

When Holly moved in with me for the summer it wasn't because she had fallen in love as well. It was because she thought not paying rent would be awesome. She ate all my food and drank all my beer and used up all my nice shampoo. Once she even had sex with a guy in my living room.

I was far from being an expert on lesbianism or relationships but was pretty sure the carnal act violated the terms of both contracts.

A rumor circulated in the lesbian community that battling my bush was akin to slicing through the wilds of the Amazonian rain forest. While the rumor wasn't entirely false, there could only have been one source. Only one person other than myself was privy to the upkeep of my pubic region at that time. Holly had told everyone that my lady cooch sported enough hair to be beaded and braided on a tropical vacation. Being the philanthropic patron of pussy that she was, she apparently thought she should receive some sort of governmental hazard pay for breaching the untouched territory of my clam to claim it for lesbianhood. Had she been able to find bare skin through my thick thatch of netherhair, she likely would've staked a rainbow flag to flutter in the breeze.

Let's be honest for a second. If Holly had been any kind of a decent person at all, she'd have been able to see the good lay for the trees (I admit, the forest was thick). If she'd really been the clitoral aficionado she claimed to be, she never would've let a little hair get in the way of prime pussy.

Now, years later, as a grown-ass woman, I am happy to say that the trees have since been treated by a professional arborist. Shortly after learning about the shitty talk, I screamed at my mom for not telling me this one very fucking important thing about sex and did some self-maintenance. I'll admit that I felt ill-equipped to handle such a giant undertaking with no years of cosmetology under my belt to help with the actual situation under my belt. Nevertheless, this girl persisted, and my pubic region is now a glorious sight to behold. Read these words and weep, Holly: No thanks to you, my fucking bush is now a place of mystical wonder. Monks weep at its very door. Every morning when I wake I find lotus flowers scattered outside my bedroom and I think, *Oh, goddamn. This golden muff sure does have a strong following, even after all these years of married monogamy.*

My ex didn't get to the good part though. Nope. She bounced before I came into my own. Instead of showing me the ropes, she ate my Walmart-bought Toaster Strudels and acted like I was the anti-dyke, burning copies of the *Lesbian Manifesto* and manufacturing environment-murdering diesel trucks in my tiny apartment. She could've helped me instead of slandering my wilderness bush to her elitist friends.

At summer's end, Holly packed her shit into her SUV and moved across the country. We had lived the lesbian U-Haul dream for only a few months when she jumped at an opportunity to go to veterinary school as far away from me as physically possible. It was a tale as old as time: girl becomes obsessed, other girl cheats on girl repeatedly while devouring the entire contents of her pantry, girl turns a blind eye, other girl spreads fucked-up rumors and runs away to Vermont. The story's screenplay is currently under contract with Pixar for their next animated smash hit. If you thought *Finding Nemo* was awesome, just wait until this baby makes it to theaters!

I did get my revenge though, and it was sweet. A year or so later Holly showed back up at my door with flowers and sweet promises of doing things right if I gave her another chance. Apparently, Vermont and all its gorgeous fall foliage and girlfriend-stealing animal-saving schools had crushed her soul. It was too late though; I had met the most amazing woman in the whole world in her absence. A new girlfriend had entered the scene not long after Holly trashed my vagina's name and square-danced on my heart. She, a sexy-ass non-amphibian totally worthy of kissing who would eventually become my wife, had a much more worldly perception of my vagina. She thinks it's awesome no matter its level of disarray. Though she prefers moderate pruning, she appreciates the opportunity to make its acquaintance no matter its state. You know what they say. One dyke's pubic dumpster fire is another lesbian's treasure.

Chapter Fourteen

Roller Rink Wreck

I've never been much of an athlete. My body type back in my twenties suggested that I should/could be, but for whatever reason, my pieces and parts don't communicate well. My brain will tell me to run, and my legs will send me careening on a death path. My arms try to shoot a basket while my feet stumble over each other in an attempt to put me in the hospital.

My mind signals, *This silly bitch wants to work out!* as the rest of my body begins looking for the nearest cliff to pitch me off of. It's an unfortunate malady, but acceptance of it has saved me a ton on sports bras and exercise bands over the years.

Before I got old and turned potato shaped (as people who only eat Taco Bell Nacho Fries have a habit of doing), I had what appeared to be an athletic form. I was five foot eleven and strong (not "strong for a girl," but strong as in "I'll kick your ass if you call me 'strong for a girl'"). My stocky frame was but a farce though. The truth was that despite its outward appearance, my body was mostly made for margarita drinking and napping.

I vowed to change all of that on one fateful Friday. A flash of inspiration made me want to rewire what twenty-two years of athletic failings had proven to be unchangeable.

I have to backpedal now to explain my motives.

When I met Carley Hall at a party, I was immediately fascinated by her. Make no mistake, despite my newfound obsession, I didn't want to date her or see her naked. The girl sported a ratted mullet, had wishy-washy feelings about showering, and could have crushed my entire body with her armpit. She would lift her ass cheek midsentence to let out a repugnant fart without so much as a blink or a blush. I was equal parts amazed and horrified by most of the things she did. Nonetheless, she was one of the coolest people I had ever met. When she entered the party, the sea of wobbly drinking people parted to slap her back, fist-bump her, and compete to get a word in with her. It was my first time hanging out with that particular group of lesbians and I was still reveling in the fact that my vagina was the most anticipated new release of the summer of 2005. I was a bit perturbed to see that the spotlight had been taken off of it and all of its glory to shine on someone else.

Still relatively green to the local lesbian party scene, I had been shocked when Carley approached me through the thick of it.

"Who's this hooker?" she sneered, staring straight into my eyes as her gritty voice carved out my lowly station in the echelons of dancing dykes.

Fuck, had she somehow peeped my Glamour Shots? How did she know?

"She's cool," another girl said with a shrug, handing Carley a red Solo cup filled with beer.

That was all the convincing the ruffian needed. She grabbed the beer and my hand and parked us on a sofa, where we spent most of the night talking.

"Hall, you were amazing last night!" a nearby voice called. Its owner's hands delivered a pair of fresh beers to our couch. My new friend nodded dismissively and sucked her teeth before gulping the foamy beer from both cups.

My cheeks burned in shame as I looked for a place to hide my half-drunk hot-pink wine cooler. I was a committed drinker with plenty of practice hours under my belt, but Carley Hall had clearly peaked at expert level.

"Your girlfriend?" I queried, trying to sound nonchalant.

"What?"

"She said you were amazing."

Carley laughed loudly before burping and chucking her empty cups in the general direction of the trash can. "No, she's talking about the bout last night."

I nodded my head knowingly even though I had no fucking clue what she was talking about. Carley watched me, a smirk playing on her lips.

"Roller derby," she finally said, mercifully letting me off the hook. "I'm a Hardwood Hellion."

I won't lie. The words that Carley uttered gave me a giant lady stiffy. The girl who had been ridiculously interesting thirty seconds before that statement had become a fucking legend in my mind. I knew my mouth had dropped but I didn't care.

"Do you skate?"

Did I skate? Well, it had been a couple of years (like, sixteen-ish) and I hadn't been especially talented at it in elementary school, but I wasn't going to let the damned truth stop me, and certainly not in front of the raddest person I'd ever met. The last time I had been on roller skates had been for my second-grade birthday party, when I had spent one afternoon as the permed queen of the rink. I had rolled over that slick floor in my stone-washed overalls like birthday royalty to Digital Underground's "The Humpty Dance" like the eight-year-old badass I was. Whether or not my pineapple lace-ups would still fit didn't matter; I was sure there was a skater inside of me still.

"Yeah," I answered as coolly as possible. "I skate."

"Come out to our practice tomorrow," Carley answered. "Our teams are always looking for fresh blood."

Dismissing my niggling concern about her word choice, I nodded. I would be there—with skates on.

When I woke up the next morning, I was slightly less intoxicated than I had been when I had agreed to what would likely be an attempt at suicide by sport. I had several more reservations that morning than I'd had while on the couch with the first roller girl I had ever encountered. The rest of the night blurred in my mind, but I had hazy memories of Carley and me promising each other eternal friendship, a grand announcement to the room that I was an up-and-coming roller derby star, and polishing off a bottle of blue raspberry Mad Dog 20/20.

"Goddammit, Jess," I muttered, liquor vapor from my morning breath burning my eyes.

I flopped over in my bed and began plotting how I would take back all the promises I had made that I was the roller-skate version of Olympian Michelle Kwan.

I snagged my phone from under a half-eaten bowl of ramen noodles and glanced at a new text.

7 p.m. @ Starlight Skatesphere. Bring sk8s.

Unless Carley wanted me to bring some over-the-shoe click-ons borrowed from my childhood, there were no skates to bring.

"Fuck," I groaned again. As a second-year community college

student living mostly on student loans, maxed-out credit cards, and promises to my landlord that I'd "pay next week," I was too poor to even consider buying myself a pair of skates.

Despite a multitude of pressing problems and the hangover that was trying to kill me, I somehow mustered up the balls to get myself to Starlight that night. Waves of nausea undulated over me as I watched the seasoned roller girls whirl around the curved skating rink like the pros they were.

Several glanced toward me as I stood paralyzed with my mouth agape in front of an air hockey machine. Their eyes passed over my frame in amusement, pausing at my pink duffel bag (which was practically empty but I had thought was legit) and leggings.

"I recruited this bitch last night," Carley grunted as she joined me rink-side. Before jumping back onto the skate floor, she punched me in the spot where my nonexistent biceps should've been.

I looked around, quickly realizing I was "this bitch," and put on my bravest face. A sea of mohawks and tattoos stared back at me. Once again in life, I found myself in way over my head. Dangling from my left hand was a pair of beaten-ass quad skates that I had rented from the gum-popping teenager at the entrance stand. They smelled like an athletic cup that had been left in the summer sun for too long. Truth be told, they smelled strikingly like Carley, who was engrossed in picking her nose as she soared around the rink.

And, despite the intense excavating she was doing in her left nostril, she was goddamned magnificent on those skates. The wind from her sheer speed blew her mullet away from her neck to reveal a trail of tattoos. Her long calves stretched with each fluid motion. When the finger finally departed her nose, the dazzling skater lifted her hand to flip me off where I stood on the rink's stained carpet.

Heeding the roller girls' cajoling, I at long last laced up my skates and wove an unsteady circle around the rink.

"I might've exaggerated a little about my skills last night," I admitted to Carley as she urged me on.

"It's cool, girl, you got the heart for it."

I was pretty sure I didn't have that either. I had loved the idea of the badassery of roller derby, but there, on that skating floor, sucking albuterol through an inhaler I had borrowed from a friend, I knew I was about as fucking out of my league as humanly possible. No matter how hard I tried, and how much more comfortable I grew on the quads, I was always a lap behind the teams. For the most part, I looked like an octopus having a grand mal seizure.

"It's probably just those," one of the team captains said, explaining my poor performance by pointing at my rickety rented skates.

Carley threw an arm around my sweaty shoulder, almost spilling me on the floor with her unexpected weight.

"I've got an old pair she can have," she said. "You think she'll make the cut?"

The team captain assessed me as I panted pathetically with the top half of my body sagging over the rink wall. I had never actually seen someone die from a stitch in their side, but I was certain it was about to happen. My aching legs shook as my ankles rocked precariously inside the skates.

"Not a chance in normal times, but Brawllipop broke her leg in three places at our last bout. We need a warm body for Saturday. Fuck it, she can play."

Goddamned great. I had been inducted into the Hardwood

Hellions on a technicality. One of their members had been broken in fucking half, and I was meant to fill the hole that her mangled-ass body had left.

"I'm actually not sure that I'm cut—" I protested, watching sweat pool on the floor in front of me. My sentence was aborted when Carley slapped my back, sending me downward onto the kneepads I had borrowed from an absent player's locker. Pretty certain that I had swallowed my own tongue on impact, I spluttered dramatically.

"Shut up," she said. "She's in."

In? Really? The bout was in five days, and I skated like a preschooler on one of those walkers made from PVC pipe they offer at the rink.

"I'll get you into derby shape," Carley vowed.

And she did. Or tried to at least. The pair of us spent every single night at the skating rink practicing. I learned to skate, start, stop, and drill. I still royally sucked by the end of the week, but at least I didn't need the walker anymore.

"They're going to fucking kill me out there," I observed after practice one night, swigging some grape Gatorade.

"Probably so," Carley agreed. She stopped picking her butt long enough to snatch the drink from my hands and finish it off.

On the night of my first bout, I was overjoyed to find out that I would be working the penalty box instead of actually competing. I happily climbed into a tiny leather skirt (not my first), fingerless gloves, sparkly spandex, and a new pair of skates. The new gear meant I would now be late on my rent, but I looked legit. With the thunder of a rowdy crowd as my background, I ushered skaters from both teams in and out of the box to serve their time.

The penalty box was warm and safe with no impending threat

of concussion. While I was inside, my life wasn't in jeopardy even once. As with skating, I fucking sucked at keeping track of time, but I still loved it.

A few months and millions of practices later, on the night of the first bout I would actually skate, I was more nervous than I had ever been. I put makeup on in the locker room slowly, not believing that I had followed through on becoming a roller girl. More than that, I couldn't believe I had actually shown up to the arena that night to play.

"Nervous?" Carley grunted, elbowing me out of the way of the mirror so she could smear black marks beneath her eyes.

"Yeah."

She thrust her beaten water bottle at me. "Drink before you pass the fuck out."

Grateful, I sucked a huge gulp through her chewed-on straw. I gagged as the mouthful of cheap liquor sloshed down my throat.

"Are you goddamned kidding me? Vodka?" I spat, wiping my lips with my jersey. "Seriously?"

Carley scratched her crotch with a puzzled look on her face. "What the fucking hell else would I put in there?"

There were a few things I knew to be true: There was a high probability that I was about to die. The months of practice had shown that no amount of hard work or determination could turn me into an athlete. Also, I was positive that I was in deep motherfucking shit.

"You've got this," Carley said, her voice conveying unjustified confidence in me that I certainly didn't feel. She skated away, shaking her head.

I followed my friend into the arena, trying not to add punctuation to the back of her helmet, which said, "DIE BITCH." An eloquent poet she was not. I listened as the emcee called her chosen roller girl name. She skated through the tunnel, her mullet waving gloriously, as her theme song knocked from the speaker.

My breath hitched in my throat when I heard the promoter announce my derby name. The song I had chosen, "She's a Bad Mama Jama," wailed from the sound system.

"Now let's welcome Milli Vakilli to the pack!" he shouted. Something about the drunken crowd's riotous roaring forced my gelatinous legs to push me forward into the arena. With my hands waving over my head, I skated a full circle around the rink as the spectators cheered me on. The only thought that floated through my head was, *Oh my god, they're chanting my freaking name. They don't know how bad I suck yet.*

I'm not being self-deprecating here. I'm really not. Even after months and months of practice, I was still impressively horrible. I loved the outfits. I loved my teammates. I loved the attention at bars and free drinks. I loved the idea of being a roller girl. Regardless of all of it though, I was still really, really bad at the sport.

I know that you likely want this story to have a hero's end. Maybe I should've changed it to me being some magical roller girl star who found her inner champion on the skating rink and dominated, surprising myself and everyone else who thought I couldn't make the cut.

But I'm not fucking Rudy and this wasn't a Notre Dame football dream. I was just a mostly inebriated girl with a one-night dream of being a roller derby star. I had no business being there and my fickle fantasizing had officially fucked me straight into the danger zone. As it turns out, my inner champ is, I don't know, like a snail that some dick kid has sprinkled salt on.

You know on World Wrestling Entertainment when the beat-down wrestler is grappling to somersault over the ropes so he won't be finished off? Like, when he's sweating bullets and his arms are shaking and he's trying to drag what's left of his body away from the carnage? So that the pulverization can end? But then the way-better wrestler grabs him and rips his fingernails from the ropes, and you just pray that either they kill him fast or he faints and goes into a coma so that he won't remember any of it? That was me during my first bout, only in an itty-bitty skirt, fishnets, and skates I could barely operate.

I didn't have a Rudy moment. I was pounded mercilessly. Every single time I tried to come up for air, my slow, wholly inept ass was knocked down. I was run over so many times that later, when I was able to drag myself to a mirror, I saw literal skate marks on my face. Literal. Yeah, like in a cartoon.

My friends, my family, and a packed auditorium of complete strangers issued "ooh" sounds and grimaced each time someone made impact with me. I suffered through it all. Finally, a tiny pivot blocker for the other team finished me off. I heard Kilbo Baggins approaching from behind long before she reached my battered body. She glided through the other skaters with her eyes trained on my broken, limping form. I was supposed to be protecting the jammer, but because I knew that one more blow would kill me, I skittered to the side of the rink, as far from her as possible. But Kilbo didn't want the jammer, she wanted to slaughter me.

I like to think it was a merciful act meant to end my piteous suffering.

When the crowd started chanting, "Kilbo! Kilbo! Kilbo!" I knew I was about as fucked as a person could be. In a moment of pre-death clarity, I realized that we had reached the point in my annihilation when the other wrestler grabs the metal chair and pounds the piss out of his victim.

I was a weak, bleating calf futilely trying to shake flies out of my eyes while being circled by a ravenous carnivore. I might as well have just spread myself with ketchup and lain prone on the arena floor. The process would've likely been less painful, and I would've left with more dignity.

The worst part though? Before she took me out, the skater, who was barely five feet tall to my five foot eleven, apologized.

"Sorry, Milli," she grumbled just before squatting to the floor and ramming into me as hard as she could. Please note that this is the moment when my soul escaped through my asshole.

As soon as my upright body took the full force of the wrecking-ball-like thrust, I went airborne. Kilbo knocked me so hard, in fact, that I flew into the arena air with a trajectory leading straight into the stands. The hit was so impressively forceful that I had actual time to think about my eventual landing as I soared over spectators. With my legs cranked over my head porn style and my arms akimbo, I noticed that a woman had covered her young child's eyes to shield her from the gruesome impact made to my body.

What felt like minutes later I landed in a tangle of skates and knees and soft pretzels and spilled soda. Someone (probably me?) was crying. I heard the distant sound of someone murmuring the rosary. Every single part of my person hurt. When the onlookers pulled me upright and turned me back to the rink, the crowd roared again. They had been the instigators, the ones begging for the folding chair the whole time. They had craved the finishing move like an alcoholic in rehab craves mouthwash. Barely able to open my eyes, I lifted my arms into the same air I had just flown through.

After all the lessons that Carley Hall had taught me over the months, I was finally going to emulate her perfectly.

To the echoing sounds of the crowd chanting, "Milli! Milli! Milli!" I raised my middle fingers and flipped them all off.

Fuck you, audience.

I am dead.

Chapter Fifteen

Magic Mike Set the Bar Too High

There were penises everywhere, just as I had planned. They hung from walls, were pasted to furniture, and were fanned across the coffee table. I had located a variety of sizes, shapes, shades, and textures, as can be found in the wild.

I stepped back, crisscrossed my arms over my chest, and stared at my creative display in awe. Over the last few weeks, I had spent a lot of time perusing the shelves of sex shops and peeling back the black plastic magazine covers at our local Hastings looking for the perfect pornographic accent pieces. In my pursuit, I had viewed more dildos and licorice thongs than any one person needs to see in a lifetime.

Being a lesbian was not going to deter me from hosting the most phallus-infused bachelorette party ever. My best friend was getting married, and as the maid of honor, it was my duty to throw her a smutty party to end all smutty parties.

In the months leading up to her big day, we had pregamed heartily with visits to bars and nightclubs. It seemed only right, to balance out all the buttoned-up dress fittings and dainty cake tastings we were forced to spend our spare time on. We weren't going to let something so silly as her impending nuptials stymie our debauchery. Somehow, in her journey to settling down, we had grown increasingly wild and inebriated.

A couple of weeks before the bachelorette party, I heard a rumor that some traveling strippers were winding their way down south and would visit our local country bar. The radio announcers guaranteed that the "one night only" performance featuring the "sexiest strippers in North America" would be "a sensational show sure to singe [our] senses."

There was nothing else to be done. We planned a girls' night out. I bought tickets as soon as they went on sale to guarantee that we had admission to the act that promised to be a once-in-a-lifetime experience.

Upon my coronation as maid of honor, Caroline had made me swear that I wouldn't invite strippers of any gender to her bachelorette party. For her, the very thought of a gussied-up stranger groping her like a honeydew at the grocery store was akin to torture. She liked being in the know and always had a finger on the go button, but when shit went down, she preferred hunkering in the nearest corner to watch.

You know how some people (me) say, "Hold my beer"? Caroline is the girl who holds it while gleefully spectating from the safe and sound outer ring.

Knowing the hives that would ensue if I hired live entertainment for her pre-wedding shindig, I had begrudgingly agreed to promise there would be no strippers at the party. The escape clause in the whole contract, however, was that I hadn't agreed there would be no strippers in the days before the party. If we weren't going to have a leopard-spotted man-thong shaken in our faces on the night of her actual party, we were sure as hell going to have it happen beforehand.

Caroline and I had been to a couple of lady strip clubs before. The memory that had melted itself into my brain was of one particular visit when I had just graduated high school. Two of Caroline's nerdy guy friends joined the pair of us on a trip to South Padre Island. As a joke, Caroline and I dragged them into an eighteen-and-up strip club. The guys, who were older than us but had likely never been near boobs other than the ones attached to their mothers, were reluctant to enter the archway of pink flashing lights.

We insisted.

Once we were inside, everything changed. Alex (the dorkier of the two, who would've probably passed out if one of us had uttered the word "clitoris" in his presence) became a man possessed. The power of pussy in that place was strong, and he was entranced by the musky allure. Caroline and I, who had thought the strip club stop was a joke up until that point, ceased giggling as we drank in the scene. When Alex accepted the clawed hand of a six-foot-tall stripper and followed her into a back room for privacy, we began frantically searching for an exit.

Miles, the more self-controlled of the pair, smugly reminded my best friend and me that we were the ones who had released the loin beast in Alex. The least we could do was wait while his wildest dreams were being realized in a low-lit room papered in cheetah print. We had arrived in one car, and it had become a ride-or-die situation. Miles was thrilled that his friend was potentially getting laid (no matter the cost to his college fund) and was just as happy that Caroline and I were learning a valuable lesson.

Much later, when Alex and his lady friend emerged from the

seedy back room, our no-longer-innocent math prodigy was much changed. His once impeccably parted hair stuck out every which way and his eyes had taken on a feral gleam. His skin was a bouquet of reds, and his breath came out in quick pants.

To Caroline's and my horror (and Miles's amusement), the former captain of the chess club allowed himself to be led to a corner of the bar. His new girlfriend (whom we dubbed Chi Chi for obvious reasons) did a backbend reminiscent of the scary little girl from *The Ring*. With her spine flat on the stage and her legs splayed in a V above her, she buried sweet Alex's head against her scantily clad vagina and bucked in seizurelike movements. The worst part of the whole thing? When Alex finally came up for air, his expression exultant, the lenses of his thick-rimmed glasses were fogged.

"We're leaving!" Caroline hissed loudly. "Miles, go get him! Now!"

At eighteen years old and as the youngest member of our group, I was similarly disturbed by what I had seen, but also secretly impressed. In that instant, I knew that the vagina I was carrying around had some serious catching up to do if she would ever live up to such an amazing feat.

Though nothing so shocking had happened in the years since my first strip club visit, I attended other such bars with my classy-ass first girlfriend. She swore she only went for the chicken wings (because of my long-standing vegetarianism, I couldn't confirm the validity of her claim that they were the best in the state). Whenever my ex and I visited the Golden Dollar Strip Bar, the female strippers performed the standard tricks. There was a lot of pole circling and gyrating that didn't interest me too terribly much. I sampled the free cookies (literal cookies) and the array of dollar shots that the club offered, complimented the strippers on their rhinestone-encrusted shoes, and watched men fall in love with dancers who only gave them the time of day for cash. When they weren't shimmying their nipple tassels, I had many a heart-to-heart with the performers, who I discovered were mostly lesbians and mothers. Somehow, I killed the magical allure of the club when I would tell my ex about one dancer's uterine polyps or how another had to remove her clit ring because of an infection. She didn't much appreciate the girl talk, but that didn't keep me from sharing.

Whatever. She was never someone who was fun to gossip with, anyway.

My best friend, who was mere weeks away from her wedding, was an entirely different story. Which is precisely why when the male strip show at the Dancing Cowboy slithered across my radar, I jumped on the opportunity.

I was positive that the show would be different from bygone experiences and the ideal activity to begin the countdown to my bestie's wedding.

On the evening of the show, Caroline and I dressed to impress. The boys of Thunder Cocks (or whatever the hell the tour was called) were sure to be mesmerized by our excessively glittery shirts, off-brand heels, and costume jewelry that was guaranteed to leave us itchy by night's end. Because we're fancy, we drank discount liquor out of plastic bottles at Caroline's house before heading to the show. She needed the alcoholic courage and I needed to take the edge off the prospect of watching men shake their hairy asses for dollars.

At the doors of the Dancing Cowboy, we were shocked to find

hundreds of women stuffed into outfits not unlike our own. They wriggled in excitement (I'm assuming from the anticipation of seeing exposed man meat) and chattered amongst themselves. They checked their cleavage to ensure their sixty-dollar push-up bras were doing their jobs, and once satisfied, they then smoothed on extra layers of lipstick. The camaraderie in the cackling line was palpable. We women had united for a common purpose (that was actually pretty uncommon if you really think about it). We were there to objectify men, and it felt amazing, exciting, and new. We were going to catcall and slap asses and make lewd comments about package sizes in a fucked-up, reverse-culture sort of way.

I actually heard a woman screech, "Bring out the beef!" just as we were entering the cowboy bar.

In that line, during that particular moment, there were plenty of things I wanted (a burrito, my ex to grovel for another chance, a daiquiri with one of those teeny umbrellas, comfortable shoes, world peace).

Beef wasn't one of them.

Caroline was nervous, and I was pretending not to be. Despite our ages, we tittered like second graders as we were squeezed into the smoky bar by the churning mass of people.

The Dancing Cowboy was packed to the gills with women of every shape, size, and age. Some girls barely looked old enough to be out so late, and some women looked like they were one hip fracture away from a permanent rest home.

Because we are chickenshits, Caroline and I found a table at the back of the room, as far away from the glitzy stage as we could get whilst still being in the club. We put our bedazzled clutches on the tabletop and commenced guzzling cosmopolitans like the refined ladies that we were.

When music started to thump from the speakers around us, Caroline began drinking faster and muttering to herself.

"Oh, Jesus. This is my worst nightmare."

The funny thing about it? I knew it really *was* her worst nightmare.

Our nervous laughter trilled across the barroom to comingle with the raucous hooting coming from the rally of women. Lecherous comments soared through the air, which smelled of cheap perfume. My mouth popped open in surprise when I saw a woman at a nearby table grab a generous handful of the waiter's ass as he served her a drink.

"It's nice that they found them a spot close up," Caroline commented around her straw, nodding at the small group of women in wheelchairs who were parked right in front of the stage. I agreed but also pitied the ladies for their front-row view. Though I hadn't been to many male strip shows, I was concerned about the potential for biologicals (a.k.a. sweaty semen droplets) to whip through the air into their rapturous faces.

As the music grew louder, a group of muscled men began making their way to the stage. Assembled in front of the screeching throng of women stood oiled firefighters, policemen, cowboys, a ninja, and one who appeared to be dressed as a plumber (which I hadn't previously considered a sexy profession). Caroline dropped her head to her hands and moaned loudly, barely able to watch the spectacle in front of us.

"No," she muttered miserably. The word slipped through her fingers. "Please, no."

Her appeal went unanswered. Dongs on Parade had officially begun.

The situation only worsened from there.

In turn, the dancers began swiveling their hips and tearing off pieces of their flimsy costumes. As each piece of clothing hit the face of a hot and bothered onlooker, the squealing in the building intensified.

"Jess, we need to go."

But I knew we couldn't just leave. I had already contemplated escape by then and had scoped out the bar exits. There were strippers at each point of egress. We were fucking trapped.

"We're fine," I answered, trying to conceal my panic. "This is totally fine."

As the words were leaving my mouth, I saw a woman who appeared to be dressed for Sunday church services bolt from her seat onto the stage to grope the faux construction worker, who had just juddered out of his pants.

"What in the actual hell?" I whispered, unsure if I had just witnessed a reverse baptism or if my eyes were playing tricks on me. The woman and her tongue were manually removed from the glistening body of the dancer, and she was plunked back into her chair. Her matronly friend, wearing a floor-length floral skirt paired with hose and open-toed sandals, high-fived the deviant as she was deposited back at their shared table.

The subsequent scene was equally disturbing. The next stripper to take the stage appeared to be dressed like either a zookeeper or a man about to go on safari, it was unclear which. With the crook of a forefinger, he summoned a woman from the audience.

We watched in a state of bewildered shock as she faced the crowd and he embraced her from behind. The brawny performer then flipped the woman upside down so that her head was at the level of his knees and her legs wagged over his shoulders. Her cries of delight were substantial, especially when he pretended to eat her crotch (exposed by her upended dress) as a snack.

I won't lie. My first thought was one of sheer horror.

My second, more delayed thought was that I needed to loosen up on the late-night nacho trips to Taco Bell if I ever wanted to be handled in such a way. In the same instant, I promised myself that I would buy nicer panties in case any such thing ever happened to me organically or spontaneously. Just imagine the embarrassment if someone tried to flip you over for a vagina meal only to not be able to heft you all the way up. Even worse? What if during the hoist the excess fabric of your voluminous granny panties wafted over the lifter's face, causing a cataclysmic tripping incident?

"Is she okay?" Caroline, always the women's advocate, shouted at me. "Does this seem unwanted to you? Do we need to intervene or do something?"

I stared at the upside-down blonde as she dry-humped the stripper's face. "I think she's good."

We both looked toward the front entrance of the bar, which appeared blissfully empty. We threw cash on the table for our tab, scooped up our purses, and made to leave. Just as Caroline was pivoting on her heel, she bumped right into a stripper. He was a sneaky little fucker of only about five foot one and had crept up to our table from behind.

The tricky teensy-weensy bastard had one-upped us.

He lifted an eyebrow at me and licked his lips.

"Oh no. We're good. Thanks though. I'm gay," I spluttered, hoping my declaration of lesbianism would make clear my aversion to his basic anatomy.

"You gay?" he said, winking at Caroline.

Her face crimson, she twisted her engagement ring. "Uh."

That was it. That was all she could say. She couldn't for one moment claim an ardent love for muff diving, thereby she failed the pop quiz. She looked like she wished a car would drive through the wall of the club and kill her on the spot.

Stepping forward, the stripper looked up into her face and smacked his lips. In what seemed like slow motion, I watched him swirl a finger around the low neckline of her glittery tank top and . . . and . . .

"What the—what are you—" Caroline clearly hadn't recovered her ability to form words.

I stood frozen to the sticky floor, utterly flabbergasted, as I watched the miniature finger skate around the rhinestones of my friend's shirt top.

"You can't do that!" Caroline finally blurted, squaring her shoulders as if she was proud to have recalled the English language.

My only thought was, *Oh my god. My sweet, docile friend is about to beat this tiny stripper's ass.*

"Yeah, I can," he answered.

With a salacious, Cheshire Cat–style grin on his tiny face, he dunked his index finger into her cleavage. Spinning on his itty-bitty foot, he twirled around and sashayed back toward the bar.

Tucking our bags under our arms, in a true act of solidarity and maturity, we both ran for the exit. It wasn't until we had caught our breaths in the parking lot that we spoke again.

"He was gay though, right?" Caroline asked, her question coming out in pants.

"I mean, for sure," I answered, still trying to figure out how our night had gone so horribly wrong. "So, like, he probably didn't enjoy it any more than you did."

Despite the wild lead-up to what I planned to be a truly spicy bachelorette party, I admit now that Caroline's big night before the big day fell a bit flat. Sure, I papered the hotel room walls in penises. Sure, the hurricane mix that I had shipped from our favorite New Orleans bar was delightful. Sure, our friends showed up in their best low-rise jeans and dress-up platform shoes ready to party. But my planning was for naught. The imported liquor fruit punch, though divine, paired with a homemade shot that could only be drunk after the top floater was lit on fire (it was a good thing we all tweezed our eyebrows into nonexistence back then, considering the flammability of our beverages), did Caroline in early. Her ability to walk went first. Then followed her capacity to form coherent sentences. As our pregaming wound down, so did Caroline's ability to see without squeezing one eye shut. She began mumbling things about needing a nap and her fiancé. The plan to hit the streets to play cutesy bachelorette games where strangers gave us their boxer shorts and bought us drinks soon became a nonreality.

But because both I and the night were young, I didn't take my bestie's brush with near alcohol poisoning seriously. With the help of our friends, I basically propped Caroline up *Weekend at Bernie's* style and trotted her around our town's bar district until I was literally carrying her.

"Jess!" she whined miserably at two a.m. "I need fucking food."

With the nearby pizza spots closed and a bestie who had turned a greenish hue, I sagged Caroline against another of our friends and ran into a diner, where the bus girl was stacking chairs atop tables to mop.

"We're closed," she griped, taking in my smeared eyeliner and hair still damp from dancing my face off.

"I just need something, anything, to eat!" I said, panicked. "My friend is sick."

She gestured to a glass case where what appeared to be day-old pastries sat waiting to be thrown away. "Take whatever. Just get out," she said.

She was both a nice girl (free food) and also kind of a dick (ejecting me from the diner). Her personality had a lot to unpack. If I'd had time to form a crush, I might've taken the opportunity. I didn't though. Dammit. I had a task to do!

Muffins or bear claws. Muffins or bear claws. Muffins or bear claws. My thought process was slow-motion sluggish from drunkenness. The options were limited, and neither seemed like the right carb to soak up amaretto and Everclear.

Screw it. Blueberry crumble it was.

"Oh thank god!" our waiting friend said as I darted out. She pushed a snoring Caroline back toward me. Though I was a mobile shit show, I tended to be the most responsible of the group on any given night. Apparently, the assignment of making sure Caroline didn't swallow her own tongue for five whole minutes had been too much for Andy.

"Here," I said. "I got food."

My friend's eyes fluttered open. Despite her nausea, she gave me a sweet, grateful smile. "Thank you," she whispered in a shaky voice.

I stuffed a piece of the dry muffin into her mouth.

As soon as the stale dessert hit her tongue, Caroline began spluttering and choking.

"What the fu—" she screeched, suddenly very much awake. Pieces of spewed muffin hit my face as she sprung forward to spit the offending food out.

"FUCKING PIZZA! I WANTED REAL FOOD! WHAT IS THIS?"

"A muffin?" I asked. It wasn't a question really, but I was a bit confused. We had grown up together. I had seen her eat goddamned muffins.

"What drunk person in the whole world has ever been helped by a muffin, Jess? What the fuck?!?"

I didn't have an answer. I was also covered in hunks of fruit and what I assumed to be a mixture of brown sugar and butter.

With my outfit ruined, our bachelorette party participants disbanded, and the bride-to-be too feeble to walk without wheelbarrow support, the night was done.

Much like on the night of the teensy stripper, we had found our festivities at a forced end. Any future career as an event planner I had once considered was gone. I was done bacheloretting. I retired.

Chapter Sixteen

Boomerang Burnout

I have to preface this story by saying I got over my fear/terror of marijuana fairly soon after my mom didn't send my middle brother to rehab. I went to college, and, well, my early twenties happened and the rest is history. More than once, I awoke ashamed of unfortunate choices made whilst crazed by the post-toke munchies. I remember distinctly once waking up next to a mostly eaten peanut butter, green olive, and mayonnaise sandwich and wondering how in the fuck it had tasted so orgasm-inducingly delicious while I had been as high as a kite.

I had different groups of friends back in those days that I did different things with. I had margarita friends, movie friends, and brunch friends. Heidi was my smoke-myself-useless friend.

One Sunday, I had had a lovely eggs Benedict with a side of sausage on the patio with brunch friends. After bidding them good day and forgoing the nap they were all heading home to have, I decided to call H. Years of our being close had taught me that Heidi didn't rise earlier than noon, but at eleven a.m., with nothing to do, I decided to ditch the niceties and wake her up.

Imagine my shock when she answered on the first ring.

"You have to come look at something," she whispered on the phone. Her voice pulsed with excitement. "Come over. Now."

When I knocked on her apartment door, she pulled me inside. With a skip in her step, she led me to her bedroom, leaving a trail of patchouli in her wake. Inside, she grabbed a giant Rubbermaid container from her closet and peeled the lid off.

My hand flew to my mouth when I saw what was inside. Hundreds of perfectly formed nuggets of marijuana crowded against each other as if elbowing for room. I could tell that the cannabis was top quality by the rich, earthy smell that emanated from the box.

It wasn't a "stay two nights in county" amount of pot, it was a "get shipped off to Folsom Prison to spend the rest of your days as someone's bitch" quantity.

"What in the fuck?" I finally gasped, searching the room for the nearest escape. I guessed we were seconds away from an entire platoon of drug enforcement officers parachuting their way through her roof. I knew that just my presence in the fancy apartment, a mere whiff away from the millions of dollars' worth of bud, would make me culpable. And, unlike my friend, my family didn't have money. I know it's hard to believe, but registered nurses and on-again-off-again farmers aren't exactly stuffing their mattresses with spare cash. If I ended up in jail, an alcoholic public defender with daddy issues was all I could afford to ever make it out.

"I'm gonna sell it," Heidi said, her eyes gleaming as she stared at the dried emerald buds.

"What the—?!? You're a drug dealer now? But, Heidi, you're rich."

She frowned at the comment but didn't disagree.

Heidi's dad had one of those jobs that old white guys have that make them rich (stock market, corporate CEO, oil tycoon, school janitor, something like that). Their family owned a beach house and had a maid. Bunched at the back of the closet were cashmere sweaters and shoes that cost more than my college education. Despite Heidi's dreadlocks, the ten-cent incense cones she burned, and her home-rolled cigarettes, there was no mistaking that she had come from money. She had tried to shake the appearance of it but failed miserably when her parents furnished her swanky uptown apartment with all-new furniture. No damned beaded curtain and Bob Marley tapestry hung above the couch were going to take twelve years of prep school stink off her.

She also couldn't stop using her limitless American Express Gold Card. No matter how independent and destitute my friend wanted to be, the flashy card had a way of inching itself out of her woven hemp purse to purchase everything she wanted. The employees at the head shops where she bought her pipes and bongs were always surprised when she slid the heavy card across their counter.

"I'm not rich, my dad is," she replied. She brushed the tips of her fingers over the weed lovingly.

I exchanged a look with her five-thousand-dollar custom-ordered Persian cat as it lolled on its back next to me. Gigi and I generally didn't acknowledge each other, but in the current circumstance, considering Heidi's stupidity, a shared look felt appropriate.

"You're going to go to goddamned jail," I said. "This isn't, like, a little bit of weed, H. This is enough to supply fucking Jay and Silent Bob for an entire year."

For once in my life, I wasn't exaggerating.

"So, you don't want any, then?"

I gazed longingly at the gorgeous nuggets.

"Of course I do, dammit," I snapped back. "But if this is one of those things where you try to rope me into helping you sell for some drug lord or ask me to fly to Brazil with five pounds of weed up my twat, you can forget about it."

It was fair of me to make such allegations against the friend I'd had since high school. A week prior, I had joined Heidi and two of her stoner friends on a trip to a lake in the woods dubbed Nipple Creek by locals. Knowing that the hideaway was a forty-five-minute drive, I had been reluctant to ride with Heidi. Too broke to fill up my own tank and bored enough to lend H more trust than she deserved, I had grudgingly agreed.

I piled into her Land Rover, splattered in "Coexist" decals, an NPR logo, and stickers from the local grocery co-op (didn't matter how much of that "I'm one of you" shit she plastered on it, hers was still a $70K luxury vehicle). Next to me sat her friend Arlo, who loved telling me how murky my aura was. Riding shotgun was Allison, Heidi's friend who was always the girl crying at the bar at the end of the night (you know a version of this girl or did in your twenties at least). Anyway, long story short, the three assholes I journeyed to Nipple Creek with started acting super strange when we were about five minutes away from our destination. We had smoked a couple of joints, but they hadn't been more potent than Heidi's normal stash.

I was concerned.

"Heidi! Come here!" I barked as soon as we unloaded from the car. I made it a point to avoid watching Arlo as he slid out of his peasant skirt and threw his tank top and puka-shell bracelets in the lake.

Heidi started giggling uncontrollably.

"What is going on?" I hissed, regretting like hell that I hadn't taken my own car.

Allison had stripped down as well, and she and Arlo were cooing and touching each other's faces.

"The three of us ate some mushrooms," Heidi cackled. "We didn't offer you any because you don't do that stuff, but . . ."

She trailed off and her mouth slackened as she watched a moth flutter overhead.

"Beeeaaaauuuutttiiifffuuuulllll," she murmured, her eyes unfocused.

"GodfuckingdammitHeidi! Is this a fucking joke?"

I knew that it wasn't though. She heeled off her shoes and threw her bra at the headlights of the car. Before her shorts hit the ground, I grabbed them and swiped her pocketed car keys.

For the next several hours I dipped in and out of the lake, snacked from our cooler, and cursed her stupid name as she and her idiot friends ran barefoot and naked through the woods petting rocks and tasting dirt.

So, you can see why I was hesitant to trust Heidi again. It had only been a week since the shrooms incident. She was still peeling from the sunburn she'd gotten all those hours she'd communed with the squirrels or whatever the fuck she was doing.

I forbade my eyes to wander back to the near-overflowing bin of pot that had begun to hum my name.

"We will just smoke a little," she protested. "They're fine with me sampling the product. How else can I be a good saleswoman?"

It was like she was reenacting the exact plot from every single drug-related movie I had ever seen. Every drug abuser skims a little off the top at first, until their use flies out of control and they eventually have their knees bashed in by one of the boss's muscle-men. I could envision a prosthetic leg and an eye patch in Heidi's very near future.

The practical side of me screamed that I should take back the frozen pizza I had brought and hightail it out of the apartment. But then there was the other side.

"I was never here," I grumbled. I knew she kept her rolling papers in her nightstand drawer, and I reached to fetch them.

"No," Heidi replied, her expression serious. "For our inaugural dip into this fine stash, we're using Betty."

My eyes widened. Betty was an absolutely enormous, intricately etched pink bong that looked like it had been crafted by Cartier. I was certain that the thing cost more than all my grandmother's silver and fine china combined. And like my grandma's showy baubles, Betty only came out for very special occasions.

Betty combined with Heidi's choice crop dealt us the kind of mind-melting high you'd not be surprised to wake up from wearing a unitard and a helmet and finding your panties running through the short cycle in the dishwasher.

My next coherent moment came the following morning while I tried to get my fuzzy head together enough to get to work. Before I left the house, I spied a polished-off pan of brownies next to empty Thai takeout boxes that should've been thrown away weeks before. Too bad my high ass didn't think to munch on some penicillin, considering how sick I'd probably be from the ancient leftovers.

With my hair askew and my clothes wrinkled, I raced out of the house, vowing to never smoke with Heidi again. I preferred cheap weed. I liked the kind of high that wore off in a couple of hours after a few fast-food chalupas, not the kind that punched holes in my consciousness and made me skip backward down a busy interstate.

"Never again," I muttered, trying to draw eyeliner on at a stoplight. If I was going to look like a steaming pile of trash at work, I at least wanted to look like a steaming pile of trash that had tried.

I glanced at my phone as it chimed with a text notification.

C u at break? Heidi texted, chasing the message with another that featured a chain of exclamation points.

I pictured my friend in a cloud of dank pot fumes waiting for me to join her couch-side during the middle of my split shift.

I blinked away chunks of the dollar-store makeup that swam across my eye.

"She's crazy," I muttered.

As a medical historian at the local plasma center, I didn't necessarily have to be sober to perform my job functions. Basically, I spent my shifts asking folks if they'd engaged in sex with wildlife and medically turning away people for smelling so bad that they made other patients pass out on the donation table. If a donor had a visible human bite mark or admitted to fucking a camel, they were sent away for the day. Essentially, it was the perfect job to be high at. But no, I wasn't going to smoke weed anymore. I had sworn off it that morning when I had awakened in a sea of orange-juice-soaked Frosted Flakes, with morning breath reminiscent of a used tampon. I especially wasn't getting high with Heidi anymore.

Screw that.

She texted a smiley face (made out of a colon and parenthesis because it was 2004 and real emojis were still a bit out of our small-town reach).

No thx. I'm out. I answered, taking approximately seventeen hours because my hot-pink Razr phone was . . . well, a hot-pink Razr phone.

Whatev. 12p.

I sighed, staring at my smudged eyeliner in the rearview mirror. My resolve to become a more responsible member of society wilted. I thought longingly of my friend and her water bong and her perfect smoke rings.

K.

I jerked the wheel in the direction of a grocery store, making a pit stop before getting to the plasma center.

If Heidi was supplying the weed, the least I could do was provide the freezer egg rolls and grape jelly.

Chapter Seventeen

MySpace Mismatch

I met Bailey at a bar. She stalked me on MySpace (yep, I'm that old), saw my plans to hit up the local gay dance club that night, and swooped in for the kill.

I was fresh out of a terrible relationship with a woman I was pretty certain I was madly in love with (I wasn't). To deal with being broken up with and miserable, I had made it a personal goal to soak myself in as much liquor as humanly possible. My friends tried to offer helpful distractions; Heidi and I went to clubs every single night of the week and danced off our beer and margarita carbs with few cares in the world. We'd end the nights screaming the lyrics of popular songs in the streets and searching for more hot pepper flakes for our slices of pizza.

I think Bailey thought I was just the girl she was looking for (I wasn't). I had a pulse and a presentable face, and that seemed enough to satisfy her checklist.

On the Saturday that we met, my friend and I made plans on my public MySpace page. A viewer patient enough to wait for my page to load while listening to my theme song (Kelly Clarkson's

"Since U Been Gone," because fuck you, ex-girlfriend whom I most definitely wasn't trying to get attention from) would have easily discovered that I'd be at our town's only queer bar that night.

Bailey suffered my song, flipped through my ever-evolving top eight friends, spritzed on some cheap cologne, and parked herself at the edge of the club dance floor to await my arrival.

This sort of prep for someone you've never met may seem like a bit much, but in a small town like where I lived back then, it was a necessary practice. Before my ex left me, she had explained that upon her departure I would be considered fresh meat by the local horde of lady gays. Because I hadn't yet cycled through the native lesbian crowd (sexually or emotionally), I was like a new, exotic pet that had been released into the wild. I hadn't screwed my way through the area lesbians, and I didn't have a cache of ex-girlfriends. My vagina was a much sought-after fresh start for the gay women who had sampled the rest of the local fare. Excuse the expression, but my pastures had yet to be grazed upon.

For the moment, I was a hot commodity.

Not caring much about Bailey's presence, I breezed into the bar like the celebrity I thought I was. As was our usual practice, my friend and I made a beeline for the dance floor, where we took shot after shot of whatever was offered to us.

"Hey, isn't that the girl who has been cyberstalking you?" Heidi asked, nudging her chin toward the perimeter of the dance floor.

It wasn't exactly a full-on predatory situation, but Heidi was a shit-talking connoisseur. I regretted mentioning the one private message from Bailey that said she hoped to see me at the club that evening.

"Uh, maybe," I shouted back over the beat of the Pussycat Dolls. What I lacked in rhythm I made up for in confusing gyrations and intense facial expressions. "I don't know for sure. The internet made her look taller."

Unfortunately, the internet had lied. Bailey wasn't tall at all. In fact, she didn't much look like her profile in any other way either. The girl we stared at had long blond hair gathered into a low-slung ponytail. She wore a pink polo with the collar strategically popped.

"You don't do girls in pink," Heidi commented, already disapproving of my admirer before giving her a fair chance.

"Or with long hair," I agreed.

Heidi shook her head, her eyes widening as Bailey did a strange, offbeat shimmy in our direction.

"Nooooo," I moaned. "Shit, she's coming over."

"Hey, you," Bailey hummed. "You're as gorgeous as your profile makes you look."

Well, that makes one of us, I thought sourly, strongly resisting the urge to ask where the butch version of her from online had gone.

I liked butch. I liked androgyny. What I didn't like was a slightly less feminine version of myself. I have never, ever hoped to go down on someone who would later ask me to flat-iron their hair and gab with me about when I think Justin and Britney will get back together. In sum, I don't want to date anyone who knows more about Kate Bosworth's skin care routine than I do. It works for some people, but it's not for me.

I knew in the club that Bailey wasn't going to work. I knew that I wasn't interested and that my friend already hated her (and that the others would soon follow suit). By the same token, I was certain there was no way I was ever going to allow her tongue entry to my mouth.

All those reasons are precisely why I shouldn't have let her peel me away from my friend for the night and why I shouldn't have agreed to go out with her the next day. But, because I was young, a proven nongenius, and desperate for attention after yet another bad breakup, I followed her to an empty table to chat.

Excitement with Bailey was limited. In the weeks after our meeting at the bar, we went to dinner at Chili's (her favorite) enough times to put me off the restaurant for the rest of my life. She ate chicken fingers and chips and salsa by the pound while I guzzled Presidente margaritas like I was trying to consume the entire world's supply of tequila (I was).

Things with Bailey weren't going particularly well. We didn't have much to talk about. We weren't even mildly attracted to each other. We didn't have the same friends or like the same foods. She was a nondrinker and was into fitness, and I was a heavy drinker with the mission of fitting as many Hostess cupcakes into my body as possible.

If the sex had been phenomenal, my young brain might have forgiven all our grave differences. Who am I kidding? My old brain would do the same. But in the two months we dated, we didn't even kiss. It never occurred to me that we should, and Bailey was too grief-stricken over her own lost love to consider making any moves.

The chicken strips and chips had clearly taken her libido to a very dark place.

Bailey cried. A lot. Like, a lot, a lot.

She had recently been broken up with by a straight woman (go figure) with a kid and missed them both terribly. On our dates at the house her wealthy parents had bought her to get her and all her tears the hell out of their basement, I mostly watched her play Super Mario Bros. and cry.

It wasn't the best time I had ever had, but the embarrassing truth is it wasn't actually the worst time I'd ever had either.

Because our nonexistent relationship was going so poorly, we decided to ratchet it up a level. On one Saturday, when I thought I was driving over to Bailey's house to watch her cry over her heterosexual ex again, she surprised me.

"Let's get a dog together," she sniffed.

Why the fuck would we do that? I wondered even as I gathered my bag and keys.

A dog? Hell yes, we should get a dog. Of course we should! I reasoned. *It will get us out of Bailey's house for the afternoon and maybe stymie the tears for a couple of hours. Sorry, Luigi! We've got better shit to do today than help you rescue Princess Peach!*

Besides, I knew that the local pound was far away enough from Chili's that Bailey's depression would get the best of her before she was willing to drive twenty minutes across town.

We ended up at an animal shelter, where we looked at row after row of pitiful pups pressed against the fence line practically begging for a home.

"What about him?" Bailey asked. She reached a puny arm (another false advertisement from her online profile) upward to pet the giant head of a mangy, snow-colored dog.

"He's huge!" I exclaimed.

The shelter employee approached us from behind and nodded.

"He's a Great Pyrenees," she said. "This big guy weighs in at a hundred fifty pounds."

I stared at Bailey, whose expression had taken on a look of sheer worship.

"He's the one," she whispered. "Hercules is supposed to be ours, Jess."

At that moment I was surprised by a couple of things. The thing that shocked me first was that she remembered my name. The second was that she had seemingly already named the freaking dog.

"He's—he's so big," I stammered.

When I'd realized we were going full lesbian and getting a dog together after two months of dating, I had figured we'd be getting something much smaller. I was thinking more Pomeranian than Great Dane. I was thinking we would rescue a ratty Yorkie that we could carry around in a purse instead of the biggest dog at the fucking pound.

Eventually breaking up with a million-pound Great Pyrenees and a crying lesbian seemed less manageable than abandoning a snippy Chihuahua, as I had previously planned.

"Bailey, maybe we should talk about this," I spluttered again as I watched her pass the worker her mom's gold-hued credit card. "I'm not really a dog person, and—"

Bailey pressed a finger against my lips to shush me, proving that she didn't fucking know me at all. I am not one to be shushed, especially not by a goddamned finger that had spent the morning scratching the mangy under-ears of stray pups and pulling ticks from their bellies.

We had never even bumped lady bits, and suddenly, we were sharing ownership of a dog. It was more than I wanted to deal with on a hungover Saturday afternoon.

With my face burning and my eyes wide, my first thought was to punch her in the throat. Instead, I backed up and tried to push my newly adopted goliath dog out of my vagina, where his nose had taken residence.

I don't know if it was the canine so willingly diving into my bits and pieces or the thrill of adopting together that effected a change in Bailey, but something sure as hell did. As soon as she had the leash in hand, she turned from a sullen victim of a broken heart to a horny beast of a woman possessed.

"Let's get to the car," she growled, tugging on the dog, who appeared to be as confused as I was. The pop of her hand against my ass rang out, causing the shelter employee to hike an eyebrow in surprise.

What in the actual shit is happening? Is Bailey one of those fetishists whose proclivities involve including animals in her romps?

I was into a lot of stuff, some of it off-kilter, but there was no way that I was going to be a party to a threesome involving a hundred-fifty-pound dog. I'm by no means judgmental of other people's sex lives but I'm wholly into consent. Hercules was in no way capable of agreeing to whatever weird kinks my pseudo-girlfriend had in mind. I was ready to call the police and, no matter my landlord's opinion, take sole ownership of the adoptee if I found out Bailey was that kind of an asshole.

Admittedly, I was nervous when we got back to her house. I had no idea what to expect as we pulled into her graveled drive. I also knew that I didn't really want our relationship to go much further than it already had. The Chili's dates had been casual, and watching her cry had occupied time I could've spent obsessing over my own ex. She was something to do, someone to be with, and that was about it. But now the events of the day, specifically the dog adoption, were fucking next-level serious. We were officially neck-deep in water I hadn't intended to tread.

Bailey all but threw the dog into her backyard, slammed the

gate, and grabbed me by the hand to drag me to her bedroom. Her breath rasped in short gasps as what I assumed was passion overtook her.

In moments, she had flung me onto her bed. Her bra hit the ceiling fan and she wriggled out of her gym shorts (her deep-depression wear for the season).

"Uh, Bailey?" I asked, craning my head from my spot on her lumpy bed.

"Yeah?" she answered throatily, peeling her boy shorts off.

Fuck, nudity had just happened. I was looking at a bare-naked woman and wishing she was instead in a full snowsuit, boots included.

"Uh, what's the plan here?"

I had spiraled into full awkward-Jess mode and there was no turning back.

"What kind of lube do you want?" she panted.

"Huh?"

My eyes bulged at the drawer she had opened. It was brimming with a variety of half-filled, crusty-lidded lubes of various shapes, sizes, and flavors. The festering drawer had clearly been through many a girlfriend.

Now, in my forties, I wish my then-twenty-two-year-old mouth had accumulated the life experience to say something along the lines of "I'm in my prime, bitch. My vagina needs no assistance."

But it didn't. I just continued to gape in wonder at the grotesque display of emollient. Some of the contraband in the drawer looked like it had been manufactured the same year as my grandparents.

Bailey gave up on waiting for my response. Apparently, the

situation had just become a "chef's choice" scenario, as she grabbed a bottle to her own liking and hopped up on the bed. The girl that I had previously known to have the energy of a three-toed sloth sure seemed to have found a fount of vitality.

"Should we check on the dog?" I asked, ignoring her blatant state of undress. I was about as turned on as a patient undergoing a root canal. "Maybe we should check on the dog."

"After," she murmured breathily. "After."

Fuck it, I thought resignedly. *At least we're not at Chili's.*

Desire burning in her eyes, Bailey sprawled next to me on the bed and poured a generous amount of red gooey liquid from the grimy bottle onto her spread vagina. She made a guttural moan as the liquid trickled over her exposed parts.

The sound was frighteningly similar to the one she made when she was halfway through an order of Chili's chicken fingers.

Oh, sweet Jesus, make her stop! my brain shrieked. I had the fleeting idea to remind her of the tragedy of the lost hetero ex. For the first time since being in Bailey's company, I wished that she would start crying.

Once she had buttered herself up like a Denny's short stack, she turned to me.

"You want to put it on, or should I?"

In that instant, I could think of nothing other than the bottle's previous users. The crimson ooze sloshed inside its plastic container. I didn't need the lube. I didn't want the lube. But if I had, I certainly wasn't the type of girl who would accept that my girlfriend thought it was all right to offer me a used-ass bottle. Was I not worth four dollars and a trip to the fucking Walgreens vaginal-itch-cream aisle? What in the hell was wrong with her?

So, with my twenty-two meager years of maturity and panic clawing their way through my chest, I catapulted out of my girl-friend's bed.

"Where are you—"

I didn't even let Bailey finish as I grabbed my keys. I stopped by the back gate to pat the dog that I had co-owned for less than an hour on his scraggly head and rode off into the sunset.

I never paid any sort of pet support to Bailey or ever even talked to her again after that fateful day. I did hear, however, through the lesbian gossip mill that I was a prudish bitch who probably wasn't worth the lay anyway. I certainly wasn't worth the last little glob of lube from the best bottle she had. That was for damned sure.

Chapter Eighteen

Cross-Country Chronic

The other day I was curled up on our overstuffed sectional, wearing my nipple-high Target mom jeans, online buying Fourth of July décor while I texted my friend Matt about bygone days.

Can we be young again for like five minutes? Please? Like, you wear those weird fuckin' shiny club pants, and we sit on your couch that smelled like pee and eat mozzarella sticks by the dozen?

How did we never end up in jail? was his response.

And here's the thing of it. We belonged in jail. We really did. We did so many ridiculous, reckless things. We weren't menaces to society but we definitely would've been safer on the other side of some iron bars. Not forever, just for as long as our early twenties were in full swing.

Remember THE pot brownies? I asked.

Which ones?

THE FUCKING POT BROWNIES!

Again, how did we never end up doing jail time?

Remembering that I was fun once, I chuckled and added some patriotic pillow shams to my Amazon cart.

Lemme just say, for the particular incident I'm about to describe, Matt and I most certainly should have spent an overnight in jail. Not because of the pot but because we were an actual danger. Granted, a very slow-moving, hazily focused, go-with-the-flow kind of danger, but a road hazard all the same.

In 2007, pot was still a big deal. Possession of it wasn't some namby-pamby, no-biggie sort of thing back then. You didn't want to get caught with any amount of it. You definitely didn't want to get caught with it crossing state lines if you were the type that wouldn't fare well in the slammer.

With me being the pussy I was, and Matt being a bit of a cupcake as well, I have to say that neither of us would've exactly been a gang leader on the inside. Within hours I would've been designated oral giver to the entire cell block. That's a lot of cunnilingus to parcel out for a girl of my particular level of laziness. My very jaw aches at the thought of all the forced rim jobs I'd have been expected to give. I'm an organized person, so a schedule would've been enacted to marshal the lip service, but it would've certainly been more exertion than I was in physical shape for.

With that at the forefront of our thoughts, we still decided to spend the lion's share of our paychecks that week on a king's ransom of marijuana. Even worse? We had been shopping with a purpose. We needed the pot not to sell but to smoke our minds senseless on the trip to Colorado to see my brother that we'd been planning for months.

If you haven't been counting the crimes, please tally with me: 1) We bought not only a little weed, but enough that if caught we could have gotten a felony charge of intent to sell. 2) We then decided to travel with it across the country.

Like Betty fucking Crocker on chronic, I tied my apron strings, dug out my best whisk, and got to work. What money wasn't being saved for road trip gas, Matt and I pooled for baking supplies. In the two days leading up to our departure, I made weed brownies (hashies, space cakes, grandma's special brownies, whatever you wanna call them). We sampled and critiqued and tweaked recipes until we had the perfect stockpile of travel treats.

Matt loaded a cooler with the makings of sandwiches and sodas, and we set off in his car. The trek from Northwest Arkansas to Denver was a long one but we cared little. We were packed with enough munchies and pot to last us far longer than it would take.

To be frank, I don't remember much of the trip to Colorado. Upon asking Matt, I learned that his memory is murky as well. Normally I wouldn't have smoked such a steady stream of blunts whilst munching magic brownies, but we were on vacation! Nothing mattered but having fun! I do recall that much of the thirteen-hour trip involved me turned around in my seat as I slapped cheese and mustard between two pieces of Great Value bread. Marijuana ingestion was a hungry business, and as the passenger, my primary duty was to keep everyone high and fed. Luckily for me, steadied precariously on my knees with a knife in hand, Matt never exceeded fifty miles per hour (even on the highway). Minivans filled with soccer moms sped by and flipped us off, and we sniggered and waved as they left us in their dust.

"Why's everyone going so fast?" I mumbled lazily.

Shaking his head and inhaling his sixth sandwich, my friend shrugged. "Dunno. They need to just chill."

We, on the other hand, were chill as fuck. We were so chill, in fact, that we probably should've been wearing adult diapers.

Which is likely why the drive took nearly seventeen hours. It's also probably why we didn't give a shit that we were still driving four hours after we should've arrived at my brother's doorstep.

My brother was thrilled with the payload of pot we delivered unto his Friday. I don't remember much of the weekend, but I know that partying ensued. The theme of our Colorado getaway was to remain as liquor plastered and weed bombed as possible, and we absolutely remained in character.

Surprisingly, when we loaded back in the car on Sunday, Matt and I were a bit over the drinking and smoking. In an effort to send our trip out with a bang, we had stayed up the night before partying. By the time we said our goodbyes, we were done. Though young, our bodies were wrecked from the forty-eight straight hours of depravity. Sleep-deprived and nauseous, we were ready to get home. We tried to refuse the giant plate of leftover weed brownies my brother shoved into my arms, but he insisted we take them home.

"I'm going sober on Monday," he said, looking longingly at the fudgy leftovers. "I can't have the temptation."

Matt and I groaned but agreed to take them home to freeze. Surely someday we'd want to be high again (like the following weekend). With our teeth and hair freshly brushed for the first time since we'd crossed state lines, we tossed our hungover asses into the car and set off.

We had just polished off a pair of bagels and some non-spiked OJ when we saw police lights in our rearview mirror. Matt eased the car to the side of the highway and put it in park.

"Dammit," he said, knowing the stop would delay our getting home. He had begun fishing in his pocket for his ID when I heard his breath catch in his throat. "Jess!" he hissed. "The fuckin' brownies!"

Motherfucking Christ. We were in so much trouble.

The cop was still pulling in behind us when I realized what we had to do. I had a genius epiphany but it had to be enacted immediately to work.

I grabbed a fistful of the leftover contraband and stuffed it into my mouth. Urging the plate into my friend's lap, I told him to do the same.

"I can't!" he said, his eyes, bright for the first time in days, shining with tears.

"Prison!" I mumbled, weed brownie spilling from my mouth. *"The Shawshank Redemption. The Green Mile."*

His mouth unhinged and in popped a pair of thick chocolate squares stubbled with the upmarket marijuana our combined checks had bought.

I watched the cop in my side mirror as I choked down a fourth brownie. Matt wolfed down a third. My fifth brownie felt like a cinder block as it undulated down my throat. Turning green, Matt gulped another. We heard the cop's boots crunch on gravel as we stared at the final wedge on the plate.

"I'm driving," Matt reminded me. He stared pointedly at the last piece of evidence.

Fuck.

I crammed the sugary hunk into the back of my throat and willed myself to swallow while my friend tossed the bare plate into a sea of suitcases and fast-food containers in his back seat.

"Son, do you know what you were doing wrong?"

We had done a lot of shit wrong. Like, a whole lot. I stared at the smug-looking state trooper as he doubled and then tripled in my drug-addled vision. It took all my mental fortitude to stuff down the giggle that was threatening to soar out of my mouth. I chomped the inside of my cheek to keep the psychotic laughter at bay.

Perhaps the drugs shouldn't have taken effect that quickly, but given the long weekend lacking sobriety and the fact that we had smoked my brother's stash into the early hours of the morning, the megadose intermingled with my hangover and slammed into my brain like a freight train.

While I corked my urge to cackle maniacally, I watched my friend squint at the officer with what appeared to be an attempt at seriousness on his face. His somber air landed us nothing more than a warning citation and instruction to "at least maintain the minimum posted speed limit." Consciously reminding myself to keep my mouth closed, I glanced at the nearby road sign. Sure enough, just below the maximum limit was a minimum of thirty-five. Apparently, the state of Colorado was well used to motorists such as me and my bestie. All these years later I still don't know what the hell we had been doing wrong other than being higher than Willie Nelson at a Snoop Dogg concert.

The cop sauntered away in his cop boots. Through my soupy, pot-blown eyesight I swear he turned into a unicorn and jumped into one of those greenish tubes that transport Mario and Luigi to different worlds. However, some of the details of this particular story are difficult to confirm. When I have repeated it to others, I have often heard, "Weed can't make you hallucinate."

The fuck it can't.

Matt was so baked that I recall him crying over how unjust it was that our patriarchal society expects women to wear bras. With my mouth stuffed full of Red Vines licorice, I sobbed with him as we bawled remembering the newly released ASPCA public service announcement featuring Sarah McLachlan's "Angel" crooned to scenes of matted, malnourished animals. We were both strict vegetarians at the time, and though we have never talked about the incident (out of pure fucking shame), I know for a fact that we stopped by a Whataburger and ate some beefy double stacks that afternoon.

That was the day that I died. My mind left my body and floated far, far away. I know I mentioned haziness regarding memories of this entire weekend before, but I'm serious now. I quite literally have not a single recollection of what happened after the cop issued a citation for "driving in the left lane too long without getting over" or some such bullshit. There were no handmade sandwiches on the way home because I was too fucking busy reminding myself to breathe. The memories from there on are nonexistent. All I know is that we eventually made it home and that I'm now forty-one (proof that I survived).

That is all.

Chapter Nineteen

Burned Barista

There are a million cool jobs out there. People work as surf in-
structors, for goodness' sake. They may risk being eaten by a shark
each time they clock in, but they're tan as fuck and can swim
away from their boss any time he acts like a dick. Some folks
make a living from skydiving. Like, they collect a paycheck by
helping folks fling their terrified bodies out of an airplane fourteen
thousand feet above the ground. Do you know how much I would
pay to push some people I've met from the gaping mouth of an
open hatch? Spies do spy shit (see the original Bourne movie or
any of its ninety-two sequels for a more detailed description).
People are Olympians, and an entire group of women does high
kicks as Radio City Rockettes each Christmas. In that same vein,
there are artists who dress up like fucking cats and skulk around
stages singing about goddamned Rum Tum Tugger six times a
week. There are private-island caretakers (truly), waterslide test-
ers, and professional sleepers (pretty sure I was one of these, sans
the pay, my freshman year of college). I have a friend who is a
brewmaster. He's a drunk who made a lucrative business out of

his inability to lay off the juice. Other than the potential for bullets whizzing past your forehead and slicing an artery, being a fighter pilot seems fairly fucking awesome too.

There are shitty jobs too, though. Roofing in Louisiana in mid-August ain't for the faint of heart. I once saw a lady standing in front of Walmart with a leaf blower whose entire purpose was to keep detritus out of the store in forty-mile-per-hour winds. She looked like she would've been happy to have been hit by one of the cars trying to find a parking spot. There are people who masturbate barnyard animals for a living, others who work as elves in the mall, and supersmellers who sniff armpits for twenty dollars an hour. Some poor bastard somewhere squeegees the ejaculate off portable toilet stall walls during music festivals.

I've had bad jobs. When I was sixteen and still reasonably innocent, I worked as a hostess at a Denny's that was connected to a drive-up motel. You'd be surprised how many pantsless people holding dildos answer their door to accept room service orders. I know I certainly was.

You can understand why, then, when I was a teenager employed by a greasy spoon, I thought working in a record store was the pinnacle of coolness. À la the casts of the 1995 cult classic *Empire Records* and 1986's *Pretty in Pink*, the edgiest, most alternative, freethinking people held employment in such places. A job sorting vinyl and recommending CDs was the career of gods. They were all wearing vintage leather jackets and plaid skirts and saying things like, "Here, try my favorite Clash underground album," while I was serving double onion patty melts at an oily diner with volcanic zits on my chin.

I liked record slingers. I liked their music. I liked their clothes. I got their angsty teenage problems. I was obsessed with how effortlessly awesome they were. But I wasn't one of them. With my Doc Martens laced to the lip and overalls cuffed, I applied to their type of jobs, I just didn't get hired. Considering my postnasal drip and never-ending campaign to secure the McRib a permanent spot on the McMenu, I suppose I just didn't have the right stuff to make the cut.

But there was this one time when I did get hired for one of those jobs. One of the cool-kid jobs.

Or at least I thought so at first. You see, seemingly out of the blue one day, my bestie Matt and I decided to find gainful employment together. Well, maybe the situation wasn't entirely out of left field. If I'm being honest, we were both so broke that we had actually smoked catnip for lack of marijuana the night before. Even Phillip, Matt's overfed orange cat, was disgusted with the pair of us. We were at rock bottom with no means to get high. Thus, we set out to make some cash.

A new lesbian club had opened near our apartments and we knew they needed help. The bar was on the wrong side of town (away from literally everything), too near a police station for party-goers to do any real drinking if they planned to drive home (this was pre-pre-pre-Uber), and, two weeks after opening, already known to be poorly managed.

The only neighboring business was a "juice bar" next door. The glitzy marquee with a long-legged cartoon woman wearing little more than a cowboy hat flickering outside made sure that potential customers didn't bring their kids inside expecting a version of Jamba Juice. For those of you who still have ideas that this place was a good spot to get a shot of wheatgrass, allow me to explain. Juice bars are full-nude strip clubs. Like, you get the entire beaver experience without having to pay extra in a splooge-covered back room. I don't think that there's a male version of this type of club because no woman anywhere wants to ogle naked dicks for fun. Because the dancers are completely naked, they aren't allowed to serve alcohol. However, at this particular juice bar, the toothless patrons were welcome to bring coolers full of liquor. The frequent fliers knew to bring a large enough ice chest not only to store their PBR and jerky sticks but also to serve as a seat, as the semen-speckled furniture was sparse in the tiny establishment.

Believe it or not, when we walked into the lesbian club next door, Blazing Lips, we were hired on the spot. It was a Friday morning, and save for the mulleted owner, Sheila, the bar was empty.

"Be back tonight at seven p.m. to work the door," Sheila said, studying Matt closely.

"My friend too?" he asked, jutting a thumb in my direction. I pulled at the hemline of my Save Ferris T-shirt and smiled nervously.

"Yeah, whatever," Sheila answered, sighing at me.

I had been hired to work in a lesbian bar! I was so, so excited. I had wished for a cool job since I had been of working age and it had finally happened. My newly out self practically burst out of my Birkenstocks. Later that night I would be face-to-face with an entire town's worth of queer folk and I couldn't wait.

Matt and I hurried home. He took a nap, and I washed and hung my nicest Hot Topic tee for the occasion.

When we arrived later that night, I bounced on the toes of my scuffed Converse in excitement. I couldn't believe my luck. Yes, I realized I'd ridden the coattails of my much cooler friend to get the job, but I didn't care. For once I wasn't standing in front of a fryer full of pig fat or behind a register refusing expired pancake coupons.

Matt and I walked through the front door of the still-empty club. Sheila and her partner waved us over.

"I'm so excited to work the door!" I blurted, sounding like I'd downed eight gas station uppers on the way to the bar.

"No," Sheila said, barely even looking at me. "You can't be in the bar."

"I'm twenty-one."

"Yeah, no," she replied, squinting at me. "You're going to work in the coffee shop in the back."

"There's a coffee shop?" Matt asked incredulously. Our city wasn't huge and we hadn't heard that such a place existed. When we weren't taking siestas and eating mozzarella sticks, we were generally keeping up on the news of our small town.

"As of tonight, there is," the owner's girl said snidely. "Now that we have someone to run it."

She grabbed my arm and led me through the club, under the strobe lights, beyond the stocked bar, and into an attached room at the back.

I sighed pathetically as I surveyed my surroundings. Indeed the coffee shop existed.

Motherfucker.

"We just set it up, so there might be some inventory issues," the bitchy girlfriend said, flicking on the lights over a makeshift bar top. I saw a toaster oven, a scratched Crock-Pot that was an exact match of my mom's, and a giant refrigerator. The coffeepot was a standard twelve-cup that looked like it had seen better days. Beyond the poorly stocked kitchenette were a few tables and a mismatched array of chairs. In completing the tour, we visited the adjoining bathroom, where there was a stool in front of the toilet. The girlfriend kicked it to the side.

"That's for my son," she explained. "He's potty training."

In a nightclub?

No, wait, I reminded myself. *We aren't in the actual bar, we are in an unnamed fucking coffee shop connected to a fucking shit bar.*

"What do you, I mean, we, um, serve?" I asked, my hands swaying at my sides awkwardly.

The mohawked girlfriend handed me the restaurant's sole hand-fucking-written menu, which included bagels, chicken salad sandwiches, biscuits and gravy, and bags of chips. There was also a sprinkling of things like bottled water (I wasn't allowed to serve water from the tap, at least not for free), sodas, and bottled juices. The coffee shop didn't appear to have much to offer as far as coffee shop fare was concerned. There was nary a latte or an espresso in sight.

"And I would, like, make this stuff?"

She looked at me as if I was as stupid as I felt at that moment.

"I don't know who the piss else would," she snarled. "You're the only one who works in here."

Wishing I was back at Denny's with their multiple fancy laminated menus and line cooks, I gnawed my lip. I couldn't bail. I had ridden in with Matt, and I was sure he wouldn't abandon his awesome new post at the front door.

"Is the shop open now?"

"At two," she answered. "When the bar closes. Jesus."

She flashed me another look of disgust and slammed back through the door that connected the café to the club.

In a time before cell phones, and a million miles away from the side of town I was used to, I was in a real conundrum. More than anything I wanted to flee like I was on fire, hit up the nearest Taco Tico, and sprawl out in my stretchy pants in front of my TV at home. But I was sure Matt was already flirting with and giving free admission to pods of cute boys lining up to get into the club. There was no goddamned way I would con him into ditching the new job. Besides, we really did need the money. Afroman (a rapper made famous by the 2000 hit "Because I Got High") was coming to town (again) and we wanted to buy tickets.

Because at twenty-one I was utterly spineless, and because the closest place that I would find a phone to call for help was at the birthday-suit brothel next door, I decided to make the best of the situation. Ergo, I decided to suck it up and figure the job out.

As I discovered that the toaster oven could only fit four biscuits at a time and that cooking gravy in a Crock-Pot was a truly disgusting task, dread enfolded me. The coffee shop hadn't been equipped with utensils to scoop the chicken salad, but that was okay, because the only bread I could find to put it on was the moldy-ass bagels that I uncovered under one of the cabinets.

With no utensils and only a paint stick to stir the congealing gravy, I felt about as fucked as a girl in her fanciest mall-kiosk cargo pants could be.

Pissed, I decided to exact a bit of revenge by helping myself to as many of those expensive whole-fruit smoothie drinks in the fridge as I could fit into my body. If I was going to do the stupid job, I was at least going to stick it to the fuckers by consuming fifty-eight dollars' worth of juice at their expense first. In reality though, I was the one who paid, in lava diarrhea for the next few days, as no human is meant to consume seventeen pears, twenty-two apples, eight bananas, five mangoes, and a kiwi in one sitting. Sure, the coffee shop had to cover the cost, but my asshole was the true victim.

Once I had sucked down seventeen thousand calories' worth of fruit pulp, I gathered myself and waited.

By the time two a.m. rolled around, I was certain I wasn't ready for the bar rush that Mohawk had promised would arrive. I had no flavors for the coffee and had only been able to cook twelve biscuits (all of which needed to be rotated back into the toaster oven because the café was without heat and roughly forty-five degrees).

I held my breath, praying that no one would show.

To my utter horror, some of the bar attendees had been talked into visiting the café. The first couple of customers took pity on me and ordered only coffee (it had to be black because I didn't have cream or sugar) in lidless foam cups.

"Eight dollars, please," I whispered, my head dipped in shame as I took the single menu back from another customer to read the price of the scalded brew.

The night didn't get better. The more drunken customers, those searching to soak up the Boone's and Mike's Hards they had spent the night downing, were less gracious with their orders.

"Chicken salad sandwich with chips," one slurred.

"I can do the chips," I offered. "But I don't have bread."

"How 'bout on one of them?" the lesbian jeered, pointing at my waning tower of cooling biscuits. She looked like she needed to puke. I didn't judge too harshly though because at the moment I likely looked the same.

I nodded curtly and pulled the chicken salad out of the mildewed fridge. I remembered at that moment that not only was I without a knife to slice the biscuit, I also didn't have a spoon with which to smear the chicken salad. I used my body as a shield to cover up what I was doing from the small gathering of foot-tapping customers. I tore the biscuit apart and attempted to use one half of the crumbly bread to scoop the mostly frozen, likely expired chicken mash onto the other side of the makeshift bun.

"Fuck me," I muttered, feeling heat creep across my neck as the betraying biscuit disintegrated in my shaking hands. I was painfully aware of the hot-ass group of women giggling to each other behind me.

"No chicken salad," I repeated through gritted teeth.

The famished drunk wasn't giving up though.

"Try that stick in the Crock-Pot," she hiccuped helpfully.

Wishing my appendix would burst and kill me on the spot, I pivoted on my heel and grabbed the paint stick out of the gravy sludge.

Laughter erupted in the small café as I sawed through yet another biscuit and began to ladle the hunks of chicken, mayonnaise, and egg onto the pitiful roll. Like a focused Bob Ross, I used teensy strokes to keep the mess of the slathering to a minimum (especially because, despite my searching, I had yielded no broom, mop, or napkins).

The job that I had started the day thinking would be so amazing had quickly gone south. Every single minute was sheer torture.

Finally, when I was near tears trying to work a register that I hadn't been shown how to use and sick of looking for normal café supplies that had never been purchased in the first place, customers stopped coming in. The last stragglers only showed up to see the rumored struggle of the girl working in the new coffee shop.

Much to their delight, I proved the talk true when I had to refuse to sell any more items because someone had pocketed the only menu and I could no longer look up prices.

When Matt ambled in at the end of the night, beer hot on his breath and a guy under his arm, I nearly punched him in the face.

"Will you make me something?" he whined. "I'm starving."

"No fucking way."

"Are you ready to get out of here?"

Friend, I've been ready to get out of here since the millisecond I walked in.

I nodded violently and snagged my jacket from under the counter. That's when Sheila, the bar owner, strode into the room.

"You have to clean up," she directed.

"Uh, I did," I answered, gesturing to the cleared countertop. With no hot water, soap, sponges, or paper towels, I had struggled to get the place clean, but I had improvised and used one of the two-ply rolls from the adjoining bathroom. The shredding of the see-through toilet paper had been the icing on top of the shit cake.

Sheila tossed Matt a Crown Royal drawstring bag of what sounded like coins.

"You still have to get rid of this," she said, gesturing toward the cooling Crock-Pot.

"Okay," I answered, desperately wanting my own liquor bag full of coins. I had earned the fuck out of my pay that night and couldn't wait to have it in my hands.

I hefted up the congealed pot of bullshit gravy, realizing immediately that there was nowhere to dump it. I had it on good authority that the single sink was clogged. The trash can was overflowing and there were no extra liners.

"Is there, like, somewhere I should put this?" I asked timidly, shifting the weight of the dirty pot in my arms. Matt glanced at his watch as his new friend nibbled on his earlobe.

The owner sighed at me again, letting me know that in a world full of idiots, I was the absolute dumbest.

"Put the gravy in the toe let," she drawled, her Southern accent stretched like taffy in an effort to allow me (her dipshit employee) to understand.

"Huh?"

She let out a big breath, her cheeks puffed from the effort.

I shifted again, trying to keep the slop off my shirt.

"I said, put the gravy in the toe let!" she repeated exaggeratedly.

"Where?" I asked again, genuinely confused. It was late and I was sober and tired and over it, but I really had no idea what she was asking me to do.

"Put the gravy in the toe let!"

I blinked rapidly. My stare shifted back to Matt for help.

"I'm so sorry," I spluttered. "I'm just not exactly sure—"

Now, I'm not a native daughter of Arkansas, but I had lived in the state long enough that I understood the accent. Nevertheless, for whatever reason, I could not wrap my brain around what the owner was telling me. I stood there confusedly, words and phrases that resembled what she was saying reeling through my mind as I searched for a match.

The owner seized my arm, almost tipping the grayish muck onto the floor, and dragged me toward the bathroom. She then pointed to the pee-stained toilet bowl and enunciated a final time.

"IN THE TOE LET!"

I stared in horror at the pubic hairs riding the rim of the off-white commode and looked back into the slimy gravy.

With my hostage money at the forefront of my mind and Afro-man just behind, I tipped the archaic slow cooker toward the dirty hole to pour. Because I hadn't been mortified enough that night, the disgusting slurry, solidified from hours of not being stirred and the icy temperature of the café, didn't budge.

The owner and I locked eyes. She jingled what I assumed was my payment for the night from fucking hell in her pocket and hiked an eyebrow.

With my self-worth so far fucking gone it had likely taken a citizenship oath in Antarctica, I slunk back to the Formica countertop where I had left the used painter's stick and returned to the grimy bathroom. Cloudy chunks of gravy plopped into the toilet lazily, making the foggy water below splatter on my shoes as I scraped the inside of the Crock-Pot with the stick. The final shreds of my dignity rested in a mass in the bottom of the bowl along with the gravy lumps, the remnants of cigarette butts, and the potty-training-toddler shit smears that had taken up residence there.

The owner nodded contentedly as the last chunks of leaden gravy made their descent. She handed me my bag of coins.

"Same time tomorrow," she grunted.

I accepted the bag, a foggy Ziploc instead of the whiskey bag Matt got, because of fucking course it was, and nodded my head.

"M'kay."

After everything that had happened, after a night that had made me want to drink a trough of arsenic with a kerosene chaser, the worst hadn't happened yet. This portion of the story is the truly fucked-up part of the tale: Armed with cutlery from my own kitchen, and aware that I had only been paid $13.26 for my evening of suffering, I, with my nonexistent self-esteem and an earned sense of impending dread, freaking went back the next night (and the one after and the one after). In fact (I'll take it a step further and go full, dignity-stomping disclosure here, because I might as well), I went back and back and back to that job that paid pennies until a representative of the health department moseyed into the makeshift café one day, looked around, and said, "Aw, fuck no. Not ever," and closed the place down.

Chapter Twenty

Skinny Bitch

There was a time in America when anal leakage was all the rage. Dribbling oil from your rectum was not only socially acceptable— it was wildly popular!

As someone in their early twenties, I was quick to jump on any bandwagon that rolled through my neighborhood. Lace-up jeans? Sounds fugly but I'm in! Tattoo choker necklace? Why the hell not? Hats that should only be worn by people who drive semis? Take me and all my money to the closest truck stop so I can stock up.

Spurting grease via my poop chute seemed like a bit of a stretch, but I wasn't going to break ranks when it came to following trends because of a teensy-weensy fear of irreparable damage to my intestinal tract.

I'll admit that when chips came out containing olestra (a chemical described by the dictionary as "a synthetic cooking oil used as a calorie-free fat substitute in various foods"), I was mildly worried by the rumors that the manufactured additive made one's booty freely trickle. Nonetheless, I wasn't willing to let my common sense (or medical concerns) get in the way of enjoying guilt-free snacks.

Lay's WOW chips first became available in the late 1990s. By the time I graduated high school, the chips could be found in all of America's beloved flavors in restaurants and supermarkets everywhere. You could lick nacho cheese powder from your fingers without having consumed a single gram of fat.

Did I care that olestra blocked the absorption of most vitamins and other nutrients, including those that prevented cancer? Hell fucking no I didn't. Not if it meant that Cool Ranch and Jumpin' Jack white cheddar flavor could be on the menu every single damned day without making my ass the size of a parade float.

Ready to take on the trend, including its promise to induce loose stools and intense abdominal cramps, I dove right in. As a lifetime lover of trash food (think dumpster raccoon), I ate those chips with finger-lickin' fervor.

What do I want with my foot-long sub? Why even ask? Ring me up for three bags of diarrhea Cheetos, good sir!

Basically, if you were living in 2003 with a cornhole that wasn't just a few salted treats away from a greasy, panty-ruining leak, you were hardly living at all. You saved the calories from eating the fat on the front end, and on the (literal) back end, you lost even more when your gut began to cramp and the lava began to flow. Thanks, WOW chips!

Heaven forbid a person cough after a generous olestra-laced snack. Such an abrupt motion could hose down your private crawl space for the foreseeable future. Olestra days were not white-pants days. It also shouldn't have been ingested on first or second dates (for obvious reasons).

I suppose it was either because I didn't consume enough of the treats or because my butthole was resilient with youth, but I never experienced the fecal emergencies that some of my peers (I promised my mom I wouldn't mention her here) encountered.

The wild abandon with which I ate olestra never caught up with me. But that doesn't mean I didn't suffer from other gimmicks.

The planet and society had told me that skinny was beautiful. I had learned via *Seventeen* magazine and waiflike models one gale away from extinction that the extra pounds I carried were unacceptable. Gaunt was in. Nourished was way out.

So, by the time poo chips came around, I was no stranger to fad dieting trends. In fact, years before, I had watched my mom speed around our house with a mop and a bucket of bleach for three sleepless months shortly after she had been prescribed fen-phen. The drug was basically legalized crystal meth (remember when I say these things that I am no scientist/doctor/person of any useful knowledge) targeted at middle-class white ladies. I don't remember my mom blinking (or eating) even one time during her clash with legal crack. Without exception, she scrubbed floors, snorted Diet Cokes, and guzzled pairs of the little blue and white pills. She would trail off when talking to stare at invisible things in the air in front of her. Minutes later she would restart midsentence as if there hadn't been a Grand Canyon–sized gap in the conversation.

Finally, because my mom is a puss, and maybe a bit of a quitter, fen-phen's cardiac side effects became too much. Just before the FDA pulled the drug from the shelves over thousands of measly concerns about damage to heart valves, my mom threw in the towel on her prescription.

But that didn't end her search for the perfect fix for unwelcome cellulite.

We bought a belt-like mechanism that used hydraulics to shake your belly while you went about your business. You strapped it on, pushed a button, and let it jostle away. Whilst wearing it you could be like, "Bitch, I'll be up here eating Rocky Road. Keep up the good work down there."

Neither my mom nor I ever received the tightened abs that the infomercial or the product box had promised.

At the same time, several states away, my uncle rode an exercise bike that had a fan that could only be powered when he cycled. While he moved his legs in lazy circles, he ate potato chips and sucked down cases of beer. He didn't seem to lose much weight either but still enjoyed his exercise time in the basement each afternoon.

In pursuit of tiny waists, we went to great lengths. Though we feared him, we allowed Billy Blanks to make us his Tae Bo bitches. My mom even arranged with the local tae kwon do instructor to allow us girls to have a Tae Bo class in his studio twice a week. In the space, generally reserved for mediocre Karate Kid wannabes, we women gathered to snarl, kick, and box.

It was fun for the whole two months that we stayed committed to it.

The advertisements pouring out of our TVs promising a utopia of dimple-free thighs and concave abdomens held most of our attention. We took Tony Little and his glorious ponytail very seriously. When he hopped atop a Gazelle Freestyle Glider and pumped his four-inch legs, we knew shit was getting done. Albeit we all felt moments of discomfort when the fitness zealot jumped behind his female cohost to ride the Gazelle with her. We watched her smile freeze in horror as the tiny man appeared to mount her from behind like they were two country dogs in heat. Tony's wagging ponytail trailed behind the pair of them like a golden victory flag as they sprinted in unison. She looked like she was running from him. He looked like he was having the best day of his life.

Years later I would fall victim to hundred-dollar shoes that promised to reshape my ass to look like a Kardashian's. I paid money for a hand weight that would only work if I jacked it off. I purchased itty-bitty containers that determined my food portions (you'd be amazed at how many cashews a hungry woman can stuff into one cubic inch of space).

My fanatical dieting didn't stop there. I was determined to lose my excess weight with as little physical movement as humanly possible. I juiced, I made smoothies, and I invested in a thermal suit that closely resembled the thing you put across a windshield on a sunny day to protect a car's interior.

In a desperate act, I finally bought P90X, a video series that even at my very fittest I could never make it through a full six minutes of. As Tony Horton and his bulging thighs and mile-deep dimple urged me to push past the agony, I lay on my living room floor in a twisted pile of pain.

"Fuck off, Tony," I moaned, feeling the quiver of my seldom-used muscles as they dealt with the aftershock of my heart rate being above eighty-two.

It was on that very carpet that I determined that I was done with the bullshit of physical torture. I had tried it and had been nearer death than I had ever been before and wouldn't do it again. I had seen the sweaty light, had been delivered unto Satan's fiery clutches, and I wouldn't voluntarily go back.

I carefully considered my options. My mind was a flurry of choices (none of which seemed all that attractive). One of my friends had recently offered hard drugs as an option for weight loss. I hadn't been sold on the idea when it had first come up but spent another moment considering it.

"You know," Heidi said, around a bite of greasy cheeseburger, "if we really wanna lose weight, there's a pretty easy option."

I raised an eyebrow as my fistful of seasoned fries took a generous dunk in the ramekin of ranch on my plate. "Okay."

"We could try crack."

I choked on the melted goo of my own burger. "Heidi! We're not doing real drugs."

I had my standards, after all. A blunt or two after work or a good hit off a bong was acceptable; shooting heroin in a bar bathroom wasn't. I was fine with slippery slopes and all, but not the kind that would lead me to offer blow jobs for actual blow.

"Crackheads are skinny as fuck," Heidi responded matter-of-factly. "We should just try it."

"Dude, you don't just try crack," I protested. "That's, like, the whole thing of it. If you could just try it once, crackheads wouldn't exist."

"We'd lose weight."

"And our hair, and our teeth, and maybe our homes and eventually our families."

She shrugged a shoulder. "You're being dramatic. Besides, you live in a shithole basement apartment. It wouldn't be that huge of a loss."

She was right, I *was* dramatic. Drama was sort of my trademark.

The comment about my four-hundred-dollar-a-month abode wasn't entirely false either. My mind flashed to the slick layer of black mold that was creeping up my bedroom wall. I coughed into my hand and scowled at my friend.

"No crack," I reiterated. "And my apartment is not a shithole."

"Pussy," she snarked.

She tossed a bottle of pills at me.

"Legal crack, then?"

I stared at the bottle, recalling that rumors had recently linked a well-known celebrity's death to to the oblong, lethal-looking pills inside.

"Fuck it," I said, gulping down a pair of the capsules.

In the days shortly after I started chowing the pills, pounds began to melt off my body. Hearing that there was a threat that the medication was under investigation and soon to be banned in the United States, I stockpiled the shit like a doomsday prepper storing pinto beans, like my aunt Bert hoards garage sale panties.

I lost and lost and lost until my ribs stuck out and my hips came to sharp points. Heidi taught me how to rest my forearm over my midsection to test whether there was a sunken space between the skin of my arm and my now-nonexistent belly. If there wasn't sufficient room, I gulped extra demon pills.

I did this until I was in a relationship with my current wife. I hid the pills from her until one day my purse fell open and the scarlet tablets scattered over her linoleum apartment floor like roaches. I dropped to my knees and frantically began to gather the tiny, toxic treasures like fucking Gollum grabbing at his precious.

"Uhhhh . . . ," my future wife said, her mouth ajar. "What the hell are those? Because if they aren't fucking blood pressure pills we've got a real goddamned problem."

I rocked my almost-lost babies in my arms, whispering

apologies. "Uhhh . . ." I stalled, my mind fractured between answering her and counting the slimmers to make sure I had collected them all. "They're, sorta, like appetite suppressants or whatever."

V shook her head slowly. "Diet pills?"

"Well . . . I mean . . . sort of . . . ," I said, trying to defend myself.

She snatched the beloved stash from my clutches. I watched in horror as she marched over to her garbage disposal, flipped the switch, and sprinkled my diet crack into the dark, grinding hole below.

I couldn't protest because I knew how psychotic and how utterly addicted I would sound. Besides, fuck it, I knew I had a supply at home big enough to make a grown elephant weigh forty-three pounds.

V grabbed her keys.

"What're you doing?"

"We are going to your apartment together to get rid of the rest of this shit," she said.

Fuckity fuck fuck. What in the piss?

"The rest?"

"I've seen them in your closet," she said. "I thought you were in one of those pyramid scheme things and selling them to rich white ladies or something. But they're all for you, right?"

"Uh . . ."

We went to my apartment, and V walked straight to the closet and emerged with armloads of my legal crank arsenal.

"You are perfect just the way you are," she said. "You can either keep dating me or keep taking these."

Let me explain something: As much as I loved my Happy

Slims and as much as they had helped me shrink into near non-existence (again, the thing that society had told me to be/do), they hadn't done much else for me. After months of sucking down the pills, my stomach burned at the very sight of them. V did a whole lot more for me and had proven to be especially skilled in ways that her mother wouldn't like me mentioning. The idea of her no longer sharing her particular gifts with me wasn't one I loved.

Thus, I helped her unscrew the caps and systematically flush my reserve. Still, canned-corn broke, with a bullshit job, I couldn't help but point out how much I could make from selling the banned-in-America supplements to rich white ladies.

"Well, Jess, you're a crackhead now," V commented. "Crackheads can't avoid sampling from their stash."

I hung my head. She was right.

It was then that I realized that I had come full fucking circle. In that very instant, I thought of when I had judged both my brother and Jessie Spano so harshly for their drug use. I had been a smug girl on the brink of teenagerhood, full of self-righteousness, with no thoughts of what my own future could hold. When I handed Cody, a wayward smoker of marijuana, a wad of cash for a life at large as a cartel leader, I had never considered such a possibility for myself. Similarly, as I watched the *Saved by the Bell* starlet fall from cum laude grace and imagined her in a double-penetration situation with her principal and the class president, I didn't pause to think that I might be in her position one day. I had known both could backslide into addiction at any given moment but never contemplated my own eventual deviance caused by dependency.

But there I was, fervently praying that one of the crimson pills had escaped the purge and skittered behind the toilet. I didn't clean my bathroom enough to eat things off the floor, but in the current case, I would certainly make an exception.

Short on cash flow and jonesing for my weight-loss fix, I could have become the one blowing Belding. I could only hope that the educator-turned-dope-peddler would accept my poor excuse for deep-throating as payment. As a lesbian I wasn't particularly gifted or practiced in the realm of working a penis into a lather, and I certainly wouldn't be doing any of that ball-cupping business that seemed to be all the rage. For a thirty-count of my slimmers I would do a lot, but the scope of my abilities was what it was. Sorry, Belding.

Instead of calling up a bygone nineties icon (I knew David from *Beverly Hills, 90210* also had drug access and would likely trade for sexual favors), I bucked up, admitted that I had developed a real problem, and sweated out the next few days feeling like I was going to puke. I spent hours thinking about nothing other than getting my shaking little hands on a fresh bottle of my trashed supply.

Despite societal pressure to stay thin enough to be see-through when light was shone at me, I let the dread of weight gain lose out to the thought of a breakup with the person I was certain I wanted to marry. I knew that she would walk away, taking what I had already planned for our future and her in-the-sack giftedness with her.

Being thin was awesome, but being screwed on the regular by a master in the art of fucking was even better.

Chapter Twenty-One

Cooter Bone

I sat in a rickety swiveling office chair with my back ramrod straight. I sure as hell wasn't qualified for the job that I had been tasked with, but I was faking it as best I could on a hangover from a two-day drinking binge and a breakfast of stale Dunkin' Donuts crullers. My expectations of my abilities for the day were set low—just as I liked them.

My hand-me-down hospital-issued scrubs bore a faded splotch of what appeared to be blood. Send-out laundry had been a poor nemesis for whatever hemorrhage the previous owner of the shirt had encountered. This didn't matter to me. I was basically wearing pajamas that made me look like a *Grey's Anatomy* cast member. Sure, I was an emergency department unit secretary with absolutely no training, but outwardly I appeared to be someone who could defibrillate a wonky heart or crack open a chest.

Now, the job was shit, and the hospital I worked at wasn't much better. I had been employed there for six months, which, considering the number of my coworkers who had been fired for smelling like rum, made me a senior employee.

It wasn't just the secretary pool that had run dry; there was also a grave shortage of nurses and other employees of the medical professional assortment. The people needed to render medical attention were few and far between, making the facility less than ideal for handling any type of situation that could kill someone.

I mean, the housekeepers, elderly maintenance men, and I were in good spirits and could host a kick-ass potluck—but we weren't necessarily the ones you wanted by your side if your breathing got sketchy.

The scarcity of qualified practitioners was the precipitating factor that landed me in the hot seat that day. The wobbly chair where I perched was stationed at the front entrance of the emergency room. When patients entered through the double doors, I was the first person they saw.

My job was seemingly simple enough. I was to get the patient's information, jot down their chief complaint, and then triage their issue. Therein lay the main problem. I wasn't actually qualified to triage patients. Sure, I'd seen enough TV to know that a spurting artery was a problem. Obviously, a newborn baby bungeeing out of its mom's vagina was cause for concern. An eye hanging from the socket by that stringy thing seemed serious too. Disembowelment or body parts separated from the host were also reasonably alarming. But the stuff that appeared more minor, that maybe wasn't so minor? That was the scary part.

Can an untrained, disinterested, hungover twenty-one-year-old who identifies as a writer but last worked at a diner spot internal bleeding? How about symptoms of a burst appendix? Does she know what a pulmonary embolism looks like?

No. Nope. Not a chance. Absolutely fucking not.

Now, generally, the things that walked through the front door were bullshit. On Sundays, a lot of folks sauntered through fishing for work excuses with supposed migraines and abdominal issues. The emergency department saw a lot of sore throats, minor sprains, and falls from the toilet. People convened in our hospital waiting room with complaints ranging from pubic lice running rampant to weeklong bouts with constipation. Tampons were sometimes lost in vaginas, and the occasional potato or can of hair spray accidentally got stuck in a rectum (I mean, it happens. Right?).

One evening, as I watched the clock tick closer and closer to the end of my shift, a scantily clad stripper approached my window. She lifted the tiny scrap of fabric that was her shirt and pressed an oozing nipple against the glass. She explained that the yellow dribble was a result of a backstage piercing gone wrong. Perhaps it was nonemergent in nature, but still, I was rightfully concerned. I have little education in exotic dancing but knew the woman's nipples were a major part of her livelihood. I can't imagine that a one-nippled stripper makes nearly as much money at the Golden Dollar Dance Holler as her more able, dual-nippled counterparts. I scribbled down her information, squeegeed my window, and pushed her name to the top of the list of people needing to be seen. As for the waiting twenty-two-year-old frat boy who had reported that he "nearly fucking died" from a serving of ghost pepper hot wings? Well, it wasn't my fault he was dumb enough to sign a waiver to eat chicken. Nor had I chosen his idiot friends who were hooting loudly at his expense next to him. He would have to wait.

Whatever the issue, I was to collect information and relay it directly to the registered nurse on duty. The more serious issues were to be reported immediately. Runny noses and itchy balls could wait. If I intercepted a real emergency, I was allowed to interrupt the nurse's urine-dipping and blood-pressure taking in the adjacent booth to raise the alert. If she agreed with my assessment, she would kick the less pressing matter out of her cubicle to prioritize the emergency.

On that particular morning, I was happy that the ER was relatively quiet. We had a few people feigning pain in hopes of scoring some narcotics, but other than the occasional, well-timed yip or moan, I was free to text my friends from my hot-pink Razr about the happenings at the bar the night before.

Want to die. I h8 alcohol, I texted my friend. *Where 2nite?*

I considered hitting up the vending machine for a snack while awaiting her response. Just as I began combing the bottom of my purse for change, the automatic door swished open to reveal a disheveled-looking woman. From her right hand swung a Fiesta Taco bag. When she smiled at me her lack of teeth hinted that she had spent some time on the side of town that was rich in crystal meth.

Fuck. My snack would have to wait.

She plunked the rumpled plastic sack on the counter in front of me. My stomach turned. Fast-food was two a.m. food, not ten a.m. food—everyone knew that.

"Go ahead and test that," she said pointedly. She responded to my shrinking away from the imitation-beef fumes by pushing the bag closer to my side of the desktop.

"Do what?"

She sighed loudly and scratched at her arms. "Go ahead and test that burrito in there."

She tapped her foot on the floor and glared at me, clearly pissed that she had been faced with the biggest idiot in the state.

She wasn't wrong. I'm not exactly high ranking on IQ tests, nor was I invited into the Gifted and Talented program in school. Nonetheless, I had no fucking idea what was going on.

"Get going, girl. Test it."

I felt like I had missed part of the conversation. "Test it for what, ma'am?"

She rolled her bloodshot eyes. "Cum!"

Having that word shouted in my face by a random vagrant while she gestured wildly at a burrito nearly broke me.

"Like, actual cum?"

"I need to speak to your supervisor."

Most unfortunately for her (as per the staffing shortage), that was me.

"Just explain it to me," I said slowly. "Why would you cum in your burrito?"

Her eyes widened, and she slammed a palm onto the Formica. "You idiot! I didn't cum in my burrito! The dickbag cook came in my burrito."

Oh. Obviously.

The nurse in the adjoining booth, who was handing a patient a sterile cup for a stool sample, raised an eyebrow at me.

"And what kind of a test do you want?"

"Goddamned DNA test."

"But why a DNA test if you already know it was the cook?"

I don't know why the hell I was acting like those kids hunting down Carmen Sandiego with my line of inquiry. What the hell did I care?

"Christ almighty! For the goddamned court of law when I sue his sorry ass."

Okay, I'd bite.

Besides, I was dying to hear the rest of the story. I happened to love that taco shack, and if there was a danger that my future snacks were going to be jizz loaded by a disgruntled line cook, I had the right to know. Upon my recent admission into lesbianhood I had adopted a strict no-sperm policy that I wasn't comfortable violating.

"Our lab doesn't really do that," I said, peering nervously into the potentially semen-sullied mess of refried beans and cheese. "Like, we don't test Mexican food for, um, you know . . ."

"Spunk!" the nurse called out helpfully, but still refused to join me at my stall.

"Yeah." I nodded. "There isn't a specific jizz test."

I wasn't sure if what I'd said was true, but it felt true.

The damsel sneered at me, scooped up her leftovers, spat at the window between us, and flipped me off as she backed out of the door. I can't say for sure, but I'd guess she ventured off to find a facility better equipped to test male ejaculate.

And though I never saw that fair maiden again, I do think of her every time I eat a loaded burrito. A true impression, she made.

As if the brush with Cum Shot Magoo weren't enough, a few days later I ran into a similarly awkward exchange. Again, I was sitting in my booth minding my own business with my attention trained on my sweet-ass flip phone when someone came barreling through the front door. A woman, dressed in rain boots and torn sweatpants, with her hair in a side ponytail, gasped for air.

"Sweet Jesus! My daughter! My baby! She broke her cooter bone!" she howled crazily, tears streaming down her face. "Do something! Please!"

Goddammit, sonofabitch. This was it. The time of reckoning had arrived. All the bullshit complaints and false alarms I had screened in the preceding months had prepared me for this exact moment. I had been told to treat pediatric patients with utmost caution. The day of a true emergency was finally upon me. My anxiety intensified when I saw a man trailing behind the frantic woman with a girl of about seven in his arms. The child lay still, her eyes smashed shut as she quietly whimpered.

"She was on her bike and comed off and done busted her cooter bone!" the desperate mother shouted again.

With community college anatomy and physiology still a semester away and a pitiable foundation of medical terminology, I didn't know what in the hell function a cooter bone served or where in the shit it was located, but I did know that the situation was really fucking bad.

Starting to breathe heavily myself, I pounded a fist on the partition between my station and the one occupied by the on-duty nurse.

"I need you!" I shouted. "There's an emergency! I need you!"

Instead of waiting for her to put down her nail file and meander in my direction, I flew to her, covering the distance in milliseconds.

"There's a little girl in the lobby," I gasped. "Her cooter bone! It's broken!"

The nurse blinked dumbly. "'Scuse me?"

"Her freaking cooter bone!" I hissed, remembering patient confidentiality and noting the guy in her booth leaning forward in interest. "She fell off her bike!"

"Put it in the computer and then come with me!" the nurse said. "Quickly."

Thinking it odd that the nurse wanted me to fuck with the computer in a time of such calamity, I scurried back to my workstation and typed in "F, 7 y.o., broken cooter bone." The computer system was designed so that as soon as I entered the intake information, all the doctors, techs, and nurses in the emergency department could see on a central screen what was waiting in the lobby. The snippet of information gave the crew in the back a snapshot of how to prepare for incoming patients and disasters.

As soon as I keyed the information, the nurse grabbed my hand and tugged me toward the double doors leading to the trauma rooms.

"What are we doing?" I asked.

"This is serious," she huffed. "I want you to tell the doctors so we can get her treated ASAP!"

Why in the fuck? That wasn't normal protocol. Not once had I ever been led to the back of the house. I certainly didn't have any contact with the doctors. I was a goddamned admin assistant, and a poor one at that; I wasn't meant for passing reports to physicians.

"Dr. T! Dr. Ellis!" the nurse screeched as soon as the pair in white coats emerged from patient rooms. "Our secretary has a serious situation to tell you about."

I glanced around silently, noting the smirks and hushed titters coming from the nurses' station where the generic patient information was displayed.

Still losing my shit over the unattended, likely deadly injury that we'd left behind in triage, I raced toward the physicians.

"There's a little girl in the lobby who broke her cooter bone!" I shouted demonically. "It was a biking injury, and she broke it!"

The doctors pursed their lips and nodded gravely.

"Have you told X-ray?" Dr. Ellis asked. "Please go notify them immediately if you haven't."

"Everyone else too!" Dr. T urged, rolling up his sleeves. "Hurry.

Tell everyone so we can prepare to handle this. Tell them to ready the trauma bay!"

And because I was young and gullible, I did. Impressed with my newfound importance in a department of people who didn't even know my name, I ran around that ER like that poor fucker in a three-cornered hat who had been forced to scream "The British are coming! The British are coming!" or whatever the hell.

Paul McCartney? Paul Newman? Paul Rudd?

Whatever. Nobody cares.

Anyway. Thinking I was saving a life and doing some damned good in the world, I informed quite literally everyone I saw.

Soon, as my heart began to slow its thunderous beat, I noticed that not only were the medical staff not rushing to save the girl's life, but that everyone was laughing hysterically, pointing at the monitor and muttering "cooter bone" whilst shaking their heads. Instead of swooping in hero style to save the injured child, Dr. T was dabbing tears from the corners of his eyes. Dr. Ellis leaned across her mobile workstation laughing so hard that she could barely stand.

Awash in a feeling of dread, I turned to the cackling triage nurse beside me.

"What *is* a cooter bone?" I asked slowly, knowing that I had spent the last ten minutes making a complete douche out of myself.

"It's redneck for 'vagina,'" she answered delightedly, gasping to breathe between peals of laughter. The bitch was actually slapping her fucking knee in the throes of hilarity.

By the time I had scraped my dignity off the floor and returned to my little spot at the front entrance, the hillbilly trio who had gotten me into the mess in the first place had left. Apparently, as

I learned when I asked the others in the waiting area, while I was making a scene of epic proportions in the patient area, the little girl had been offered ice cream, which had somehow been a miracle balm for her vaginal pain.

Her mom in her galoshes, her dad in his overalls, and she in her post-cooter catastrophe had skipped happily into the sunset with the promise of double dips while I had to face an entire building of coworkers who had just learned that I was the biggest dipshit who had ever lived.

I didn't work at that hospital for many more shifts, as that day I had earned the moniker "Cooter Bone." Though I desired a consistent paycheck to support my drinking, there was no amount of money worth being made fun of relentlessly every time I dug a fork into a Lean Cuisine in the break room or waited for my Bugles to pop out of a vending machine.

Twenty years later, still living in the same town, I'm now an actual licensed medical professional charged with teaching future practitioners. When I go visit my students in training at the hospital of this fateful incident, I still sometimes hear the tale of a young, idiot secretary and her emergency cooter bone misadventure. Incredibly mature and worldly now, I chortle right along with the gossipers retelling the yarn of the silly girl of yore and think, *Fuck you all*, as I slide my frozen dinner into the scummy staff microwave oven with the comfy anonymity of a woman that no one remembers as "Cooter Bone" anymore.

Chapter Twenty-Two

Betrayed by Singing Austrians

Getting pregnant wasn't supposed to suck so much. In fact, a lot of people have a great time conceiving. That was our plan too.

We ordered some sperm from a cryobank, laughed hysterically at the giant subzero tank it came in, lit some candles, and went to work. My wife rolled up her sleeves (not figuratively, *literally*; she wasn't trying to ruin a flannel shirt with a sperm sample splashed in the wrong direction) and got down to business.

We set the scene with champagne and chocolate-covered strawberries. I wore a sexy nightie. We were making a baby! What could be more special?

Well, a lot of things, it turns out.

Using a plastic pipette to guide sperm into my nervous cervix was actually way less romantic than it sounds. The sample, which had warmed in my armpit for the required fifteen minutes, had an orangish hue that made both my wife and me cringe.

"Is it supposed to look like that?" V asked incredulously.

"I don't know!"

"Well, I've never actually seen it. You're the experienced one in this area."

(Gold-star lesbians are the worst with all their superiority and "I've never had jizz in my mouth" shit.)

We reread the fourteen-inch-thick stack of paperwork that had shipped with the sample and determined that though the color was extremely off-putting, it was normal.

"Which donor did we pick?"

I blew hair out of my face and sighed. I was pantsless in our drafty bedroom and didn't exactly want to be talking about donor 862134 again.

"The Hispanic biochemist humanitarian with blue eyes," I reminded her.

"And why would an altruistic blue-eyed Hispanic genius want to jerk off in a cup for a couple of lesbians again?"

"I don't know, V. Maybe his rent in the biodome was due. Who fucking cares?"

She sighed and repositioned herself between my legs. The romance had fled. She looked like an electrician trying to sort a tangle of highly volatile live wires. I had witnessed the exact same type of high-intensity concentration whilst watching Keanu Reeves defuse a bomb during a chase scene in *Speed*.

"I'm going to need some actual light," V muttered, staring at my exposed vagina.

Cool, nothing makes a girl feel more cherished and adored than a floodlight on her snatch. Things were quickly going from easy and fun to clinical and uncomfortable. We'd been married for a while and V had spent plenty of one-on-one time with my vag, but something about her examining it like it was a Sudoku puzzle was making me want to punch her.

Despite the newly introduced light, she squinted as she inserted the pipette. I half expected her to call out for her "readers" in the voice of an elderly woman. We had both begun to sweat. She bit her bottom lip as she expressed the sample into my waiting uterus.

"That should do it!" she said, patting my belly like she had just finished an oil change. She helped me tilt my pelvis toward the ceiling, making sure the pillow slid beneath my hips was my own (because of, you know, the fear of me sneezing and sending the $930 sperm flying across the room). I lay there with my chins doubling as my body arched upward, hoping the spunk potion would seep into the right crevice and result in a positive pregnancy test.

Can you imagine someone doing that after a one-night stand? Like, amid the postcoital glow, you throw your legs up on said stranger's wall to lock in the trickle of semen?

"James, is it? Yeah, sorry about my feet on the picture of your mom, but I'm in my mid-thirties and I've gotta get this shit moving. Time's a-tickin' and gravity helps!"

Despite our initial attempts at fanning the flames of desire, the insemination felt strictly practical. Sadly, romance had fled our own baby-making efforts. I had been taking my temperature, examining discharge, and charting my ovulation like it was the key to finding the Lost World for months. Despite my spouse's enthusiasm for all things sexual, she was likely getting sick of staring into a vagina that seemed to be broken and out of warranty.

I shifted uncomfortably, staring at the popcorn ceiling.

Technically I had been inseminated, but I felt like my wife should offer me one of those punch cards you get at drive-through coffee shops. Or at least hand me a baby.

Neither happened. Nor did a pregnancy from our humdrum mating ritual that day.

We aren't quitters though. So, we kept trying. But at a literal grand a pop, we couldn't afford to be do-it-yourselfers anymore. This wasn't a thirteen-dollar flea market coffee table we were trying to give a makeover; we were dealing with a set of uncooperative fallopian tubes that were quickly spending all our savings.

So, I dug in and read every single thing on the internet about fertility. I was ready to do any kind of anything to make a baby stick. I started downing eight-dollar wheatgrass shots from the natural grocery store each morning. I saw an acupuncturist twice a week. I ate pineapple cores, macadamia nuts, salmon, and other weird shit that magazines promised would make my insides flower like a goddamned lotus.

Then, after a million more vials and no proliferation, we invited a gynecologist to join in the good times. That's when shit really got real, because gynecologists have drugs, the kind of drugs that fuck with your hormones and make you crazy.

I quickly became a monster of epic, fertility-drug proportions. V learned to only enter the house bearing chocolate and flowers, and she agreed to revoke her remote-control rights for the duration of the treatment.

One particular drug, taken midway through my cycle, made me so crazy angry that I had to be taken off of it after I almost committed homicide at Target one sunny Sunday afternoon. I mean, the lady who took the last bag of jalapeño chips obviously had it coming, but the words I said to her should've put me in the pen for at least that day. I can't even imagine what I looked like as I tore that fucking snack out of her grip. Actually, I can imagine it. I was wearing stretched-out yoga pants, a T-shirt sporting accidental bleach spots, and furred Uggs in the summer. I looked as nuts as I felt. Sobbing against my steering wheel minutes later, the victorious smell of jalapeño dust lingering on my fingers, I called my doctor and had my meds changed.

I worked as a respiratory therapist in a neonatal intensive care unit at the time (because what better job for a desperate woman struggling to conceive than to take care of infants?), and my hormones raged. With my hands in a heated incubator, treating my tiny patients, I would sweat, my head would spin, and tears would well. I saw babies all day, rocked them, whispered to them, and made them feel better, but none of them were mine. I watched asshole crackhead moms doze off while holding their babies in the NICU rocking chairs and heard stories from security guards about their boyfriends and husbands getting caught doing actual, literal, for-real motherfucking crack in the hospital parking lot.

The experience was a special kind of brutal.

One day, I lay on the acupuncturist's table, repeating in my head, *Free your mind, free your mind, it only works if you believe it works*. The problem? I didn't believe in acupuncture. I didn't think it would help. I thought it was expensive and a little painful, and I hated the fucking sound of the waves crashing against the shore that my medical acupuncturist played during each session.

My brain was near implosion when I finally spoke up.

"Can you turn that crap off? Please?"

"Excuse me, ma'am?"

"The waves, the scuttling crabs, the birds. Can you turn the ocean off?"

"It's relaxing."

"Well, not for me!" I barked, my voice snapping through the tranquility of the room. "The seagulls sound like they're circling some poor kid to steal his Cheetos. It's complete chaos!"

The sound machine stopped, and the acupuncturist tapped her foot.

"You might not be in the right state for this," she said quietly, packing away her supplies.

She was exactly fucking right. I was in no state to have needles poked into my feet. I was in no state to listen to sea vultures hunt children. I was in no state to be allowed in Target alone. I was in no state to be taking care of drug addicts' infants. I was in no state for anything.

On my way out of the office, the well-meaning receptionist (none the wiser about my breakdown in the back) grinned at me.

"You have a doctor's appointment this week, right?" she asked. My acupuncture appointments were timed around the gyno visits.

"Yep," I said, my blood still boiling.

"Sweetheart, I have eight kids," she said, leaning forward. "Lemme tell you the secret to making a baby. Any time you want one, watch *The Sound of Music* before you do the deed. Seeing all those adorable kids singing in their precious curtain outfits? Worked for me every time."

I stood blinking at the woman, who was clearly so fertile she could get pregnant from across the butcher counter at the grocery store. I pictured my barren body flying across her desk, over the photo of her fucking soccer team of a family, to pummel her smug face.

But I was also intrigued. Of the two of us, she was clearly the expert on baby-making.

A few days later, a couple hours before our gyno appointment, I presented V with the idea, with a new copy of *The Sound of Music* in hand.

"Isn't that a goddamned musical?" she asked, her eyes flicking to the softball game she had just turned on.

"Uh, yes?"

I explained the receptionist's theory.

"I don't watch musicals," V replied. "It looks fully terrible."

My lip quivered. "But she said that this is the thing that will work."

"No," V answered staunchly. "Not a chance. Not a musical, Jess."

"But it's not a bad one," I argued. "It's World War II era. They all die at the end. It's actually pretty gruesome."

I could tell that my wife's attention had been lured in. She's a huge action movie fan. Basically, if an eyeball is plucked from a socket or someone is shot, she's in. She also likes roundhouse kicks and beheadings. She laughs hysterically each time an actor gets punched in the penis. Basically, she has the refinement and movie taste of most nineteen-year-old guys.

"All of them die?"

"Well, all except the dad."

She raised an eyebrow and cast one last look at the ball game. I grabbed a beer out of the fridge for her and started the nearly three-hour movie.

"It's too bad the dad makes it," she muttered, staring at the flickering screen.

As the musical droned on (and on and on and on), she sort of got into it. I think the thought of Maria being eviscerated was what helped her through the melodies and jaunty dances. We were approaching the end of the movie, and our appointment time, and hopefully my blossoming fertility, when she gave me a sideways glance.

"When do they die?"

I guess she hadn't exactly become as attached to the von Trapps as I had hoped she would.

I watched as Liesl's boyfriend, Rolf, betrayed the family to serve the Nazi Party.

"Soon."

As the movie ended, with the still-intact von Trapps frolicking through the Alps, away from the Nazis, their guns, and any chance of beheadings, V's mouth fell ajar. The very-much-alive family who had very much escaped death were singing their towheaded hearts out.

I felt V's laser stare sear my skin. No gunshots rang out as the credits rolled across the screen.

"Are you goddamned kidding me?"

"I thought you'd like them so much after three hours you wouldn't want them dead. This was for the baby."

"A baby built on lies!"

She stomped a foot and tossed me the keys to drive to the clinic.

Not many people can say they've been cockblocked by Maria and the von Trapps, but I can. No baby was made that day.

I have never felt warm feelings about the film (or Germany) since.

Chapter Twenty-Three

Earning My Big-Girl Panties

I didn't go to respiratory therapy school to be a hero. I certainly didn't want to play any part in battling a pandemic or be a person with a shit-ton of responsibility. Moreover, it wasn't exactly my lifelong dream to be covered in sputum. I'm more of a hands-off kind of lady instead of a dive-into-action girl. In short, I didn't become a respiratory therapist to make a difference. I had no such aspirations. I just knew the medical field was aswim with jobs and stability.

That said, seeing my mom's career had steered me far from nursing. Many of her work stories told over Domino's pizza at the kitchen table ended with me saying, "I sincerely hope you make a gazillion dollars an hour, because your job is fucking disgusting."

I went to RT school because, as it turns out, writers don't get paid shit. I had worked for a newspaper for three years, won multiple literary awards, and still couldn't afford more than one thing off the McDonald's Dollar Menu on payday. I watched layoffs start rolling out in the newsroom, saw colleagues tug pushpins out of yellowed comics and stack stained coffee mugs into boxes. I saw them head home with envelopes touting shitty severance packages and dashed dreams. I wanted to go out on my own terms. When my pencil skirt and I moseyed out of the newsroom for the last time, it would be when I decided. Sure, my days were numbered as fuck, but I'd always have the satisfaction of knowing that the last story about the local school board I filed was my decision.

It was time for a career change. So I walked into the local community college to have a frank discussion with an advisor.

"So, my GPA is okayish. Which program can I most definitely get into?"

I steepled my fingers at my chin and awaited her response. I had plans to meet a friend at Applebee's for lunch and didn't want to fuck around with much more of my time. There were appletinis to drink.

The advisor sighed at my lack of purpose and pushed forward a short list of options. I redirected my train of thought from sour apple liqueur long enough to skim the Post-it. Physical therapy assistant was most certainly out. I could barely bend and move my own aged body without effort and pain; I wasn't up to helping others strengthen theirs. As mentioned before, nursing wasn't an option either, as I would never be willing to slither a catheter into a stranger's urethra.

"This one," I said, tapping the words scrawled at the bottom of the note. "I'll do that."

Said advisor sighed even louder, gifting me with a breathy puff of the tuna salad she'd had for lunch, and looked at my completed list of courses.

"You can actually apply for this program today," she said, seemingly surprised that my unmotivated ass had such a large cache of fulfilled prerequisites. Like certain members of the Duggar family collect children and criminal charges, I had accumulated courses over my many years waffling in and out of associate's degree programs. I was inches away from being either a welder, an interpretive dancer, a potter, or an expert in the field of Western civilization (limited through the year 1650).

I heeded the weary advisor's advice and applied. A couple of weeks later I received an acceptance letter in the mail.

"Well, I'll be fucking damned," I muttered, staring at the letter. I traded my nonprescription glasses (which I thought made me look more reporter-y) for T-shirts and flannels. I was back in school.

I worked the night shift as a secretary at a local neonatal intensive care unit. With only an hour between the end of my shift and the beginning of class, I slept in the college parking lot each weekday. It was goddamned brutal, and my sole daily purpose was to avoid falling asleep in a puddle of drool in front of my classmates. I studied at bars and crammed what information I needed to make it through. Before I knew it, the two-year respiratory therapy program was over and I had passed my national boards.

This is when things got sketchy as hell. The moment I found myself standing in scrubs in a hospital as a new RT was one of the scariest of my life.

Who in the fucking world really believed I was qualified to take care of living, breathing patients? Actually, would you like to know the best way to kill a perfectly healthy living, breathing person? Assign them a shitty, unprepared, shaky-skilled RT who desperately wishes she'd never left her writing desk in the first place.

Needless to say, I spent most of my first year after school completely fucking terrified. I worried that I would be the only medical professional in a room where someone started to die. Yes, respiratory therapy school had taught me to deal with such situations. Yes, I had passed all required exams and demonstrated the necessary skills and competencies. No, I was in no way ready to be or capable of being at the helm of any kind of lifesaving shit.

Because I'm a crafty, resourceful bitch, I looked for a quick resolution to my fear. I soon decided that I needed a cushion of sorts. I needed a respiratory mentor whom I could enlist as a buffer or bodyguard. I needed to buy myself more time before I had to be the guy in charge of throwing down when shit went south. All indifference aside, I had no interest in committing manslaughter via my own glaring ignorance.

Believe it or not, people weren't exactly lining up to be a new grad's meat shield. But Mitch, a sixty-seven-year-old, rough-around-the-edges veteran of the field who stole people's lunches in the break room and cussed at patients, took a liking to me. I followed him like a magician's assistant and started to learn what I needed to know. Our shifts matched, so there was seldom an emergency that happened while I was working that my personal savior wasn't there for. Whilst silently crapping my pants, I watched my vocational Miyagi stick his meaty finger into red airways when tracheostomy tubes popped out. I helped him tow asthmatics back from the brink of death. I saw him wrestle long-time smokers, delirious from high levels of carbon dioxide, into breathing masks. I listened to him lecture the same thirty-year smokers about the dangers of lighting up, even though we both knew he was dying for his next cigarette break.

I quickly learned that the adult population of patients wasn't my cup of vodka. As lovely as many of them were, and as sorry as I was to see them suffering, others were outright dicks. For any readers not associated with the medical field, allow me to explain a few things. Some adult patients attempt to grope their respiratory therapists whilst receiving a breathing treatment. Others throw actual shit that they've removed from their own assholes at the people trying to help them. Some people (I won't mention names here) rip out their own catheters and chew on them while staring medical staffers dead in the eye. In a fit due to lord knows what kind of hallucinogens, some fellas even cut off their own testicles. Imagine that fucking unfortunate surprise when you finally come off your high days later.

"Bill, this going to be a bit hard to hear but you lost most of the month of August. Also, your right nut."

I quickly determined that such debacles weren't for me. I'm not a thrill seeker. I don't want to see an oozing gunshot wound. I'll be over here in the fetal position waiting for your sawed-off leg to heal into a nice, clean stump, thank you very much.

In all of my petrified, what-the-fuck-is-wrong-with-our-devolving-species revulsion, I did eventually find that there were some patients I really, really liked. I found my true home in respiratory therapy after a rotation in the neonatal intensive care unit. Not one of my snuggle-muffin infant charges in that unit called me a "fat-ass cunt bitch whore," nor did any of them attempt to gnaw off their restraints (one of the real benefits of toothless patients). The premature infants that I cared for helped me find an actual passion for a field that I was mere days away from parachuting the fuck out of. Their mewling cries, warm little bundled bodies, and problems I actually cared about (far more than those of the drug seekers and ass squeezers) balmed my otherwise growing determination that the world would be better off if humans just handed the planet over to hamsters.

Mitch didn't follow me into the NICU. He claimed that he didn't give two shits about babies and their bawling, but I knew otherwise. I was positive that under the Marlboro haze and "I'll fucking murder you" glare lived a softie unwilling to care for patients who could melt his icy demeanor. It was probably for the best though, because I can't imagine that many neonates would fare well from the nicotine contact high my mentor likely would've gifted them.

The NICU wasn't without its problems. One of the major roadblocks to my vocational bliss was the part that wasn't baby related. If you're at all familiar with infants, you know that they generally have parents. Sometimes those parents, while worrying about and staring at the person they love more than anyone in the universe, go a bit ballistic. It's fair behavior and defensible but can still be tricky to work around. I'm not gonna say that these parents can be assholes (because I don't want to be shot at or maimed), but I'm also not going to say that they're the most pleasant group of folks. For all their assholery, they are justified in losing their fucking minds.

Another part of the NICU that wasn't so bright and shiny? Attending vaginal deliveries ranks high. I say that birth is beautiful and magical and miraculous, but let's be honest, it's also totally, wholly fucked up. Whoever it was who was creating humans and deciding how people would make other people, they were clearly at a loss when they came to this part. There was some real sadistic dialogue happening. I'm sure it went along the lines of:

"This obviously can't be a job for men if we want to keep the species chugging along. They'd never do it. I'm gonna go ahead and push this duty off on women, which is super on-trend right now anyways.

"*Janice, take note: while they're working at cracking glass ceilings and begging for basic rights, I'll have them be solely responsible for the propagation of the human population as well. That being said, I don't want them to get a whole lot of credit for it. That seems totally fair and reasonable. Now to the nitty-gritty of getting babies out into the world.*

"*How should birth work?*

"*Maybe the ear canal? Should I make a person come out of there?*

"*Nah, that could really fuck up a lady's face. We want them to still look nice.*

"*The butt? Yeah, maybe the butt.*

"*No, still not quite right. I gotta think this through.*

"*The mouth seems like a reasonable evacuation point. This is where I plan for them to rid themselves of excess vodka and spoiled Spam. It could work. Ugh. But that just goes back to royally fucking up all those lovely faces.*

"*No, wait! Shit, I have a seriously awesome idea! How about I hide a dime-sized hole in the vulva? That would be hysterical. Yeah, let's put it there. We will make it only stretch so much and then during actual birth, it can split open like a rotten pumpkin that's been sunning on the porch ten days post-Halloween.*"

At this point, whoever was planning this bullshit likely smashed a Pabst Blue Ribbon can on their forehead and drank the crumbs from the bottom of a bag of Doritos before burping.

The ill-conceived idea was then handed over to a goddamned prehistoric design team to handle all of the fleshy logistics. (Then the idea originator was freed up to piece together a hedgehog or whatever.) Once the team had a mockup, with the birth canal located in the most fucked-up, painful, inconvenient place, they rolled the prototype out.

Without any scientific resources backing my theory, I'd say that some of the details may be askew, but what I've described is the basic reason that the highway to birth is what it is.

As glorious and magical of a marvel as birth is, it is a shock to witness (even when you do it for a living). When I began working with mothers and babies, I really had to adjust to the spectacle. More than that, I had to train myself to not wear facial expressions reflective of what I was feeling. Harnessing horror became a daily task. Like I had with the general patient population, I hung back in vaginal deliveries for as long as I could. I assisted when instructed but didn't take much initiative.

One day, I didn't have much choice though. This is the day that I really became a medical practitioner. My experience was odd (as you've likely come to expect) but uniquely formative.

I was on night shift and was called into a delivery room where a mother was having difficulty with a vaginal birth. I was the only RT on duty that night and felt the familiar creep of fear when I realized that I was the responsible person in a potential emergency. When I entered the room, I spied a young woman who appeared as afraid as I felt. Her legs were splayed enough for an entire doctor on an entire stool to park between and she was surrounded by nurses.

I avoided eye contact with her. I felt the smallest amount of comfort knowing that the nurse who had joined me from the NICU was an expert (capable of actually saving people). I breathed slowly as I readied the bedside warmer where we would receive the newborn.

"Mi coño está en llamas!" the expectant mother shrilled.

Okay. I don't speak a lot of Spanish, but I do know that she had just said her pussy was on fire. From my vantage point, she wasn't far off base. I hadn't had children of my own yet and her high-pitched screeching certainly postponed even considering such things.

The gaggle of white women surrounding the patient nodded and patted her hand.

"You're fine, dearie," a nurse said in unnecessarily loud English. "You're fine."

The young woman panted, her eyes wide with panic. She was the opposite of fine.

She shrieked an impressive tangle of Spanish swear words and thrashed on the bed. I was pretty sure she was planning an escape. It seemed to me like an inopportune time to flee, but what the shit did I know?

Swallowing against the fear that had gathered in the pit of my stomach, a gut feeling reminiscent of a Malibu-and-pineapple-juice hangover, I glanced around the room. I realized that the patient was without friends or family, and that there was no one present who was fluent in Spanish. Dread digging deeper, I admitted to myself that I was two things in that room: a) the sole respiratory therapist, and b) the only person who could speak any Spanish other than the panicked woman delivering a baby. Don't misunderstand me, my Spanish is total shit and based entirely on the dirty words and slang I learned from my wife's family during drunken card games, but it was the second best in the room.

An unfamiliar (and absolutely unwelcome) sense of responsibility enveloped me as I listened to the woman scream about her flaming pussy. The nursing staff was trying to explain to her how to push the baby out in English. I could see on the fetal monitor that the baby's heart rate had dropped and that we were nearing an emergency situation. The longer it was taking the young woman to deliver, the more peril the baby was in. The more goddamned peril the baby was in, the more likely I was to have to use my respiratory therapy skills.

Fuck.

"We are going to have to go to the operating room for a stat C-section if this doesn't happen in the next two minutes," the doctor, who was beginning to sweat, barked.

Fuckity fuck goddammit. Fuck me.

I listened to the ominous sound of the heartbeats on the fetal monitor spaced further and further apart and the English squawks of the women in scrubs as they tried to coach the patient into delivering.

"Okay," I said, swiping at my sweating forehead with the rubber gloves I wore. "Fuck."

I left the radiant warmer and pushed my way to the front of the room. At the bedside, I grabbed the laboring patient's hand and stared into her eyes.

"Yo hablo español," I said slowly. "Un poquito. Un poquito."

Tears of relief streaked the woman's face as she reexplained the situation of her blazing vagina.

"Tell her to push," the doctor shouted at me. "Tell her to push with her butt!"

"Uhhhhhh . . ." I trailed off.

Agony splashed across her face; the woman screeched to me in Spanish more quickly than my slow brain could translate.

"Um, okay," I said again, guzzling a giant mouthful of air. "Puje con su cola. No. No. Lo siento. Empuja con tu culo. No uses tu sucio coño."

My face was turning labia-red as the woman began to giggle. Without the proper Spanish vocabulary backing me, and after

years of hearing swear words slung across the table during domi-
noes by my in-laws, I had pieced together the one phrase I could
come up with to tell the woman to push with her butt.

Essentially, in broken-ass Spanish, I had told her, "Push with
your asshole. Don't use your dirty pussy."

At the moment, I didn't know that I had called her vagina
dirty. Truthfully, it was as clean as a vagina can be in such a situation. It took an internet search of my phrases later to realize the
full horror of what I had said.

Impressed with my language prowess, and ignorant of my
trash-mouth swearing, my healthcare-worker peers grinned and
clapped me on the back in congratulations.

"Empuja con tu culo. No uses tu sucio coño," I urged again.

Whatever the translation, it worked. With her eyes still locked
on mine, her only ally in a room full of English speakers, the
woman squeezed all the blood from my hand, sucked in a big
breath, and began to push.

"Bien! Más! Más!" I shouted. "Empuja con tu culo! No uses el
gatito!"

Now, the impressive part to me in this whole thing is that I
couldn't have come up with the proper Spanish word for "kitchen"
if the doctor had held a scalpel to my throat, but I sure as hell
knew multiple translations of the word "pussy."

As the baby slipped out of the angry-looking vagina (which I
had just called both a cunt and a kitten), the woman cackled
loudly. The final push resulted in the miracle of life as well as the
howling laughter of a patient to whom I had just said some of the
most terrible things that had ever come out of my mouth.

Still whispering curses under my breath, I took the baby
that the doctor offered me to the warmer, checked him over,

determined that he was fine despite the rough start, and returned him to his exhausted mother. When the new mother and her baby, both healthy, locked eyes in instant love, it was almost as if some foul-mouthed white woman hadn't been shouting Spanish obscenities throughout the duration of the delivery. There is little doubt in my mind that the birth story is now the stuff of family legend and has been retold over many a family dinner.

"I had no idea you spoke Spanish!" the NICU nurse exclaimed as we took our leave to head back to our department.

"I don't!" I said, still frazzled. "I really, truly don't."

And that, my friends, was the first time I took initiative as a healthcare worker. I still had a ton to learn, but after that I was less afraid. I had finally stepped up, pulled my big-girl panties on over my kitten, and made a difference. And though that woman and I likely share PTSD from the experience, together we delivered a beautiful, healthy nine-pound kid who went on to live another day.

Now, many years after the fateful delivery, I feel a responsibility to speak up about the events of that night. I eventually birthed two children of my own. As excited as I was, I remember the moments as being wholly terrifying. I can't imagine how amplified that fear would have been if none of my assigned healthcare providers could speak to me in my native tongue. There are resources and translators (both human and technological) available in hospitals (even back then) that should have been used to help that poor woman have a more peaceful delivery. She deserved that. Sure, we were busy as hell, and many in the delivery room were burned out from careers of long hours and not enough pay, but it's still bullshit that no one took the extra step to accommodate our patient to make her experience less traumatic. I'm going to go ahead and give everyone in that room (minus the patient and her newborn) a big fat fucking F on being decent humans that day. What a bunch of douchebags. I'm also super stoked/grateful that the patient didn't decide to sue my ass for all the slanderous sailor speak about her vagina. I'd like to state again, for the record, that it was neither dirty nor deserving of being called a "kitty" whilst performing one of life's greatest miracles.

Chapter Twenty-Four

Bargain Mart Baby-Making

The thin paper covering the table crinkled loudly as I shifted my weight. I dreaded the moment when I would have to hop down to get dressed, knowing there would be a sweaty ass print left behind and likely shreds of tissue stuck to my thighs. It was like my butt's own version of a Rorschach test, only instead of indicating whether or not I'm a serial killer, it betrayed just how fucking nervous I was.

My vagina wasn't happy with me. I didn't feel particularly happy with me either. Infertility was a real bitch. I was the one in ten or whatever the fucking statistic is. I was finally special but all it meant was that I had won the no-baby lottery.

Like in the summer of 2005, when she had been a fresh young debutante being introduced to lesbian society for the first time, my vagina was once again a popular topic of conversation. Unlike before though, none of the talk was awesome. My body would never achieve pregnancy without some serious medical intervention. I was the disappointed owner of ovaries that were about as functional as a celibacy vow at a college party.

I'm not going to try to make infertility funny, because it isn't. The years spent trying to baby-make while failing miserably were soul crushing. But today, with a few kids who finally came to be, I can recall some shitty moments that were tinged with hilarity. I didn't laugh at the time because I was too busy stomping on my feelings with handfuls of Chili Cheese Fritos and cake, but hindsight has given me the gift of amusement at my former self.

I thought I'd be awesome at getting pregnant. Since just before my eleventh birthday, I'd had my period regularly. Blood came out, chocolate went in (my mouth, not my vagina), and so on and so forth. No glitches had been detected. Everything with my nether parts appeared to be going exactly as planned.

Basically, I expected my body to be more like a vending machine when it came to having kids than it was proving to be. I had always assumed that once I made the right deposit (sperm), the appropriate thing would pop out (a human).

No matter though. Because at thirty-two years old I was on a fertility doctor's exam table with a speculum so far up my hoo-ha I could taste the zest of metal in the back of my throat. As my doctor mined around (as they tend to do), the normal questions ran through my head.

Is it supposed to feel like she's crammed a whole crate of Lincoln Logs up there? Is the smell of my vagina more lavender vanilla or tuna tartare? Does she hum like this for everyone or am I special? Why the fuck would someone go to school for thirteen years for this crap? And, most important and blaring, will this pile of utter painful bullshit eventually lead to us having a baby of our own?

My vagina had developed very expensive taste in doctors as of late. Ordinary gynecologists had become oh so basic. Regular brew wasn't good enough anymore. My vagina had turned pumpkin spice breve with extra whip with no intention of going back. Thus, she had begun preferring doctors that cost hundreds per visit.

"Oh, I'm sorry, you did your fellowship where? Sorry, no admission. You understand. I'm a bit of a physician connoisseur these days. No getting past this vulva unless you're Columbia trained!"

Considering all of the garbage we'd gotten through together and the trailer we'd lived in for a stretch, you'd think the ol' girl would've remembered her roots. She didn't though. She was acting like we were more caviar than Kraft (though we both knew better).

Bougie-ass bitch.

"We know the problem here, we just have to figure out what to do with it," my doctor said, her voice echoing in the cavernous depths of my vaginal canal (as voices tend to do).

Despite my biological age, my ovaries were older than Betty White's diaphragm. Essentially, Bob Barker's penis pump had more miles left on it than my broke-ass uterus (medical terms).

The doctor slid out from my undercarriage (picture one of those rollers mechanics lie on to work on your car), toweled herself off, and sighed.

"IVF is the next step. You know that," she stated.

Of course it was, because my filet-mignon-preferring beef curtains had decided so.

"We know," V said. She squeezed my hand.

But the thing was, my wife really *didn't* know. She wasn't an obsessive Googler like me. She hadn't spent jillions of eye-burning hours glued to the internet researching the cost of in vitro fertilization like I had.

Even more, my wife, who is roughly the same age as me, is

super weird about finances. She's not cheap; she's something else that's hard to explain. She grew up with parents of the same generation as mine, but instead of knowing TLC and Ricky Martin lyrics, she knows disco (this is a real problem for us). It's like she somehow missed a whole span of history that she was physically present for. When it comes to money, she's Dust Bowl era.

"We will do whatever it takes," she added encouragingly. "Whatever it takes."

I couldn't look at her.

V is amazing in ways that I probably never deserved in a partner (because of this evil empire of sarcasm I've spent my life building). She has always given me everything I want. If I asked for Pegasus mounted above our fireplace, she'd be like, "Well, this shit seems a bit excessive, but whatever you want, honey. Let's go buy a unicorn-killing gun."

But again, the price tag on IVF was uncharted territory for us. She had no idea, and then there was that weird money stuff.

Let me explain.

The thing about my wife is she has no concept of what things cost. She grocery shops and buys pants like a normal person, but then, I don't know, the second she leaves a store, she seems to forget the actual price of things. When she goes back into a store to buy a work shirt or underwear, she is genuinely blown away by the cost of things.

"Does this tag say forty dollars? That must be a mistake. I bet they accidentally added an extra zero," she'll laugh in a department store, giggling at the absurdity of the error.

"So, you think this shirt actually costs four dollars?"

"Of course!"

"No, babe," I'll answer. "I'm pretty sure it's forty dollars."

"There's no freaking way!"

Versions of this conversation between us happen often. On this matter, she is always wrong. When the cashier confirms the marked price, V will blink in sheer confusion, look at the cotton good, and shake her head like she was just transported here in her covered-wagon time machine from 1821.

The aforementioned story is just one example of many such incidents. As a couple, we have a shared checking account and separate ones as well (because she doesn't need to know my online shopping habits). For groceries and bills, we pay everything out of our joint account.

I'm going to grab some groceries for the next couple of weeks, I'll text. *Do you mind transferring some money over?*

Transferred $11. Go get your nails done too! Love you!

What in the actual fuck?

Uh, I'm not going to the general store on our lame-legged donkey for dry goods. Eleven dollars won't even cover my goddamned chip habit for a weekend.

When I correct the mistake, she's always quick to send more money, but even from afar, I can feel her utter shock at the amount requested. I'm sure she thinks I have some illicit drug problem. She likely assumes I spend the eleven dollars on nails and lattes and fourteen days' worth of food and the rest on powdery things I snort up my nose.

She grew up in Southern California and "remembers back in the day, when [she] started driving, when gas was eighty cents a gallon."

No. Just no.

Despite my internet searches that prove that gas hasn't been under a buck on the West Coast since 1998, this is a constant debate in our marriage. I got my license around the same time she did, and fucking gas was never that cheap (unless you were siphoning it from someone else's tank with a garden hose).

She talks about the price of things in the "olden days" like a weathered grandmother on a porch rocking chair.

"I remember when we only had one pair of britches made out of gunnysacks!"

Hooker, you were raised as a member of the upper middle class in a gated community in Orange County. What in the actual piss are you talking about? Like, you lived by the ocean and had season passes to Disneyland. There was no rationing of butter in your childhood.

So, when V agreed to IVF, I knew she had no clue what we were getting into. She just loved me a whole lot and knew that my heart was hemorrhaging without a baby, and she didn't care what it took to make me happy—she was going to do it. I'm sure she was already planning a trip to town in our Model T to do some livestock bartering.

When the doctor finally told me to put my pants on, I did so wordlessly.

"You want to talk to our financial person to discuss options?" she asked.

The contents of my stomach, soured by the last hour, lurched upward.

"You okay, babe? Let me get you a sodie pop," V said soothingly while handing me a goddamned nickel and steering me in the direction of the humming Coke machine in the lobby. "Is that right? Good god! When did drinks go up to a dollar fifty?" she exclaimed, flabbergasted by the blinking neon digits on the glass face of the soda machine.

Fuck me.

V was about to go question the front desk receptionist about the erroneous price of Sprite when my name was called. We followed the click-clacking steps of the finance manager as she walked us into her office.

"I already printed the pricing information on IVF for you," she said as soon as we sat down. She pushed a sheet toward me, which I gingerly picked up.

Gulping a breath, I passed the sheet to V.

Silence ensued, and the same nervous sweat that I thought my ass had left on the exam table began drizzling down my back.

V cleared her throat no less than three times before her voice finally had the ability to pass her vocal cords.

"So sorry, I'm new to all of this," she said, fluttering a hand in the air. "Is there an extra zero on this amount?" V smiled winningly and pointed at the digit at the end of the grotesquely long number on the sheet before her.

"Oh, sweet Jesus," I whispered, remembering her asking the same damned question at Banana Republic.

The financial lady knocked her glasses down from atop her head and squinted at the sheet. "No, dear."

At that moment I knew that the only way we were going to have a baby was if V climbed back in her nineteenth-century time machine to steal one from the clutches of rats, fleas, or the bubonic plague. The shilling she had offered me earlier would've likely bought us a really nice kid in the mid-1300s. With that kind of cash to throw around, we might've even been able to score a set of twins.

"All-fucking-right," V murmured, siphoning the air left in the room into her lungs. "You sure you want a baby?"

The tears I had stemmed so far now leaked from my eyes. My dreams were ravaged, and I couldn't breathe. I refused to answer.

I considered what I would do after leaving that office with no prospect of having kids. The nunnery hardly seemed appropriate with all my former debauchery and soft version of slutting around.

V, raised a disco queen with no concept of the cost of milk, snagged a pen from the woman's desk and signed her name across the bottom of the pricing sheet, which was practically banshee-screaming the outrageous price of happiness into our faces.

"Let's do it."

And just like that, the woman I loved, the one who paid pennies for dime candies and got petrol for a quarter, bought me the majestic Pegasus I wanted for above the fireplace.

Chapter Twenty-Five

Two Girls, One EpiPen

"Ma, I know it's crazy, but can we just go over it one more time?"

I tapped my foot on the floor and stared at my mother expectantly. We both knew I wasn't asking her. I was telling her. We would be going over it one more time, and one more after that even, if that's what it took for me to breathe better.

She sighed and accepted the tiny, handheld epinephrine injector trainer that I jiggled in front of her.

I was leaving our two kids, a seven-month-old and a two-and-a-half-year-old, in her care while I ran to the grocery store. My anxiety was well-founded as just a month before, shit had gotten real as fuck the moment the baby tasted a new food and nearly died from anaphylaxis. On the advice of our pediatrician, I had fed the baby a scrambled egg, and the end result had been disastrous.

A few days earlier, I had wisely asked, "But can't babies have a pretty bad reaction to eggs? Like, they stop breathing sometimes, right?"

The doctor had chuckled as he rubbed smudges from his

glasses. "We introduce high-allergen foods early these days," Dr. Turner reminded me. "Don't be such a worrywart. Go ahead and let the little guy try some good stuff out."

Listen, dick breath, I thought, his placating chortle searing my brain. *Believe me, no one wants this kid eating fucking omelets more than me, the mom whose nipples are stretched so far out from breast-feeding that they could be used for double Dutch. Pardon my caution. I'm just trying to avoid major catastrophe here. Please remember that these kids cost an entire life savings to make.*

But I heeded the doctor's advice because his medical degree outweighed my paranoia about my offspring's potential suffocation by ingestion.

Well, let's just say I regretted that when the little guy almost gave me a goddamned aneurysm about five minutes after he had eaten his first bites of the egg. The look on his chubby bubble face was nothing short of ecstasy until angry hives began to dot his chin and chest. His breathing grew labored, and my very heart was eviscerated as I realized the severity of the situation and dialed 911.

An ambulance ride and a stay in the hospital later, we were sent to an allergist, who warned that the baby was highly allergic to egg protein.

No fucking shit, Dr. Genius. Thanks for the official diagnosis. You must know our brilliant pediatrician. I'm so glad our insurance deductible could make your acquaintance.

We had left her office with an EpiPen (a terrifying little auto-injector that gives premeasured doses of epinephrine to treat anaphylaxis when shit hits the fan). We had also been prescribed a trainer EpiPen. The trainer looked nearly identical to the real-deal, med-loaded pen but it was meant for practice. When you opened the trainer pen, an automated voice walked you through the steps to administer the medication just like you would in real life. The only difference was that it didn't have a needle or actual epinephrine.

Because the baby was so young and his allergy so severe, we were given three different EpiPens and trainers to have with us and to scatter about our house. The goal was to always have a unit accessible no matter where we were. The doctor also gave us a few expired adult units to use just for practice.

"Just keep these around, activate them, and practice," she said. "You have to know how to do this in case of another emergency."

Per our allergist's instruction (and to my wife's embarrassment), I made it my life's mission to teach everyone on the planet how to use the EpiPen via instruction with the trainer.

"Jess, the guy spraying for bugs won't ever need to give him epi," V would say. "Please don't teach him."

I'd volley back a highly improbable scenario involving me having a seizure from the bug spray chemicals at the same time the baby crawled into the fridge, peeled some hard-boiled eggs, and went to town eating them. At that moment the Terminix guy, my emergency proxy in a home with no other adult, would actually be the person to assume immediate care of our kids. I wasn't taking any chances.

Which is exactly why my mom was being run through the EpiPen gauntlet for the seven billionth time. I loved her a lot and trusted her with our kids but wanted to make absolutely sure she wouldn't kill one of them while I was squeezing cantaloupe in the produce aisle.

"Okay," she said, shrugging off her purse. "Let's go through it again."

"Take off the cap and listen to the instructions," I said seriously. "I'm not gonna help you. Go through it by yourself this time."

Mom tugged the lid off the trainer, which activated the device.

"Remove the red safety guard," a robotic voice announced from the trainer. "The device may be used through clothing."

She complied, tossing the crimson piece onto the table next to her.

"Place the pen on the outer middle part of the thigh," the automated voice continued.

"Should I really do this part?" my mom interrupted.

"Do it all, Ma," I said through clenched teeth. "You have to go through every step. It's just a trainer, it won't really do it."

"Press firmly until you hear a click and a hiss sound," the trainer continued. "Hold it in place for two seconds."

Used to my anal-retentive bullshit and ready to get the lesson over with so she could greet her grandkids, my mom shrugged again and stuck the unit to her thigh. She pressed firmly.

This is the part where the situation hit the skids. Instead of nothing happening (which was normal when we practiced with the trainer), we heard the click and hiss described by the robot.

My mom's eyes flew wide, and she screamed.

"What in the actual fuck?!? That hurt! Jesus H. Christ!"

"Stop with the drama!" I shouted back. "It didn't hurt. It's a fucking trainer!"

Even as I said it, a block of dread cemented in my gut.

Tears in the corners of her eyes, my mom smacked the device into my hand and pulled down her pants (in my kitchen, right near the damned half-eaten bowls of Fruity Pebbles). A small trickle of blood oozed from her exposed thigh.

"Uhhhhhh," I said. "It was a trainer."

I glanced at the plastic box in my hand, realizing that it most definitely was not a trainer. To my horror, I realized it wasn't even a pediatric EpiPen. It was the expired adult unit given to us by the doctor.

My own jaw dropped.

"It's fine," I said, committing to the lie. I was atop the hill I planned to die on. "Totally fine."

But it really wasn't. I had just injected my mom with epinephrine, a drug that shouldn't be fucked around with, especially by a lady such as my mother, who was on a massive dose of blood pressure meds.

How would I explain such a grisly murder scene to my brothers so close to the holidays?

"Sorry, boys," I'd say morosely. "She hadn't even finished her Christmas shopping before I mistakenly injected her with a lethal dose of epi and murdered her in my kitchen."

Like a character in the movies, she turned sheet white and swayed on her feet.

"M-my heart!" she stammered. "I'm sweating. My heart is racing. Oh god!"

Knowing my mom, and being fully aware of her propensity for theatrics, I shook my head. "Your heart is fine. Just breathe."

"I AM A NURSE AND I JUST FUCKING HAD A SHOT OF EPI-FUCKING-NEPHRINE AND I AM GOING TO DIE!"

At this point, because I'm fully nurturing and kind, I started to giggle. In retrospect, I will admit that it wasn't the most sensitive thing I've ever done.

"You will not die," I said matter-of-factly. "Here, just have a sip of water."

"WHAT THE FUCK IS WATER GOING TO DO? OH, LORD JESUS, I AM GOING TO FAINT."

I pushed her onto the couch and began to mitigate the situation. As a medical professional in a small community, I knew I couldn't call 911.

What would I even say?

"Hi! I'm a master's-prepared respiratory therapist and my mom is a twenty-five-year veteran emergency room nurse. We accidentally shot her full of epi and just want to make sure she doesn't go into cardiac arrest. Any thoughts?"

That wouldn't fly. Not if I wanted to work in the community ever again without being a laughingstock.

I decided to do the next best thing. With my mom panting herself into a frenzy on the couch and guzzling the prescribed water, I called my paramedic firefighter wife.

"Hey, babe. What's up? I'm on a call. Is this important?"

"Sorta," I said, giggling as my mom checked her own pulse, her eyes bulging. "So, we kind of mainlined my mom with a loaded EpiPen and now she's convinced she's gonna die. Will she?"

"I'm sorry," V said slowly. "What?"

"Will a little epinephrine kill my mom?"

"Jessica, what in the fuck are you two doing over there?" V spat, abandoning her own patient for the moment.

"Babe," I huffed. "Is it okay?"

"You two are complete dumbasses," she muttered. I'm sure she hadn't meant for me to hear that part. I'd guess she was wondering why in the hell she trusted me to be alone with our two young children every day.

"I mean, as long as it was a pediatric dose," V finally answered. "It'll probably be okay."

"It was an adult dose," I murmured, trying to trap the words between a cupped hand and the receiver.

My mom's head snapped up from the pillow she had lolled on. "ARE YOU FUCKING KIDDING ME? MY GODDAMNED TONGUE IS SWELLING!"

"If that's her screaming, she's fine," V responded. "Monitor her vitals. I'll get back to you after we drop our patient off. Please, please do not call 911. We will never hear the end of this bullshit."

I hung up the phone and pivoted on my heel to face my mom. The melon-groping grocery trip was clearly no longer on the docket.

"My pulse is one twenty-six," my mom shouted frantically. "Jessica! I think I need to go to the ER."

"Your pulse is one twenty-six because you're losing your shit, Ma," I said, sounding more confident than I felt in the situation. "Drink more water."

I was pretty certain fucking water wasn't going to do anything, but I needed a minute, minus her panic, to formulate a plan.

Her nursing knowledge out the window for the moment, she gulped like a man dying in the desert.

"Goddammit," she gasped. "Floaters. I'm seeing floaters!"

Much to my dismay, my two-year-old had wandered out of the playroom to watch the histrionics and ask for a snack.

"Grammy's fine, nugget," I said, shooing her away from her grandmother. "Nothing to see here."

My mom lay slumped across the sofa, the back of one hand draped over her forehead. She looked like a Victorian painting of a woman swooning on a fainting couch.

"Mom! Seriously! Stop!"

I palpated her pulse. For good measure, I pulled out my

stethoscope and listened to her lung fields. To my practiced, professional ear she sounded exactly like a woman losing her goddamned mind.

I handed the toddler an iPad and animal crackers and pushed her out of the room, then I pulled my phone from my back pocket and did a quick search on the internet.

"What are you doing?"

"Ordering a fucking pizza," I snapped, finding the phone number I was searching for. "What do you think I'm doing?"

I dialed the Arkansas State Poison Control hotline and listened to the phone ring while my mom moaned dementedly on the couch.

"Poison Control, can I get your name?" a monotone voice said on the other end of the phone.

No fucking way was I giving her my name. I was certain those calls were recorded and couldn't risk my medical peers ever hearing the impending exchange.

"Uh . . ."

"Your name, please." The woman sounded tired.

"Belvedere," I shot back, searching my trashed living room for a last name. "Belvedere Pebbles."

Smelling my bullshit three hundred miles away in her office in Little Rock, the woman let out a giant sigh. "What can I help you with, Ms. Pebbles?"

"Mrs. Pebbles," I said, correcting her.

I'm a married woman after all.

For whatever reason, staring at my flailing, red-cheeked mom and listening to the droll tone of the dispatcher, I started to giggle uncontrollably again.

"Ma'am? What can I do for you?"

"So, my mom maybe accidentally got an adult dose of epinephrine via an EpiPen and I'm just wondering if I need to do anything about it?"

Mom, who had ceased flopping around on the sofa like a fish, actually started to cackle too.

"Ma'am, this is very serious," the dispatcher, who had been put on speaker for my mother's amusement, warned.

We laughed even harder. Tears began skating down our chuckling faces.

"Okay," the woman said. "God. Okay. What's your mom's name?"

Our laughing ceased, and we froze.

"Um, Penelope Stonebreaker?" I offered, the lie rolling off my tongue. I thought my mom would appreciate the tribute to her first internet boyfriend but instead she, still very much Trish Morrissey, shook her head violently.

"Sure," the woman, who sounded close to hanging up on us, intoned. "Whatever."

"Will she be all right?"

I heard a long breath sizzle out of the woman. She probably wished both my mother and I would drop dead in that moment so she could get back to QVC shopping or whatever the hell she'd been doing before we interrupted her Wednesday morning.

"I can't say either way without knowing more about the situation," the woman recited. "I would advise that you go to an urgent care."

Tittering like a pair of twelve-year-olds caught drawing dick pics, we declined the dispatcher's advice and hung up the phone. As medical professionals, we were both aware that a high dose of epinephrine can, in fact, kill you. The lifesaving medication can skyrocket one's blood pressure, resulting in both heart attacks and strokes (one following the other makes for an especially shitty week). If we had been smart, we most certainly would've packed my kids up and moseyed to the local emergency department to err on the side of safety. But we aren't that smart. Besides, other than her melodramatic seizure-like writhing and overdone gasping, my mom wasn't showing any clinical signs of distress.

"Still think you're gonna die?" I asked, watching my mom flick away her tears. I put a forefinger on her wrist to palpate her pulse one more time for good measure.

"I'm done practicing with your goddamned EpiPen," she answered. "I think I've got it figured out."

I monitored her for a couple more hours, breastfed the baby who had started the whole debacle in the first place, and then waltzed blissfully alone to the grocery store, where I manhandled the hell out of some honeydew.

Chapter Twenty-Six

Adventures in Parenthood

I don't give a crap how cute my kids are, they have made an utter mess of an already chaotic life. Make no mistake, the Shitstorm Jess Show was in full swing before they made their debut, but they certainly didn't soften the chaos.

That being said, I love them more than life. I would do anything for them. Anything. Like, if someday one of them goes on a murderous rampage and needs bodies hidden, I won't think twice.

"Come to Mama, baby," I'll say into the phone from where I stand in line at Walmart buying hydrochloric acid and ordering one of those infomercial blenders that can turn a bowling ball to dust. "I've got you."

If we need any sort of large-scale mass grave site, I will have to buy one of those digging tractor thingies, because this hooker is not doing manual labor. I do brunchtime waffles, not back-breaking shovel work.

Corpse disposal required or not, parenting is hard as hell. There's this whole army of tired, confused adults wandering around the planet trying not to fuck up any more than they already have. It's a huge responsibility, and sometimes the sharpness of it feels like a stiletto to the carotid artery.

But my wife and I are doing this kid thing to the best of our meager abilities and we're exceedingly proud of keeping these little guys alive and fed. From where we started—cussing drunks with the shared objective of drinking more and fucking—to cussing mostly sober people too defeated to even smile at each other, we've progressed a zillion miles. Nowadays, at the grocery store, we visit the cereal aisle before the beer aisle. There are egg whites and diaper rash creams in our cart instead of whiskey. I'm not saying it's an improvement, just that it's an evolution for two people who decided to grow up.

But man, it's hard sometimes. Raising a little girl with the same flair for drama and theatrics as myself is some bullshit, let me tell you that. She's perfect and wonderful and one of my favorite people on the planet, but damn, she makes me realize that my mom did not deserve the shitstorm of bombastic shenanigans that I so readily doled out. Raising a little boy whose sole purpose in life is to surprise roundhouse kick me in the vagina isn't any easier. And adopting a third baby at forty? Don't even get me started.

But I'm making it. I am fully woke and taking parenthood one day (drink) at a time. The people we're raising over here appear to be turning out pretty damned cool despite my unruly rearing.

Some days surviving beyond our three-hour bedtime routine is the only goal I set for myself.

I have to reiterate that I started out this parenting thing with the best of intentions. I really did. Our brush (scrape? Clash? Brutal-ass hammering?) with infertility made us especially grateful for this entire experience that we almost didn't have.

So, when our first baby finally skipped out of my uterus, I was like, "Oh hell yes. I am going to dominate at this domestic mom shit. I will be a gold medalist in parenting."

I would be Lance Armstrong at momming (sans the dope, as that was obviously left behind in my ~~early~~ twenties), and I couldn't wait to get started.

I had carefully observed all that my own parents had fucked up and had a clear plan.

I bought a Baby Bullet, and for five whole days, I mixed organic blends of kale and carrot purée for my beloved infant.

That BS met its abrupt end after a wailing baby proved to me that waiting forty-five minutes for freshly blended roasted beets was not going to make for a happy home.

I think parents feel the need to do such crap because of how judged we feel. Perfect Pinterest and Facebook and TikTok moms show all of us normal folk how utterly wrong we're doing things. Then, because we're crazy and sleep- and hairbrush-starved, we actually buy into their public show of perfection and believe that they're better than we are.

They aren't! They just rally their kids and bribe them into being perfect for thirty-second clips that they pass off as real life.

I'm over here eating Nutella out of the jar in my sweatpants with the ass blown out—but secretly so are they, dammit.

I love when people tell me, "The kids should really sleep in their own rooms."

My rebuttal? "I fucking agree, Margaret, but I'm goddamned tired and it's not happening. Go back to digging in your ass before I kick it!"

Yesterday my kids had garlic cheese croutons and petit fours for lunch, which seems a little bit country, a little bit rock and roll, as much as it seems a little bit rent-by-the-hour motel, a little bit

Hilton. I had originally offered them nuggets and applesauce, but they refused. Because I absolutely negotiate with terrorists, I agreed to their counteroffer of the aforementioned shit meal, and we all walked away happily.

There's no mercy in this, so I must choose my battles.

My car, once a brand-new thing of pride, is now a rat's nest on wheels. Have you ever spilled Dippin' Dots inside a vehicle? I haven't either, but my kids have. My light gray interior now features pastel-pink and baby-blue polka dots from floor to ceiling. An endless supply of Pokémon cards, sticky from melted chocolate, is fanned across my floorboard. I have almost caused death to other motorists on more than one occasion because of goddamned empty Bubble Tape canisters trapped beneath my brake pedal.

As I said, it's really hard.

So, if you see me scrubbing vigorously at the car wash, I'm not disposing of a body or trying to get bloodstains out. I'm legit scraping gummy-worm-Cheeto goo out of my floor. My kids are currently too little for homicide, but if you see me doing the same in twenty-five years, my sixty-six-year-old ass still wearing skinny jeans and a Ruth Bader Ginsburg T-shirt, it's likely the real deal.

All I'm saying is if the Donner Party had had access to the trail mix and saltines stuck within my back seat, their winter would've been way less fucking traumatic. No one would've needed to eat Mawmaw if they had the tasty offerings of my vehicle.

Even though sometimes it feels like my kids are actively trying to kill me, I'd still fuck someone all the way up if they monkeyed with them. Yes, they've absolutely made a sheer mess of things that were already hanging on by bits of tape, but this mess is one that I mostly love and one that I waited a long-ass time for.

If you're one of those Pinterest moms (how did you even find this? I'm most certainly not for you), I apologize for my crassness. I'm sure you have some super-duper helpful suggestions on how to organize my car using Ziploc bags and marbles. You could probably whip me and my GMC up in a jiffy without even a jiggle of your perfectly coiffed beach waves.

But you can fuck right off, because this ain't that kind of ride and I ain't that kind of mom.

Ozone layer be damned, we are not meant to carpool together. I wish you all the best as you continue on your Instagram-perfect journey with your middle part and Pellegrino. I'll be over here taking sips from whichever two-day-old bottle of discounted water has the fewest visible Pringle floaties from my one-year-old in it.

A true friend, the type that knows what it feels like to be judged by all the got-it-together moms at gymnastic meets, can better understand the state of my car and my life. Instead of asking whether the streaks on my passenger seat are chocolate or poop, they gladly brush away leftover Uncrustables remnants and hop in. Such a friend would never question the strange smell coming from my air vents, because they know that the source can't be precisely nailed down. Meatloaf? Maybe. A burrito? Perhaps. A corn dog? Likely. That friend, a true ride-or-die, is also the type that will accept a last-minute cancellation of plans without making you feel like a loser and will chew the proffered linty piece of gum from the bottom of your purse. She's there for the fun stuff but also for the shit show.

Make these friends and hold on to them tightly. They are a lifeline, a source of strength, and the first people who will show up with a shovel in hand if you can't rent that backhoe to dig a body-sized hole. They will be your village whether you've been too busy for meet-ups for six months or you're curled on their couch while your jumble of kids annihilates a perfectly clean house for no goddamned reason. People need people. Find some who make you laugh and help you be a better person. If they aren't the type that helps you be better, at least make them the kind that can spill all the tea. That's just as important. Sometimes better person–ing requires more energy than any of us have. But none of us are too busy to hear about that judgy-ass bitch down the street who lost her shit in line at the self-checkout at Walmart. There's always energy enough for that.

Don't get me wrong. You don't have to have a legion of people. Sure, there are times you might need an army, but so long as your sprinkling of "we ride at dawn" supporters are scrappy and true, you're all set.

Me? I have my wife, my mom, my brothers, and a couple of close friends in my inner circle. That's it. That handful of people paired with my three kids are already more birthdays than I can keep up with and the maximum number of relationships I can balance.

My wife is a fixer of all things and a fierce protector of me. She swears she will go full "Uma Thurman in *Kill Bill*" on anyone who dares hurt my delicate feelings. I can report that she has yet to have to use Beatrix Kiddo's infamous five-point-palm exploding-heart technique or kill a person using a black mamba. As a woman with thinning hair myself, I am equally glad that V has not once sliced off the top of any of my sworn enemies' scalps.

My mother cheers me on and is always on my side even when I am super wrong and being a whiny asshole. This may not seem like the most helpful thing in the whole world but I believe that everyone should have someone who will go down with them on a flaming ship that they lit themselves.

"I'm sure you had a perfectly good reason for dousing this thirteen-million-dollar yacht with kerosene and tossing a match," Mom would say. "No worries. I brought floaties."

If I tell her that a kindergarten teacher who donated both of her kidneys and all of her life savings to rescue infant elephants from a flood in the Amazon is an evil shrew, my mom will nod slowly, cluck her tongue, and say, "I always knew there was something wrong with that cunt."

My lifetime bestie Caroline is hands-down the most fabulous hype girl in the whole world. More like a sister than anything else, she sees my wins as her own and cheers me on even when I feel done and defeated. It doesn't matter that we both got old. If I need a margarita or to hear some shit talk, she's at my front door with a blender, ready to unload.

Even though he would never want me to tell anyone that he's anything other than a black-hearted creature, Matt has gotten me through some of the hardest times of my life. He is proud of me always. When my confidence flickers and I'm convinced that I don't belong in a place, he props me up with words that make me feel stronger.

I am inclined to think that my brothers are annoyed by 94 percent of the shit I say, but they don't tell me that. They answer my endless stream of phone calls and feed me gossip and make me bubble up with nostalgia.

Despite my laundry list of failings, my trio of children look at me like I hung the moon (I didn't—I'm terrible at hammering and stud finding). They're perpetually ready to offer hilarious suggestions for next books and will always dance in the kitchen with me even when they think I'm low-key embarrassing.

Still more, I have a French bulldog who will listen to me talk at length on any subject as long as the treats hold out. Sure, he sighs a lot and sometimes I suspect he's thinking, *Get on with it, bitch!* (in a fancy Parisian accent), but he's there, and his attempts at appearing mildly interested in my blathering are much appreciated.

Here's the thing: I'm trying to get on with it, Hanky boy. I really am. And I understand that you're French but please don't swear around the kids.

Now that I've talked about how tiny my circle is, I have this burning desire to go find a pair of jeans that will puzzlingly fit us all. We would spend the summer passing the enchanted pants around, enjoying whatever adventures awaited inside their magical denim confines, and then giggle as we recounted the tales.

Sometimes I'm truly unnerved by my uncanny ability to generate such entirely original, never-before-done schemes.

This is the best idea ever. I can't wait to take everyone shopping.

Edited to add that the *Buddyhood of the Journeying Trousers* idea has been vetoed by my mom, who claimed she would kill herself if she wore the same size jeans as my two brothers. She might sink with me on a flaming boat, but she's not going to wear jeans that Cody potentially forgot to wash after going commando in. Screw me for even trying.

Chapter Twenty-Seven

On Wednesdays We Go to Walmart

I didn't have to apply for a license or file paperwork to keep exotic pets or anything to be able to have kids. I didn't even have to get my mom to sign a permission slip to procreate. Basically, if you have a uterus willing to host a human, you can repopulate.

If you ask me, there really should be at least a fill-in-the-blank test or an oral interview in front of a panel of stuffy judges for something so serious, but no such thing exists.

Like, one day the stars aligned, and I got pregnant, and BAM, there was a murder of babies (like crows, right?) in our house. The babies came one at a time, but once there was one, it felt like there were forty. I was round and pregnant and sort of glowy for what seemed like five minutes. People thought it was cute when I ate burritos and guzzled slushies for the briefest time. There was a baby shower, then I went to an operating room and the doctor cut a person out of my abdomen. In that instant, my grip on control in life was lost forever.

After a couple of days as an inpatient, the crazy bastards at the hospital then sent me, my wife, and a tiny baby home. Not one person cocked their head to the side and said, "Y'all got this shit, right?"

And it's probably a good thing they didn't, because we most definitely didn't have it. We didn't know what we were doing then, and now, after eight years in the trenches of parenthood, we still don't.

Truth is, I feel like someone should be monitoring us more closely, because we are likely royally screwing up over here. The baby stuff, with all of the pooping and crying and aching nipples (mine; the baby had no way of telling me if her nipples hurt), was an adjustment, but one we handled. It was rocky at first, but we jumped some hurdles, traded our beers for coffee, and made do.

Sure, we had some rough days (months), but babies are cute enough that you sort of forget wanting to run the fuck away most of the time.

But kids? Like, walking, talking kids with ideas and agendas and feelings of their own? This shit is a whole new ball game of terrifying oddities.

I mean, there's no one else in the world other than a three-year-old who could make horrific comments about the size of my areolas while standing (thoroughly uninvited) in the shower with me. Like, you joined me in the shower, kiddo, and you're openly gaping at my untended pubic area, making derogatory comments, and acting disgusted when the literal reason I'm so ungroomed is because you won't stop asking for fucking apple juice.

I mean, I genuinely wish my pubes weren't long enough for a generous Locks of Love donation, but that's just not my life right now.

I wear ratty T-shirts and three inches of eyeliner smeared under my eyes not because I'm a natural-born slob (this might be a lie) but because I haven't had four minutes to myself since 2015.

Kids are crafty as hell, and without even trying, they prove daily that it's miraculous that I manage to scrounge up the smarts to keep breathing.

My children ask questions all day long that make me feel like a complete dumb shit.

Like, "Mama, what's soap made out of?"

"Well, sweetie pie, it's obviously made out of—" *Fuck. What is soap made out of? Hell if I know. Goddammit, stop asking me hard stuff.*

When I repeat the utterly baffling question to other adults, the real assholes in the crowd always say something to the effect of "Glycerin. Soap is made of glycerin!" with an eye roll and an arrogant toss of their fringe of bangs that is poorly disguising hair loss.

Okay, Doogie Bill fucking Nye. But what else? Without reading the goddamned label off the back of a bottle of Softsoap, tell me what the shit else is in there. Please enlighten us all.

My wife is even more baffled by this process of parenting than I am. At each stage of our kids' lives, she's utterly dumbfounded by the new surprises that find their way into our existence. Her constant state of shock has turned me into the lead in this whole situation. Ergo, I am the resident parenting expert in our household. If you know me at all (or have read any of this damned book), you understand how far out of left field that idea is.

Each day I hear things like, "Babe, is it normal for him to hump so much?" and "Should we really be letting them eat chocolate cake for breakfast?"

According to my extensive research (via Google while driving), the answer to both questions is a firm yes. Chocolate cake has the same amount of sugar as Cocoa Puffs, and unless she's going to start making fucking quiche Florentine with a side of arugula salad each morning, the cake will have to do. As for the incessant humping, if it's okay for our French bulldog, I hardly think it's fair for the three-year-old to be cut off.

And to be frank, dessert for breakfast and air humps are low on the ladder if you ask me. The real problem that we're currently facing involves public interaction. Much like the rest of the world, we spent a couple of years relatively shut in, just staring at each other for a long time. We lost all the polite pieces of personality that we worked so hard to instill in our offspring. Granted, we hadn't exactly established a ton of niceties, but any that were there are now dismantled.

During COVID confinement, our household forgot the feel of real pants. We said what was on our minds at all times without worrying about our audience. Our only real contact was FaceTime calls with grandparents, and they were becoming even stranger in internment than we were. We lived in a bubble. Sure, we bitched and wished for sunny days at ballparks every now and then, but we would later remember how little we like crowds and quickly toss away the nostalgic meanderings. We had been caged for a long time and we missed people, but we had the sneaking suspicion that people were still dicks.

I retreated to teach online college courses, and our only glimpse into the outside world was through my firefighter paramedic wife. We mostly enjoyed the stolen time when everything was frozen in uncertainty and solitude.

But then, maybe before it should have, the world woke back

up. People who had been sequestered for years began crawling from their weird little holes and rejoined the ranks of the general population. With little warning, real life was happening. Ready or not, our kids, who hadn't interacted with the human race in years, were part of the planet again.

Such were the conditions for one particularly memorable day. Fresh out of quarantine, I had to take my kids to Walmart to pick up a prescription. All was fine, other than we were late to everything, everyone had cried once already, and my period had started with a vengeance as soon as we pulled into the parking lot. I wrestled with unbuckling two car seats and begged a toddler to put down the month-old French fry he had dislodged from the crack between the door and the window. Once unbuckled, his five-year-old sister had scurried to the back of my SUV in an attempt to find her "favorite thing in the whole world," which she was unwilling to identify. I couldn't chase her to the rear of the car as any abrupt motion paired with my newly commenced period would've certainly caused a waterfall of catastrophic, pants-destroying proportions. After trying to pry said kindergartner out of the vehicle via the hatchback, I threatened to leave her in the car for the rest of her life (she had no idea this is illegal). After some fairly intense negotiation, she finally resurfaced holding a mangled McDonald's toy.

Out of the parking lot and into the store, we sprinted to the bathroom like three madmen. When I told the kids that I had a potty emergency and needed to move quickly, they concluded that I had pooped my pants. Because, obviously.

I stuffed the trio of us into the nearest stall, shuffled carefully so as to avoid knocking a teensy body into the toilet, locked the door, and begged the kids not to touch ANYTHING (no, really, guys, it's fucking disgusting in here). Imagine my relief when I dug in the bottom of my purse and my hand made contact with a tampon. As I dragged the cylindrical shape out of the gummy depths of my bag, my shoulders sagged a bit when I realized it was partially opened and appeared to be covered in glitter and purple marker.

Let's be truthful here, my vagina had seen weirder, far less glamorous shit. Fuck it. In it would go.

Ignoring the school supplies dangling from the only feminine hygiene product I could find, I turned toward the wall, away from my kids.

"Mom, why you got candy?" my littlest simpered, hearing the crinkle of the pink tampon wrapper that I was trying to conceal.

"No candy, bud," I muttered, blowing sparkle flakes off the tip of the exposed cotton. "Just give Mommy a minute."

"We love candy," his sister added, putting sticky hands on my hips and trying to rotate me enough to see what I was doing.

"Baby, stop!" I barked, sweat rolling from my armpits.

Gritting my teeth and wondering what my gyno would think if I had to schedule an appointment with her for a raging sparkle infection, I inserted the tampon, pulled up my granny panties, and spun to face the kids.

"Ready to shop?"

Quite naturally our quick trip to the pharmacy had turned into a full-blown shopping event. We loaded the cart with toys, bug spray, paper towels, boxed macaroni and cheese, and Popsicles.

We had just joined the long pharmacy line, full of people impatiently checking their watches and grunting irritably, when the dreaded peppering of toddler questions began.

After a long minute of carefully studying me, my five-year-old spoke up in a voice one volume notch below the loudest sound in the universe.

"Momma, why'd you put that thing up your butt?"

Every head in the Walmart line snapped around to look in our direction. I stared back into the chocolate brown of my daughter's doe eyes and shook my head. "I didn't put anything up my butt," I said, trying to keep my voice airy.

"Yeah, you did," she argued shrilly, disregarding the horrified looks of the curious bystanders. "Just now in the bathroom. You put that glittery stick right up your butt."

"I didn't!" I practically shouted back. I made eye contact with a man nearby who wore an expression of sheer disgust. "I didn't put anything up my butt!"

His boot tapped loudly on the dull floor as he perched his hands on his hips and glared back.

"I really didn't," I whispered.

At that moment, my three-year-old, apparently feeling left out of the conversation, chimed in.

"Mommy, you did!" he yelled. "And we're not supposed to lie! You put it in your butt."

At that point (not my lowest, not even close), I glanced around the audience, looking for an ally. The pharmacy tech at the front of the line wore a sneer. The old woman with a cart full of Raisin Bran tsked disapprovingly. A middle-aged woman who was either a Sharon or a Karen flipped her bob cut and narrowed her eyes to slits.

Even the pregnant lady with a cart full of kids who should've understood my plight cast a judgmental glower my way.

Pissed at the entire line, and mostly my betraying kids, I leered back at the mom who should've been my ally. My cheeks burning in embarrassment, I let my eyes trail from the woman's one-year-old, chugging a liter of Mountain Dew, to his older brother, who appeared to be trying to lick the label off a discount pack of toilet paper.

Fairly certain that at least one of the spectators was searching the internet for a hotline to child protective services, I shushed the kids.

"Wine, huh?" I muttered, verbally jabbing at the pregnant woman, whose eldest child was sitting atop a box of Franzia white zinfandel. "Not exactly recommended for pregnancy."

I watched the onlookers shift their glares and concern to the other woman, who was clearly as shitty at parenting as I am. Then, in true cowardly form, I turned the wheels of our cart, hunkered forward, and sped my kids and our prepackaged cans of Beanee Weenees out of that hateful-ass pharmacy line.

You know what? Screw them! Parenting is hard as hell. If the only way to get through my day is to shove a glitter glow stick up my ass, no one needs to judge me. I'm raising tiny humans on no sleep, little food, and a fingerhold on sanity—a girl's gotta do what a girl's gotta do.

Instead of slinking away shamefacedly, I walked out of that store with my head held high. My grocery bags were bulging with processed shit I refused to feel guilty about feeding my offspring. My own bottle of wine, scooped up on the way to the checkout, gleamed under the fluorescent light enticingly. The kids each clutched to their chests new stuffed animals that they certainly hadn't earned during their insurgent little display in the pharmacy line. They chattered excitedly about the snow-cone-stand trip I had bribed them with to help all three of us survive the rest of the errand.

Plenty of the folks still waiting on their drugs likely would've happily listed my parenting fails. We made it through the day though, and the next one after that, and the next one after that. Now, at eight and six with a one-year-old little brother, my nuggets are happy and healthy and pretty well adjusted considering that we're making life up as we go. Despite my continued discretion when inserting feminine hygiene products, the kids still believe that I shove glitter up my rectum. They also think I'm a real-life fairy though (because I told them as much), so the art supplies up the wazoo make perfect sense. They reason that the only way such a magical pixie could sprinkle endless sparkle dust is to reload every now and then.

You don't have to tell me the obvious, okay? I'm well aware that I have some very real explaining to do before any of the people my wife and I are raising go to public school sex ed.

Chapter Twenty-Eight

Armed and Ready

"Someone's in the house," I whispered, my hand cupping the phone so my voice wouldn't carry.

My wife, on a twenty-four-hour shift at the fire department, had just been awakened by my frantic phone call.

"What? What's going on?" she shouted.

I shushed her as my eyes scanned our darkened house for the alleged prowler.

"I just need you to be quiet and be on the freaking phone with me," I growled, terrified and unjustifiably angry at my spouse, who goes to work in order to feed us and buy the kids pants and me Red Bull.

The reason for my overt pissiness? Well, I'm more of a muffin-making lesbian than a ninja lesbian, and my specific skill set was proving to be quite unhelpful in the current situation. The only tucking and rolling I could do involved making cinnamon strudels. I was pretty sure I would need to throat-chop someone in the very near future and wasn't sure if my limited whisking talents would be up to the violent task. I bake cookies and help the kids craft pumpkins and drop care packages off to sick neighbors. I buy sweaterdresses on Amazon. I'm not a search-the-house-in-the-dead-of-night-with-the-intent-of-murdering-intruders sort of dyke.

"Do you have the gun?" V asked, lowering her voice. The question made my entire body freeze.

"No!" I whisper-hissed. "Of course not!"

My searching suspended for the moment, I slid my back against the wall and tugged shut the door to our bedroom, where our two sleeping toddlers were nestled in the king-size bed. I had been with them when I'd heard the noise; the boogeyman wasn't in there.

"Hank!" I called, my voice wobbling. "Hanky! Come here!"

"Why in the hell are you calling him?" V asked too loudly on the other end of the line.

"Protection!"

Despite the severity of the situation, V snorted.

Hank, our then seven-year-old French bulldog, who was so lazy that we had to check him for a pulse multiple times a day to make sure he was still with us, was far from an armored car, but he was the only option I had.

"What?" she asked.

"To stay with the kids!"

Before sauntering my way from the laundry room, Hank lapped water from his bowl and stopped to read an entire Sunday edition of the *New York* fucking *Times*.

"Hank," I growled, making our marshmallow fluff of a dog pick up his turtle pace to a leisurely trot. Apparently, he had little concern regarding my impending death.

As soon as I shoved Hank into the bedroom, I resumed my search for the intruder.

I thought back to the moments before our three-year-old had fallen asleep that night.

"Mom, did you see that scary man in the mirror?"

Our son, who became the middle child a couple of years after this incident when we adopted his brother, is world-famous for saying creepy shit right before falling into an angelic, peaceful sleep. The evening before, he had wrapped his sweet arms around my neck and said, "I don't like it when the lady cries," and passed out with a serene smile on his heart-shaped lips.

Who in the actual fuck says things like that? I've spent my entire life trying to act like certain things aren't real, but then this little guy comes along and screws with my head and then sleeps like a milk-drunk kitten.

"Jessica, get the gun," V insisted. "The big one."

I shuddered at the thought. There was no way I was pulling that GI Joe shit off the rack V had secured to the back of the closet.

"No."

"Get the gun. Right now!"

"I'm not goddamned Vin Diesel, V!" My wife was distracting me from searching our house for an armed murderer.

"Get the little one, then. Do it."

I swallowed through the heartbeat that was trying to missile out of my chest and crept back into the bedroom, past the dog, which had abandoned his guard post and recommenced his stuporous slumber, and reached for the small gun that I knew was hidden in a locked drawer.

"You need the magazine," V added.

"A magazine?"

"Jesus Christ, Jess! The metal boxy thing next to it."

"The bullet holder?"

"Oh my god." I could picture my wife massaging her temples with her forefingers. "Just put it in the gun."

I was completely aghast at the suggestion. As previously mentioned, I'm definitely more a chocolate chip cookie gal than a semiautomatic.

"Putting you on speaker," I said, reentering the hallway to resume my search.

"Just sent you a video on how to use the gun," V said loudly, her voice echoing off the fucking walls.

"GODDAMMIT, V, NOW HE FUCKING KNOWS I DON'T KNOW HOW TO FUCKING USE A GUN!" I shouted.

I wanted the home invader to think I was a killing machine. Since I was occupied with canvassing my house for an escaped convict, it hardly seemed like a good time to watch YouTube.

Fuck it. I flipped the nearest switch upward, flooding the hallway in light. My wife, miles away at a perfectly safe firehouse, had just blown my cover and basically broadcast that I was no damned John Wick. If the late-night lurker was about to launch an attack, I wanted to at least be able to see for the hand-to-hand combat. For the first time in my entire life, I wished for a good set of nunchakus, or at least a decent katana. I had seen enough episodes of *Ninja Turtles* to use either weapon with a fair amount of confidence.

"If you're in my house, come out and let's fucking do this," I yelled.

I didn't know what "this" was, but I knew it was going to be fucking serious.

I heard Hank flip over in the bedroom, his collar clattering on the floor.

"Did you just really say that?" V asked.

"'Bout to fuck this bitch up!" I snarled.

And I fucking meant it.

Apparently, there is a little John Wick in me.

Fortunately, no masked person popped out of a closet or the fridge. I stood there, in a pose modeled after Blanka from *Street Fighter*, and waited. Still, no one showed. No one knifed me in the hip or snaked an arm around my neck to drop my ass with a chloroform-soaked cloth (this is how these things usually go).

"I think I'm good," I finally said, relaxing my stance as I determined that I wouldn't be kicking anyone's ass that night.

V stayed on the phone with me while I checked all of the closets and peeked into the showers. She made me look under each bed even though the very act of crouching on the floor and peeking beneath the mattresses almost made me crap my jammies.

"What exactly did you hear?" V asked.

"The door handle, it jiggled," I answered.

"Had the air conditioner just kicked on?"

"Maybe. Yeah."

"Love you, Jess. Watch the YouTube video I sent so that if someone ever really breaks into our house you can shoot them in the face."

In the face? Jesus Christ. What if it was a supermodel down on her luck or in between Parisian gigs who had broken in? I wasn't trying to destroy someone's damned livelihood.

When the time came, I'd definitely be aiming for the legs. Hopefully, no dancers planned on breaching our front door in the dead of night.

V hung up and I disposed of the gun (I've always wanted to say that; I actually just locked it back in the drawer). Then I crawled into bed between our sleeping kids.

Overhead, I heard the air conditioner kick back on, and seconds later the door sucked in, and the doorknob jiggled.

The sound was vaguely familiar. My wife being right was also vaguely (and irritatingly) familiar. Goddammit. I blamed the three-year-old and the alleged man in the mirror.

I just need to put it out there and say that it doesn't matter if you look like a baby dove on a nest of cotton candy; if you say terrifying crap to your mom before passing out, it's still a dick move.

Chapter Twenty-Nine

I'm Not Like a Regular Mom, I'm a Dumpster Fire Mom

I don't think anyone else has ever said this, but getting older is weird as shit. I know, I know, I'm a true think tank. I hope no one got scorched by the heat of my burning intellect. My brilliance has been both a blessing and a curse in my forty-one years. Which is impressive really, considering that I am a woman who once smoked catnip.

But really, life and its progression are weird. Getting older and growing into responsibility is one of the oddest things that I've ever done.

And if you've read the preceding chapters, you can attest to the fact that that is saying something momentous. Because odd shit is sort of thematic in this life of mine.

All I'm saying is that one year you have your tits out at Mardi Gras. You eat Pez for breakfast and drink cocktails before ten a.m. A decade later you start growing hair on your face, you need scripts for reflux, and you schedule shit like mammograms.

It used to be like, "Fuck, I don't have insurance," when a cop slowed behind my dented, barely running Camaro. Now it's like,

"Oh, goddammit. There's no way that fucker in the beater behind me even has liability insurance," as I steer my mom SUV out of the way while tsking. I sip my basic-ass nonfat white chocolate latte while looking at the 401(k) balance on my phone, hoping that the rascal makes it home without incident.

I've grown into a different, more predictable kind of life. I'm so damned adult now that I remember to program the coffeemaker each night for the next day. I'm not worn out because of a hangover and dread that I have to make it to work at the gas station in order to have money for pot. Nowadays I hobble out of bed slowly each morning because of advanced age and back pain, like that mean old bitch who threw those kids into the oven in her candy house.

Life was mostly about the next steps. I survived my crazy childhood. Next, I trudged through my painfully awkward teens. Then, the truest accomplishment of all, I made it through the third decade of my life. I mean it when I say that survivors of their twenties should be rewarded with medals. On the day you cross the threshold, some sort of momentous commencement should mark the accomplishment of not drinking, drugging, eating, or crying yourself into the grave in a ball of youthful hormones and fury.

When I met the amazing woman who is now my wife, I was a special kind of crazy. Not because I had actual mental breakdowns, but because people the age I was (twenty-four) are so chock-full of drama and emotions and tears and rage and happiness and confusion that they are always on the brink of spontaneous combustion. It's like someone took all of my fucked-up feelings, heartbreaks, and rejections; put them into a two-liter bottle of soda; popped a Mentos in; and said, "Shit's about to get real."

And it did, for about ten years, and then, one day, the drama sort of fizzled out and I settled into who I am today.

It was time for the next step.

So after years of saving, selling our starter house, and surviving a global pandemic, my wife and I built our dream home.

We bought a few acres of land, conned an architect into sketching the house plans that had forever lived in the dusty corners of our minds, and began the new adventure. V (the career firefighter with no building abilities to speak of) served as our contractor. When she wasn't running medical calls in the ambulance or chasing fire alarms in the fire truck, she was barking orders at subcontractors.

Thus, we are now country lesbians. V mows our lawn wearing flannel in a shiny new tractor that is treated better than most human beings. For no sane reason, we arrange pumpkins and hay bales on our porch in October and say shit like "Happy fall, y'all!" to our neighbors. Sometimes I think about getting chickens.

I saw child square dancers (remember, we live in Arkansas) a couple of weeks ago at the county fair. Instead of thinking, *Those poor bastards. Their parents should be shot!*, I gasped and said, "Oh my god. So cute!" In that moment, which would've truly disgusted my younger self, I meant what I said. In fact, I even picked up a flyer at a nearby table that advertised the youth classes, thinking that maybe my daughter would like to join.

For shame, Jess. For shame.

I own monogrammed pillows that I arrange and then send pictures of to my friends. Sometimes I even write strongly worded letters to my kids' teachers and threaten bullshit like "going to the administration." I have an Amazon habit that I hide from my spouse, and I book photographers for beach vacations years in advance.

But let me tell you, I like this life. At forty-one years old, I know who I am. I don't try to impress anyone but me anymore, and that is fucking freeing. When I blast music in a parking lot, it's not so bystanders can see how cool I am. It's to cover the noise of my children's fight to the death in the back seat.

I wore a two-piece at the pool this year and didn't worry about who was looking. This body of mine is a road map of memories. It housed two kids who sometimes act like douchebags but are awesome for the most part. Everything that wiggles and shakes is hard-earned.

Don't get me wrong, there are moments when I want to run away from home. Parenting and spousing can be hard AF. Living can be scream- and tear-inducing. Like all moms, I have instances when I think about putting on a cardigan and sensible shoes and making for the road. Maybe I would run as far as I could go. But I know my cunning family would soon find me one-sixteenth of a mile from the house, where I'd lie dead from exertion on the sidewalk. Even if they didn't find me, though, by nightfall I'm sure I'd venture home, missing the belly giggles, snuggles, questions about dinosaurs, and shared late-night movies turned so low my wife and I can barely hear them just so that they won't wake the snoring kids.

Sometimes I think that I would kill to spend one more night in my party days, drinking in every single rebellious moment. Maybe it would be fun to give one final body shot out of the cleavage of my twenty-year-old boobs, which hadn't yet experienced gravitational pull. But then I look at the dusty pair of knockoff Louis Vuittons stored in my closet that I haven't worn in ten years, and I remember the pinch of the toes and the guaranteed heel blisters. I longingly finger the glittery clutches that I haven't been able to part with, but then I remember that those bitches aren't big enough to hold all my vitamins or a goddamned foot-long sub.

So, I don't run, and I don't stuff my feet back into those painful shoes. These kids, with their tiny hands and giant imaginations and embarrassing comments, are my people. This wife with a firefighter's temper and a laugh that makes my heart soar is the future I wished for. She was this drunk girl that I met when I was a drunk girl, who turned into the kind of parent that makes rainy-day forts for kids and feeds my drive-through coffee habit every morning when she comes home from work. My nutso mother with all her quirks, my bestie who remains a kick-ass hype girl, my politically incorrect brothers, and my off-kilter friends are my community. They're fucked up, but they're my kind of fucked up.

I'm now a historical timepiece. I wouldn't say I'm a collector's item like the 1982-issued metal E.T. lunch box my first boyfriend gave me that I've been trying to sell on Facebook Marketplace for two years—but still, I'm something of a revered relic. I'm like the thing that someone picks up at a flea market and jabs their friend, saying, "Oh shit! Do you remember when these were cool?" before stuffing it back onto the shelf behind dusty-ass Beanie Babies and Furbys.

With the experience gained from such a life lived, I have a bit left to say. So humor me for just a spell longer.

Here I sit on my throne of hard-won life lessons. After years of binge drinking premixed margaritas and slurping cheese from a squirty can, I am now a survivor leveled up to my full glory, chugging antacids in torn flannel jammies. So, before I complete my ascension into a blur of parenthood hell (goddamned *Blippi* reruns and jelly on the leather couch I never should've bought in the first fucking place), let me chime in one last time to impart some final wisdom.

To the generation after mine (Gen Z):

Please quit telling me to stop wearing eyeliner on my waterline—y'all can fuck right off until you give up your fanny packs and stop recycling trends from my high school days. The waterline trend will follow me to my old-lady rest home, and I fully expect whichever mortician my children hire after I die to draw it on my corpse.

Also, you and your mom jeans are just begging for a yeast infection. I'm talking a serious case of vaginosis that would need Monistat shooters for days. Denim is not supposed to be worn so high that it hazards entering your vulva. That's not what Mr. Levi Strauss intended when he rolled out his first jeans prototype in the 1870s. Also, please stop calling them "mom jeans" when wearing them at nipple level. I am an authority on the fact that actual moms aren't wearing these atrocities anymore (we have given up on all pants with actual structure and only wear stretchy shit). The women who wore them first are now your grandmas (I realize that grandmothers are the original moms, but please just stay with me on this). Please rename this ill-informed fashion trend accordingly and attribute the poor example to its rightful owner (your granny who no longer gives a shit whether or not her vagina receives circulatory support).

I hear you screaming at me, telling me I'm doing it all wrong, and I don't disagree. But you're also doing it wrong. And you will keep doing it wrong. You will make mistakes just as I did, and you will repeat them expecting a different result. You'll get hurt and bruised and tired. Someday you'll miss your nights out but will love your nights in even more.

Like me, someday you might have kids, and you'll quickly realize that you don't know what in the hell you are doing.

As a mom, every single day I wonder, *Fuck, is this thing that I just did the thing that will land my daughter on a therapist's couch someday?*

Because there will be a couch and I'm sure there will be crying.

You'll likely do the same.

Because every parent who has their first child is literally just faking that they know what in the hell they're doing. The first prototype of successful conception is a literal practice kid. When Trish birthed me in 1982, likely to the tune of "Eye of the Tiger," she probably didn't say to herself, "How will I screw up this precious angel baby who just ripped apart my vagina?"

I know at the beginning of this book I promised not to offer advice, but I actually have some to give. Just remember when you're fucking up your kids that someday one of them might pick up a pencil and become a writer. If they're as entitled as me, they might think their story is interesting enough for people to want to read. Worst-case scenario? They take that misplaced conceit, and they jot down the story of their childhood and lay all your parenting shit bare.

Don't raise a writer.

Also, younger generation, stop the shouting and criticizing and judgment. Let me sit over here on my pile of fringed pillows that say stupid shit while I buy face creams online.

Please show some respect and remember when you're wearing

your upcycled Doc Martens with overalls that it was our idea first. Even more, while looking for where that bitch Carmen Sandiego ran off to again, we were rocking Baja hoodies before your parents even considered getting it on. And the two guys who created SoundCloud, providing the music you shake your poorly dressed asses to? Yeah, they're my fucking age. When you are making fun of people in my generation on goddamned TikTok, please take note that it was created by Zhang Yiming, a Chinese gazillionaire genius born in 1983. He's my people—not yours. Soak all that early millennial goodness in, guys. These nineties kids, like me, kick total ass.

To the generations before mine (Gen X and boomers):

I'm sorry for being such a dick. I really am. On behalf of my entire generation of people, which your generations made, I want to issue a formal apology. You were right about so many things. My face certainly could have frozen into one of the many ugly expressions I made at my brothers (I know this because I repeat the same phrase to my own children, which makes the adage concrete fact). You were also right when you shrilled "Because I said so!" for the 184th time. As a wizened adult, I now understand that such expressions should never be questioned.

You probably shouldn't have kicked me out of the station wagon for arguing, and you probably should've been more worried about little things like, I don't know, child abduction and maybe all of my underage drinking. But when it comes down to it, I know you were doing your best. When you let me stay up until three a.m. to talk to my internet boyfriend, and when you didn't kill me after the sleepover where my bestie infected our entire household with head lice, you were showing love in your own dysfunctional way. I can appreciate that. Today, newly in my forties and driving the twenty-first-century version of a station wagon, I understand you on a fundamental level. My feet hurt. Gas prices are too high. Why don't these fucking kids have any respect for their elders?

To my generation (millennials):

If you're also an elder millennial and you get the vibe of this book or relate in any way, get in, loser, we're going shopping. I owe you a slushy. You should totally come over and we can make friendship bracelets or have a Pog tournament (but no keepsies, because I love my shit). Let's compare which Mighty Duck we had the biggest crush on and make Goober Grape peanut butter and jelly sandwiches while our Kool-Aid hair dye soaks in. If you survived this incessant ramble, you are a special kind of person and deserving of only the best. If you made it through and related to what you read, you are my person. I am your person.

As a proven nonexpert on life, I shouldn't be giving advice, but I will say this: Things will be bad and hard and ugly sometimes. Some days it will seem easier to grind yourself up in the garbage disposal than to finish work, put the kids to bed, or make dinner. But in cases when you can, let the bad stuff be a blip, not a blight, on your path forward. Keep going, things get better. In cases when they don't, still try to push onward. You might end up with some funny material for a memoir. At the very least, your therapist will have a fresh cache of stories to sort through.

Obviously, I don't have it all figured out. We've covered the fact that I don't have my shit together. Truth be told, this entire book is about what a giant dumpster fire my life has been. There's no silver lining on the horizon and the forecast predicts that I will continue to stumble as if drunk through the rest of my days.

I see Pinterest moms and wonder how in the shit I missed the crafting boat by such a wide margin. When I drop my kids off at school, I pray that the teachers in the car line assume I'm wearing flesh-colored leggings instead of realizing that I've actually just forgotten my pants again.

I've said it before, and I'll say it again now: my messy affairs and constant state of disaster can be attributed to how I was raised and the generation that raised me.

I'm not trying to bitch more than I've already bitched here, but my life was hella hard. I lived in the trenches of the nineties. Anyone who says such an experience is for the faint of heart has no idea what they're talking about.

I had the pressure of keeping a goddamned precious baby Tamagotchi alive before I could even use a can opener. Do you think doing such a thing was easy to manage between English class and recess? It sure as hell wasn't!

You can't watch Simba's dad get trampled by wildebeests in *The Lion King* and just be expected to have a normal day after that. Moreover, no one can spend their childhood worried their parents will leave them home alone à la Kevin McCallister without developing some crushing anxiety. Because I was a nineties kid, there wasn't a single fucking day that went by that didn't have me panicked that Bette Midler, Sarah Jessica Parker, and Kathy Najimy (the Sanderson sisters) were on the way over to our house to sip my soul like it was a cup of lobster bisque. This is scary shit, guys. When I should've been learning the laws of exponents, I was wondering why the piss Reese Witherspoon gave Mark Wahlberg the code to her house in *Fear*. The bastard cut her dog's head off! Boyfriends were dangerous!

At one point, I sobbed so hard over Jack and Rose's death-torn romance and obsessed so much over the sinking of the *Titanic* (the cinematic one, not the one that killed more than fifteen hundred actual people) that my mom took me to see a therapist.

As a chubby kid, I was taught by movies like *Heavyweights* and *Camp Nowhere* that my girth was not only unacceptable but also so hysterically funny that it made me a fair target for anyone who wanted to comment on it.

I read *Bridget Jones's Diary* when I was fourteen, too young to buy the ciggies she chain-smoked or to have any real concept of her struggles with the opposite sex. The songs I hummed while gathering books for my next class were just as befuddling. Like, for years I've been trying to figure out in what setting Marcy Playground would've run into the mixed odors of sex and candy. At forty-one years old, I've never encountered the pair together but can't help wondering in what circumstance gummy bears and ejaculate ever collided in front of the late-nineties alternative rock band.

This is what I think about. Imagine my day-to-day exhaustion from having a head filled with such utter bullshit all the time.

I hope you also remembered all of this millennial dreck as you read about me. Please don't judge the stories until you weigh my lifetime of weird experiences against my actions.

When you see my friends writing letters to their dogs for their birthdays on Facebook, keep an open mind. They know that their dogs can't read. They realize their terriers don't give a fuck about the day they were born. They just need validation. They crave the attention that we millennials swear we don't want but still desperately seek. Remember that when you make fun of our embarrassing YouTube tutorials and Pinterest boards, you tear a little piece from our souls that will never grow back. We're people too.

And remember that I couldn't have been normal. Not really. None of us could have.

And our kids won't be either, because our generation hasn't developed or discovered the skill set to right the wrongs of our past. In a true perpetuation of cycles, we are going to continue screwing up the newer generation. The kids we raise will be future presidential candidates, and they too will be totally dysfunctional but in a different way than we are. We are actively stirring them into a defective broth, one that is special in its own right.

So just quit being so hypercritical of my mess over here.

This nineties girl hardly has the world figured out, but she did okay for herself. Despite what society might've thought would happen to a young person who had messed with all those episodes of *Dawson's Creek*, chokers, butterfly clips, and canned SpaghettiOs, I became an adult I'm pretty in love with.

You will too.

Epilogue

No worries if you just skimmed this book. Here's the CliffsNotes version in bullet points for if/when you are tested:

- I don't care how long I've been married to a woman or how much of a flag-waving lesbian I am, I remain wholly in love with all the *Footloose* Willards (ages and movie release dates notwithstanding).

- You're not a real nineties kid if you aren't still crying over Heath Ledger being dubbed Sir William in *A Knight's Tale*.

- I was kissing girls (and liking it) long before Katy Perry discovered how delicious cherry ChapStick is.

- I was also wearing clothes donated by the relatives of dead elderly persons long before Macklemore ever ventured into a thrift store. I was grandpa chic before it was a revered genre.

- My young kids will tell you that I have "harpies" if you run into us at the grocery store. They're talking about herpes and are referring to the cold sore I get once a year (but that was super memorable to all those living in our household and is still a hot topic of dinnertime conversation six months post-breakout). I'd super-appreciate it if you'd just smile and nod and move the conversation along.

- In the 1990s parents always threatened to "turn the car around" when you were arguing with siblings. This threat could be tossed out on a fast-food dinner run or when you were on your way to the hospital to get stitches. If that threat didn't work, they resorted to steering one-handed while the other arm blindly whacked at legs in the back seat. If you were still being a dick and in need of additional punishment, you would inevitably be left on the side of the road to walk the fuck home by yourself (parents of the nineties always came back before you were kidnapped, but not until after you nearly shit your pants).

- To Generation Z (are you really calling yourselves zoomers? Really?): Ease up on the makeup tutorials and scoffing at the liner on my waterline. I know you think your fake lashes make you look like a baby fawn, but in reality, it looks like you're one of the troubled kids who got their ass whupped in *Willy Wonka and the Chocolate Factory*. Think about it and dial in the appropriate level of respect.

- In the next twenty-five years or so my generation will begin having open-heart surgery. When the cardiac surgeons take a look inside our arteries, they will be surprised to find a unique blend of the oil from Taco Bell beef mixed with whatever the fuck that waxy shit is on Little Debbie cupcakes. We will all eventually die from this odd mixture of fast-food additives and sugar paraffin.

- Square-shaped nails cut practically short are the best shape. These younger fucks with their nineteen-inch coffin-shaped nails are living life wrong. Who in the hell are they enlisting to wipe their asses, anyway?

- If you are a mom at a swimming pool with young kids, you have to play defense at all times because there absolutely will be a moment when a pair of tiny feet find their way into your swimsuit bottom and you will have to make the decision to drown your child or keep your pants on (all my kids are still living, so you can see the choice I've made more than once).

- To the youth of America (to whom I've reluctantly surrendered my title): Stop telling me I'm canceled. You don't have the authority to decide such things and I wouldn't know what the fuck it means even if you did.

- Be warned that if you visit my home in the week between Christmas and New Year's, no one in my family will be wearing pants. We will be snoozing in postholiday leisure wear, polishing off stale peanut clusters, and not giving a flying fuck that we have no concept of the date or time.

Acknowledgments

My thanks go first to my fellow elder millennials, who like me are trying to figure out why their hair is falling out and why the fuck eye cream costs eighty dollars per ounce. We survived sleeping on our bellies through infancy and car rides without seat belts. Surely we can endure parenting and all the bullshit that comes with middle age. Thank you for reading—this book is an homage to all of us. You are my allies, my people, and the ones I look forward to high-fiving in nursing homes.

To the children of elder millennials, thanks for bearing with this book. Guys, we really are sorry. We meant well. Make sure you are well insured and find a counselor who will help you work through the majority of this mess. You can try to bill us, but it's a gamble as to whether we're financially stable enough to pay. This book was for you too—so you can better understand why your moms have so many goddamned sparkly shirts still hanging in their closets and why your dads continue wearing Volcom board shorts with flip-flops.

To Emi Ikkanda, you believed in my work more than I did and pulled the best words out of me. Thank you for picking through the dark jokes for the truly funny. Editors deserve all the credit. All. The. Credit. How did you make this thing that should've given me hives and made me cry so much fun?

To my agent, Claire Draper, you have listened to me cry. A lot. Thank you for believing I would eventually find my way while I sashayed through genres and tossed around crazy ideas. You know what the hell you're doing. It is high time you and I have some moonshine on a porch swing somewhere together.

Klaudia Amenábar, you have been such a great sport helping Claire and me drum up book titles. Please don't ever stop.

Phoebe Robinson, you are younger than me, but I still want to be you when I grow up. I'm so glad you're in my corner. Thank you for everything you do to elevate writers and creatives and for being a bright spot on this planet. You have built a publishing empire that should be an example to the rest of them. I continue to be starstruck as fuck.

To my publicist, Sarah Thegeby; marketer, Isabel DaSilva; production editor, Alice Dalrymple; copy editor, Aja Pollock; jacket designer, Vi-An Nguyen; the folks at Azantian Literary Agency; my friends at the Bent Agency; and everyone else working so hard behind the scenes at Tiny Reparations Books, thank you for making me look much cooler than I've ever had a right to be.

To V, there aren't enough words for this part of my acknowledgments. My heart woke up the minute I found you. Thanks for letting me sit around in my PJs with little notebooks and lots of coffee instead of working. Also, for understanding my middle-of-the-night writing frenzies and crazy eyes when I'm onto a great idea. Your sneaking suspicion that I could become something turned out to be true. You are my swoon. Always and forever.

PS: Yes, I want wine tonight. Stop asking. It's always yes.

Nuggets, choose to be the good that there needs to be more of in this world. I am on this planet to be your mom. Nothing else. You are better than all the best parts of me and I can't wait to see the magical things you do.

Ma, thanks for making holidays pure magic and the rest a shit show funny enough to write an entire book about. You never, ever once told me that I couldn't become whatever I wanted to be— and I believed you. Because of you, I grew up knowing that dreams are possible and that even a girl with the humblest of beginnings can rise if she so chooses.

Christian Jonathan, I'm sorry for laying all your shit bare, but god, we had a lot of fun. Maybe some good does come out of do-nating plasma (other than the lifesaving bullshit). Thank you for being on my side even when I'm ridiculous.

Caroline, how we survived the stories in this book I will never know. I'll always be sad that no one ever made a reality show about us. It's still something I would watch. Thank you for listen-ing to my stress and understanding me better than most.

To my brothers, I'm so glad the universe put our motley asses together to be the ultimate sibling gang capable of kicking so much small-town butt. Thank you for letting me share memories that are yours too.

Grandma, I have a sneaking suspicion you had something to do with all of this. I still see your red whenever I need it the most.

Pops, you were right. It takes all kinds to make this world work.

Drs. Shauna McKinney and Amy Sarver, you gave me everything I love the most and acted like I wasn't behaving like an absolute psychopath in the process. You are the true heroes walking this planet. Sorry for all the beaver shots.

Dr. Christina Dalton and the crew at Arkansas Children's Northwest, thank you for saving the very best girl, whom we just couldn't have lived without.

To anyone who gave my stories a try and read this compilation: thank you so very kindly for being a part of this dream that was forty-one years in the making. Now please stop picturing my wonder bush and puzzling over what happened to those lesbians from the cruise trip. Some mysteries must remain.

ABOUT THE AUTHOR

Jess H. Gutierrez is a speaker and former journalist whose work has been published in the *Northwest Arkansas Times*, the *Arkansas Democrat-Gazette*, and the *Siloam Springs Herald-Leader*. She has earned several awards from the Arkansas Press Association. She also won the fifth-grade spelling bee despite the fact that everyone thought that Crissy Eaton would take the title. She lives in Northwest Arkansas with her firefighter wife who is way cooler than she is, their three wild kids, a surly bulldog named Hank, a cattle-herding Yorkie-poo named Bella, and six chickens who refuse to lay eggs.